Coteaching and Other Collaborative Practices in the EFL/ESL Classroom

Rationale, Research, Reflections, and Recommendations

Coteaching and Other Collaborative Practices in the EFL/ESL Classroom

Rationale, Research, Reflections, and Recommendations

edited by

Andrea Honigsfeld and Maria G. Dove
Molloy College

Information Age Publishing, Inc.
Charlotte, North Carolina • www.infoagepub.com

Library of Congress Cataloging-in-Publication Data

Coteaching and other collaborative practices in the EFL/ESL classroom : rationale, research, reflections, and recommendations / edited by Andrea Honigsfeld and Maria G. Dove.
   p. cm.
      Includes bibliographical references.
   ISBN 978-1-61735-686-5 (paperback) — ISBN 978-1-61735-687-2 (hardcover) — ISBN 978-1-61735-688-9 (ebook)
   1. English language—Study and teaching—Foreign speakers. 2. Language arts—Ability testing. 3. Curriculum planning. 4. Literacy—Evaluation.
I. Honigsfeld, Andrea, 1965- II. Dove, Maria G.
   LB1576C737 2012
   372.6—dc23

2011043687

Copyright © 2012 IAP–Information Age Publishing, Inc.

All rights reserved. No part of this publication may be reproduced, stored in a retrieval system, or transmitted in any form or by any electronic or mechanical means, or by photocopying, microfilming, recording or otherwise without written permission from the publisher.

Printed in the United States of America

DEDICATION

We dedicate this book to our respective families who are the source of our greatest support and inspire our creativity: Howie, Benjamin, Jacob, and Noah; Tim, Dave, Jason, Christine, Sara, Meadow Rose, and Gavin Joseph. We also dedicate this work to educators throughout the world who are committed to working collaboratively for the sake of English language learners.

CONTENTS

Foreword
   Margo DelliCarpini .... *xi*

Preface
   Andrea Honigsfeld and Maria G. Dove .... *xvii*

Acknowledgments .... *xxiii*

PART I: CONCEPTUAL FRAMEWORKS AND MODELS OF COLLABORATION

1. Bilingual Students Within Integrated Comprehensive Services: Collaborative Strategies
   Martin Scanlan, Elise Frattura, Kurt A. Schneider, and Colleen A. Capper 3

2. Mainstream and ELL Teacher Partnerships: A Model of Collaboration
   Angela B. Bell and Anne B. Walker 15

3. Inclusion or Intrusion? Reculturing Schools for Collaborative ESL Instruction
   Clara Lee Brown and Andrea J. Stairs 27

4. Fixing the Implementation Gap: Creating Sustainable Learning Spaces for Successful Coteaching and Collaboration
   Anne Dahlman and Patricia Hoffman 37

5. Collaborative Interdisciplinary Team Teaching: A Model for Good Practice
   Andrew Gladman 49

6. Coteaching for English Language Learners: Recommendations for Administrators
   Jocelyn Santana, Jennifer Scully, and Shaniquia Dixon 59

PART II: DOCUMENTARY ACCOUNTS OF COLLABORATIVE INSTRUCTIONAL AND LEADERSHIP PRACTICES

7. Collaborative Conversations
   Cynthia Lundgren, Ann Mabbott, and Deirdre Bird Kramer 69

8. Barn Raising in New England: Working Together on Sheltering Spaces
   Patricia Page Aube, Bonnie Baer-Simahk, and Kelly Waples McLinden 79

9. Double-Teaming: Teaching Academic Language in High School Biology
   Rita MacDonald, James Nagle, Theresa Akerley, and Heidi Western 91

10. E-Collaboration: Connecting ESL Teachers Across Contexts
    Lan Ngo, Susan Goldstein, and Lucy Portugal 101

11. Collaboration to Teach Elementary English Language Learners: ESOL and Mainstream Teachers Confronting Challenges Through Shared Tools and Vision
    Melinda Martin-Beltrán, Megan Madigan Peercy, and Ali Fuad Selvi 111

12. Sharing Vocabulary and Content Across the Disciplines
    L. Jeanie Faulkner and Carol J. Kinney 121

13. Voices From the Field: Teachers' Reflection on Coteaching Experiences
    Judith B. O'Loughlin 131

14. Assuring ELLs' Place in the Learning Community: Leadership for Inclusive ESL
    George Theoharis and Joanne E. O'Toole 141

PART III: EMPIRICAL STUDIES ON COLLABORATION

15. Understanding by Design as a Tool for Collaborative Planning
    Laura H. Baecher 155

16. Does the Devil Laugh When Team Teachers Make Plans?
    Christopher Stillwell 165

17. Summer Book Clubs for English Language Learners: Teacher Collaboration for Promoting Academic Achievement
   Susan Spezzini and Abby P. Becker 175

18. Power Differentials: Pseudo-Collaboration Between ESL and Mainstream Teachers
   Nelson Flores 185

19. Barriers to Collaboration Between English as a Second Language and Content Area Teachers
   Beth Lewis Samuelson, Faridah Pawan, and Yu-Ju Hung 195

20. Pulling Away From Pull-Out: Coteaching ELLs in the New Latino South
   Greg McClure 207

PART IV: COLLABORATIVE PRACTICES TO SUPPORT MENTORING AND PROFESSIONAL DEVELOPMENT

21. Coteaching as Professional Development
   Francesca Mulazzi and Jon Nordmeyer 219

22. Peer Group Mentoring: Preservice EFL Teachers' Collaborations for Enhancing Practices
   Hoa Thi Mai Nguyen and Peter Hudson 231

23. Shared Competence: Native and Nonnative English Speaking Teachers' Collaboration That Benefits All
   Jan Edwards Dormer 241

24. In Our School, We All Teach ESL: The Impact of the Collaborative Work of a Teacher Study Group
   Patty St. Jean Barry 251

25. Building Communities of Practice: Support and Challenge Through Mentoring Networks
   Gabriel Díaz Maggioli 261

26. Synergizing Professional Development Through Video Recording, Critical Reflection, and Peer Feedback
   B. Greg Dunne and Sean H. Toland 271

About the Contributors 281

FOREWORD

Margo DelliCarpini

I am delighted to write the foreword to this edited volume on coteaching and collaboration in English as a second language (ESL)/English as a foreign language (EFL) settings. In *Coteaching and Other Collaborative Practices in the EFL/ESL Classroom: Rationale, Research, Reflections, and Recommendations*, Andrea Honigsfeld and Maria G. Dove have created a cohesive text that provides a solid rationale for why coteaching and other collaborative partnerships between ESL/EFL teachers should exist and be supported. The contributors, who share the research that they are engaged in, the reflections that emerge from their experiences, and the recommendations based on research, practice, and reflection, contribute to a growing literature on ESL/EFL collaborative practice and bring the challenges and successes of these partnerships into focus. Whether you are a teacher, administrator, researcher, professional developer, or teacher educator, you will find material in this volume that can add to your own understanding and practice as it relates to coteaching and collaboration. Honigsfeld and Dove as editors have compiled a comprehensive body of work that addresses a variety of aspects related to collaboration among mainstream and ESL/EFL teachers.

The strength of this book is that it creates new ways of understanding and implementing collaborative practice from a variety of perspectives. The contributors represent diverse voices which include researchers, program administrators, teachers, and teacher educators. These many voices, all contributing to our body of knowledge on the topic of coteaching and collaboration in the ESL/EFL setting, embody the theme of the work, which speaks to the strength we gain when we work together. The editors

Coteaching and Other Collaborative Practices in the EFL/ESL Classroom:
Rationale, Research, Reflections, and Recommendations, pp. xi–xv
Copyright © 2012 by Information Age Publishing
All rights of reproduction in any form reserved.

share that few resources are available to help general education and ESL teachers, or EFL teachers collaborate effectively.

Throughout my career as an English as a second language teacher and TESOL teacher educator, I have seen the need for ESL and mainstream teachers to collaborate in order to provide effective instruction for English language learners (ELLs). My formalization of this began in the spring of 2000, after having been contracted to provide a series of professional development (PD) workshops in a large school district on Long Island, NY that was comprised of about 15% ELLs, at the time, one of the largest populations in the state outside of New York City. I was working with a dedicated and competent group of secondary level content area teachers and my goals were to provide them with a foundational knowledge of the theories of second language acquisition and academic language development, as well as practical strategies that they could use in their classrooms to better meet the needs of ELLs in the mainstream, secondary level classroom.

During the second meeting, as I was discussing the differences between basic interpersonal skills (BICS) and cognitive academic language development (CALP) (Cummins, 1979). I paused and looked around at the participating teachers: Not one was an ESL teacher. Later, during a break, I asked the building level representative who had contacted me why the ESL teachers were not present. I was met with a truly bewildered look. Essentially, this PD was for content teachers. No one thought to invite the ESL teachers. I realized at that time that we can pour unlimited resources into professional development opportunities for mainstream teachers, and hold equally wonderful workshops for ESL teachers, but until we were able to create a dialog between these two sets of educators we would not be successful in reaching our goals. As I continued to work within this framework, I developed a deep understanding of how these collaborative efforts needed to be a two-way street, rather than one set of teachers telling another set what to do.

As I developed in my career, I made collaboration a critical issue in the courses that I taught, the professional development workshops that I led, and in my own practice as an ESL teacher and TESOL teacher educator. I was not always met with open arms, but I worked to develop resources that the teachers and teacher candidates I worked with could draw upon, and quite frankly some olive branches, to sweeten the pot since, as you will read in the following chapters, ESL/EFL and mainstream teacher collaboration is not always easy and not something that necessarily comes naturally.

A few years after the above mentioned incident, during a student teaching seminar course I was teaching at a large research university in New York State, I had invited a former graduate, who I will call Rebecca,[1] to speak during one of the class sessions. She returned at my request to share her experiences, first as a student teacher, then as a new teacher in a district with a large ELL population. I asked her about any coteaching or collaborative efforts she was a part of. She responded honestly:

> My district does some push-in. I'm in a K-6 building. I push-in to one class each day, and teach pull-out (free standing) for the rest of the day. When I push in, I realize this is supposed to be a coteaching situation. We worked on this in methods and student teaching seminar, so I felt that I could do this and was excited that I was actually in a school that did push-in. I wound up sitting next to the ESL students, pointing to places where the teacher was on the page, whispering the meaning of vocabulary into their ears during the lesson. Basically, I am a VERY well paid aide. Not what I wanted or expected. When I try to talk to the teacher I am supposed to be collaborating with, she really doesn't want to hear it. I'm a second class citizen to her."

Rebecca's response highlights some of the barriers that exist for effective coteaching or collaborative partnerships to occur between ESL and mainstream teachers. However, while it is true that barriers do exist, when the relationship works, it benefits all involved. In a subsequent semester, when I was teaching at another institution and had further developed the collaborative experiences that my preservice ESL teachers were exposed to, the following final reflections, one from an ESL teacher and the other from a mainstream secondary level English teacher were submitted after these candidates had worked together throughout the semester on developing collaborative skills: Kayleen, a mainstream, secondary level English teacher who was completing her MSEd in English education shared:

> I started this semester thinking that we would just be engaged in an activity that was essentially a waste of time ... that I wouldn't learn anything. I have been proven wrong. As an 11th-grade English teacher, I am responsible for getting these kids ready for the Regents [New York State standardized assessment]. I always had this suspicion that my ELLs were just not working as hard as they needed to. What I discovered this semester was that there are these stages they go through, and that just because they speak English really well doesn't mean that their literacy level matches that. Working with an ESL teacher has really helped me understand the needs of these kids ... it is more than just grouping them together so they are busy ... it is actually designing instruction with their needs and level in mind. And I found out I can do that and it isn't as hard as I thought.

Emma, a third year ESL teacher, completing her MSEd in TESOL and a classmate of Kayleen's commented as such:

> I am so glad that this class was offered. For the last three years I have been trying to work with content teachers, but in the high school it's hard. This class brought us together and really showed us why it is important to collaborate and how we can do it without taking a ton of time. I saw a real difference in my own work as a result, and I felt like a real teacher, respected by my colleagues, for the first time.

The above reflections illustrate that, despite challenges, when there is support and room for collaboration, positive outcomes occur. While not always easy, collaboration and coteaching in ESL/EFL settings change the dynamic of teaching and offer benefits to all.

However, there are considerations; Andrea Honigsfeld and Maria G. Dove have compiled a body of research in this edited volume that addresses these considerations. First, both parties need to understand why collaboration and coteaching can benefit all students that they teach; how it can foster a sense of ownership for the success of all learners, ELLs and native English speakers alike; and why, in this rapidly changing school-aged population that research estimates will be comprised of approximately at 40% ESL learners by the year 2030 (Northwest Regional Educational Laboratory, 2004), collaboration and coteaching between ESL and mainstream teachers is a must rather than an option (*Rationale*). Additionally, all stakeholders need to have a solid understanding of the process and practice of coteaching and collaboration between ESL and mainstream teachers. This enables all participants to make informed pedagogical decisions and engage in theory grounded practice (*Research*). Then, once the partners in these collaborative and coteaching relationships are working together, either in formal coteaching situations or collaborating by engaging in common planning or observing each other's practice, reflection becomes key.

In reflective teaching practice, educators essentially think about what they did in the classroom and what the consequences of those actions were, why they make the instructional decisions that they do make, and how they implement the pedagogical practices and skills that they decide upon. This benefits both the teachers who engage in the critical reflection and the students whom they teach. In no place is reflective practice more important than in the coteaching or collaborative partnerships between ESL and mainstream teachers. Farrell (2001) discussed the importance of reflection and the development of *critical friendships* and he defined this relationship as "people who collaborate in a way that encourages discussion and reflection in order to improve the quality of teaching and learning" (p. 369). What a perfect way to describe the potential relationship that can exist between mainstream and ESL/EFL teachers who develop such collaborative and reflective partnerships (*Reflection*). Finally, this reflection ultimately leads to changes or modifications to existing practice and to educators learning from each other and their practice and sharing that knowledge with others, who can then implement the ideas and best practices that emerge from the development of knowledge of content and pedagogy (*Recommendations*).

As you read the chapters that combine to make up this comprehensive text on coteaching and collaboration, it is important to see that not only have Honigsfeld and Dove selected work that adds to the theoretical and pedagogical understandings of collaborative practice in ESL/EFL settings, but also how continued work on this topic can be continued in a scholarly way. I look forward to adding this book to my own library of material on coteaching and collaboration and trust that you will find a rich resource in the chapters that follow.

NOTE

1. All names are pseudonyms.

REFERENCES

Cummins, J. (1979). Cognitive academic language proficiency, linguistic interdependence, the optimum age question and other matters. *Working Papers on Bilingualism, 19,* 121-129.

Farrell, T. (2001) Critical friendships: Colleagues helping each other develop. *ELT, 55,* 368-374.

Northwest Regional Educational Laboratory. (2004). *ELL unit focuses on growing population.* Portland, OR: Author.

PREFACE

Andrea Honigsfeld and Maria G. Dove

"Individually, we are one drop. Together, we are an ocean."

—Ryunosuke Satoro

Over a decade ago, Elmer (2000) observed that individual teachers seem to be operating in isolation from each other, without much needed opportunities for "respecting, acknowledging, and capitalizing on differences in expertise" (p. 25). He also noted that—as a characteristic of our vocation—teacher isolation seems to be a dominant experience across classrooms, schools, districts, and beyond with troubling implications:

> It creates a normative environment that values idiosyncratic, isolated, and individualistic learning at the expense of collective learning. This phenomenon holds at all levels: individual teachers invent their own practice in isolated classrooms, small knots of like-minded practitioners operate in isolation from their colleagues within a given school, or schools operate as exclusive enclaves of practice in isolation from other schools. (p. 21)

Individually, we are one drop. Together, we are an ocean. If teachers are expected—or believe they are—to stand alone charged with the formidable task of educating the next generation of English learners, they are each one drop of water, the basic essence or foundation of instruction and learning, yet limited in magnitude and power. However, when they are given the opportunity to share and build upon each other's knowledge and skills, together they harness the energy of an ocean, and their impact becomes so much more powerful.

Coteaching and Other Collaborative Practices in the EFL/ESL Classroom:
Rationale, Research, Reflections, and Recommendations, pp. xvii–xxii
Copyright © 2012 by Information Age Publishing
All rights of reproduction in any form reserved.

WHY THIS BOOK IS NEEDED

Much has been written about the cognitive and academic language needs of those learning English as a new language (be it a second language in the United States or other English-speaking countries or as a foreign language in all other parts of the world). Many guidebooks and professional development materials have been produced on teacher collaboration and coteaching for special education, inclusive classrooms. Similarly, much has been published about effective strategies teachers can use to offer more culturally and linguistically responsive instruction to their language learners. However, only a few resources are available to help general education teachers and ESL (English as a second language) specialists, or two English as a foreign language (EFL) teachers (such as native and nonnative English speaking) teachers to collaborate effectively.

WHAT IS OUR GOAL

With this volume, our goal is to offer an accessible resource long awaited by educators whose individual instructional practice and/or institutional paradigm shifted to a more collaborative approach to language education. Through this collection of chapters, we closely examine ESL/EFL coteaching and other collaborative practices by (a) exploring the rationale for teacher collaboration to support ESL/EFL instruction, (b) presenting current, classroom-based, practitioner-oriented research studies and documentary accounts related to coteaching, coplanning, coassessing, curriculum alignment, teacher professional development, and additional collaborative practices, and (c) offering authentic teacher reflections and recommendations on collaboration and coteaching. These three major themes are woven together throughout the entire volume, designed as a reference to both novice and experienced teachers in their endeavors to provide effective *integrated, collaborative* instruction for EFL or ESL learners. We also intend to help preservice and inservice ESL/EFL teachers, teacher educators, professional developers, ESL/EFL program directors, and administrators to find answers to critical questions including the following:

- What are key elements of a high-quality ESL/EFL collaborative service delivery system?
- What organizational structures and cultures are necessary to support the implementation of collaborative practices and coteaching in English language education?
- What leadership practices encourage effective teacher collaboration for the sake of English learners?

- What first steps can teachers and educational organizations take in examining and improving their collaborative practices?
- How can technology support aspects of teacher collaboration?
- What are the research-based knowledge, skills, and dispositions critical to effective collaboration and coteaching?
- How do ESL/EFL teachers enhance their instructional practices when they engage in collaborative curriculum planning, instruction, and assessment?
- How do teacher collaboration and coteaching contribute to job-embedded professional learning?
- What models of professional development are supported and enhanced through teacher collaboration?

WHAT IS UNIQUE ABOUT THIS BOOK

The volume constitutes a distinctive contribution to the field of teaching ESL and EFL for the following compelling reasons:

1. First, it is designed to be a text for use in professional development and teacher education courses by virtue of focusing on the subtopic of a unique instructional approach—coteaching, also referred to as partnership teaching—as well as other collaborative practices in the ESL/EFL context.
2. Next, it contains applied research, with a special emphasis on ESL/EFL program organization, classroom applications, and reflective practice.
3. Last but not least, the content of the book is underpublished in the professional literature. Most ESL/EFL teachers and administrators seek out resources on coteaching or teacher collaboration published in the special education context. This book fills the need for carefully documented, evidence-based ESL/EFL-specific, research-based coteaching experiences, additional collaborative practices that support coteaching, and practical implications thereof.

HOW IS THE VOLUME ORGANIZED

By organizing the chapters into four major parts, we address both theory and practice, teaching and administrative issues, ESL/EFL and content teachers skill sets, linear and global procedures to implement collaborative practices, teaching and learning approaches in the cotaught classroom, the processes and outcomes of collaboration for teaching ELLs, and the successes and challenges of ESL/EFL coteaching.

In Section I, *Conceptual Frameworks and Models of Collaboration,* we grouped together chapters that offer a theoretical and structural background to ESL/EFL teacher collaboration. In the opening chapter, based on their extensive collaborative research, Martin Scanlan, Elise Frattura, Kurt A. Schneider, and Colleen Capper take an asset-orientation approach to culturally and linguistically diverse students and assert that support services for these students should be structured in integrated and comprehensive manners. Angela B. Bell and Anne B. Walker share their research on how the professional learning community (PLC) framework led to designing their own model of collaboration in support of mainstream and ESL teacher partnerships. Clara Lee Brown and Andrea J. Stairs raise several critical questions including whether teacher collaboration and coteaching is perceived and practiced as inclusion or intrusion.

To ensure that collaboration represents inclusive practices, they invite readers to consider comprehensive reculturing efforts as they ready their schools for collaborative ESL instruction. The chapter by Anne Dahlman and Patricia Hoffman addresses the implementation gap and suggests ways to achieve a large-scale adoption of successful coteaching and collaboration practices through a systematic, organic, and sustainable change process. Grounded in his own research and practice, Andrew Gladman presents a three-mode model for collaborative interdisciplinary team teaching to guide practitioners in their efforts to create ideal conditions for effective teaming, meeting the needs of both students and teachers. In the final chapter of this section, Jocelyn Santana, Jennifer Scully, and Shaniquia Dixon not only present a framework for ESL coteaching in the form of an assessment tool, but also offer recommendations to administrators for its use.

Research-based instructional practices have become highly in demand in recent years. In Part II, "Documentary Accounts of Collaborative Instructional and Leadership Practices," scientifically based exemplary practices are introduced. In the first chapter, Cynthia Lundgren, Ann Mabbott, and Deirdre Bird Kramer present protocols for collaborative conversations between general education and ESL teachers that ensure access to content, provide explicit language instruction, and facilitate interaction between content concepts and language. Also using sheltered instruction as an instructional framework, Patricia Page Aube, Bonnie Baer-Simahk, and Kelly Waples McLinden offer step-by-step implementation procedures for teachers working together on content-based curriculum development, coplanning, coteaching, and coaching support. Rita MacDonald, James Nagle, Theresa Akerley, and Heidi Western provide evidence that successful teaching of academic language in a high school biology course sometimes calls for double-teaming—collaboration between and among content area and ESL experts, professors and inservice teachers.

Using web 2.0 technology, Lan Ngo, Susan Goldstein, and Lucy Portugal invite readers to witness the process and outcomes of their e-collaboration across various content areas, instructional contexts, and geographical locations. Melinda Martin-Beltrán, Megan Madigan Percy, and Ali Fuad Selvi examine a university–school district partnership for professional development designed to enhance pedagogical practices for ELLs and identify how ESOL and mainstream teachers confronted challenges through shared tools and vision. L. Jeanie Faulkner and Carol J. Kinney take a detailed look at how to enhance vocabulary development through content-based collaboration. Examining collaborative teaching, Judith O'Loughlin reveals the schoolwide practices that support the implementation of coteaching partnerships. George Theoharis and Joanne E. O'Toole discuss the important roles school leaders play in assuring equitable place for ELLs in the learning community through creating and supporting inclusive ESL services.

Generally, educational research is conducted to lend insight to promising school policies and practices or successful teaching and learning techniques to bolster student achievement. Our search for experimental data to support collaboration and coteaching practices for ELLs has led us to offer a distinct selection of *empirical studies on collaboration*. In Part III, Laura H. Baecher details an approach for improved collaborative planning between ESL and content teachers using a research-based framework. Christopher Stillwell documents the first year of an instituted coteaching program and the lessons administrators learned about the implementation process. Susan Spezzini and Abby P. Becker examine the effects of a collaboratively conducted summer book club for ELLs and its consequences for ELL academic achievement during a subsequent school semester. Nelson Flores qualifies the difference between pseudo-collaboration and true collaborative practices with his study of the power relationships that exist among teachers. Beth Lewis Samuelson, Faridah Pawan, and Yu-ju Hung analyze some of the challenges to collaborative practices involving administrative support, teacher attitudes, and time factors. Finally, Greg McClure shares the results of a year-long case study regarding the experiences of two fourth grade coteachers and that factors that both supported and hindered their collaborative efforts.

Research studies have found teacher collaboration to be an important component of effective professional development (McLaughlin & Talbert, 2001; Wilson & Berne, 1999). In Part IV, "Collaborative Practices to Support Mentoring and Professional Development," we underscore professional learning schemes for developing collaborative practices for ELLs. Francesca Mulazzi and Jon Nordmeyer discuss the benefits of coteaching as a professional development tool and how educational institutions can implement a collaborative service delivery model of instruction for ELLs. Hoa Thi Mai Nguyen and Peter Hudson explain how a group of preservice teachers participated in a peer-mentoring framework as a practical and effective means of support for their professional learning. Jan Edwards Dormer explores the working relationships between native English speaking teachers and nonnative English speaking teachers and highlights the benefits of their collaborative teaming. Patty St. Jean Barry shares how a teacher study group comprised of both ESL and general education teachers cooperate to discern and cultivate instructional approaches to better serve ELLs. Gabriel Díaz Maggioli documents innovative collaborative partnerships targeting teacher collaboration across different levels of a public school system. Finally, B. Greg Dunne and Sean H. Toland identify the benefits of video recordings to increase teacher self-awareness, receive peer feedback, and enhance teacher reflection concerning instructional practices.

CONCLUSION

Chapters in this book address the challenges and successes with teacher collaboration and coteaching in the ESL and EFL context, both in the United States and overseas, in the K-12 school context and at the college level. While each chapter takes on a unique perspective, they underscore the importance of establishing collaborative practices that benefit both teachers and the students they serve. Together, harnessing the energy of an ocean, teacher collaboration can make each drop of instruction the most dynamic and effectual approach to educating English learners.

REFERENCES

Elmore, R. F. (2000). *Building a new structure for school leadership.* Retrieved from http://www.ashankerinst.org/Downloads/building.pdf
McLaughlin, M. W., & Talbert, J. E. (2001). *Professional communities and the work of high school teaching.* Chicago, IL: University of Chicago Press.
Wilson, S. M., & Berne, J. (1999). Teacher learning and the acquisition of professional knowledge: An examination of research on contemporary professional development. *Review of Research in Education, 24,* 173-209.

ACKNOWLEDGMENTS

We would like to extend our gratitude to the authors who generously contributed to this volume, all of whom shared their experiences, insights, and results with collaborative teaching practices as well as their critical ideas to create successful learning environments for English language learners. As a result, we were able to document how authentic and innovative inclusive policies and collaborative practices for English language learners throughout the United States and abroad have made an impact on both teachers and students and identified an array of successes and challenges that were the outcomes of teacher collaboration.

We would also like to thank our friends and colleagues at Molloy College, Rockville Centre, New York, who continually support and encourage our scholarship efforts.

This project would not have been possible without the support of the staff at Information Age Publishing, to whom we would like to express our sincere appreciation for making the creating of this volume both enjoyable and successful.

Last but not least, we are truly grateful for the ongoing support of our families and friends who sustain and applaud our endeavors, no matter what.

PART I

**CONCEPTUAL FRAMEWORKS
AND MODELS OF COLLABORATION**

CHAPTER 1

BILINGUAL STUDENTS WITHIN INTEGRATED COMPREHENSIVE SERVICES

Collaborative Strategies

**Martin Scanlan, Elise Frattura,
Kurt A. Schneider, and Colleen A. Capper**

Historically, education has been a practice of norming groups of students based on specific disability, language, or student behavior. At the outset, we want to be clear about two premises. Our first premise is that language is an asset. Students from culturally and linguistically diverse backgrounds who develop bilingualism are better served than students who only gain fluency in English. Therefore, simply labeling these students *English language learners* or students with *limited English proficiency* is problematic because they define these students solely in terms of acquiring English. Multilingualism is implicitly devalued. This runs counter to the overwhelming evidence across numerous studies that multilingualism promotes cognitive outcomes associated with achievement (Adesope, Lavin, Thompson, & Ungerleider, 2010). In this chapter we employ the label *bilingual* to reference these students, which implicitly values linguistic diversity, emphasizing the growth in learning two languages. It does not diminish the importance of focusing on developing oral and written fluency as well as literacy in English, but frames mastering registers of academic English as a necessary, but insufficient educational goal.

Our second premise is that schools should design service delivery models that are integrated and comprehensive. This design counters historical approaches that orchestrate services for students within our schools under the umbrella of *programs*. Programmatic approaches are inefficient and ineffective, place undue burdens on individual students, and impede the capacity of adults in schools to meet the diversity of student needs. Integrated and comprehensive service delivery raise the capacity of the range of educators to accommodate student differences and do this in a manner that minimizes student isolation and curricular fragmentation.

These two premises frame our approach to this chapter. We explicitly take an asset-orientation to culturally and linguistically diverse students by affirming their (potential) bilingualism, and explicitly affirm their membership in our school communities by asserting that support services for these students should be structured in integrated and comprehensive manners. We begin by contrasting programmatic and integrated service delivery for bilingual students.

DISCIPLINE-SPECIFIC PROGRAM MODELS VERSUS INTEGRATED SERVICE DELIVERY MODELS

As we have addressed in earlier writings (Frattura & Topinka, 2006), programmatic service delivery models insidiously extend inequities:

> We as educators consistently facilitate societal oppression through educational practices in support of separateness and then mystify it in nondiscrimination acts that often discriminate through the very application of their regulations; that is, in school systems across our country, we have constructed a normed group of students whom we label "general education students." By the very nature of the title, we also have defaulted to another group of students, loosely labeled as non–general education students. Non–general education students are those students who do not meet the criteria of academic, language, physical, emotional, social, or behavioral success of the normed or dominant group, the general education students. Consequently, when a student has deviated from the dominant group, we as an educational society look for another subculture in which to track and marginalize the student who does not meet the normed parameters. Yet, the most startling fact is that throughout the years we continue to increase the number of students that we send to the sidelines of our educational institutions (Thurlow, Elliott, & Ysseldyke, 1998; U.S. Department of Education,

2000; Ysseldyke, 2001; Zhang & Katsiyannis, 2002). Such programs include, but are not limited to, special education programs, at-risk programs, English as a second language (ESL) programs, teenage parent programs, reading and math programs, Title I, and so forth. (pp. 327-328)

Often such types of social oppression are created through *program models* that may impede the array of educational needs of children who are and are not bilingual. Common characteristics of program models include:

- overlooking the individual needs of students by fitting students to a specific *program;*
- separating students with language needs from their nonbilingual peers and from core teaching and learning;
- exceeding natural proportions of students with language needs in one classroom compared to those without English language needs within the school and classrooms;
- fragmenting students' daily schedule by moving them from location to location to receive services and expecting the child to synthesize the information;
- isolating teachers and inhibiting the sharing of expertise between general education and bilingual staff; and
- requiring bilingual students to attend specific schools.

Conversely, a proactive system of supports is grounded in the understanding that ESL services are not a location. Therefore, the bilingual teachers are aligned with a range of differing support staff (Title I, at-risk, special education, and so on) by grade level in full collaboration with general education teachers to bring appropriate instructional supports to each child in an integrated environment. Resources are allocated for the development of teacher capacity rather than the institutionalization of bilingual resource assistance as permanent band-aids to or replacements for continuous staff development.

By contrast to program models, common characteristics of integrated service models include the following:

- considering the range of learners within every classroom and grade/cross grades;
- integrating to core teaching and learning seamlessly;
- eliminating classrooms/schools that are set aside for labeled kids— all schools and classrooms allow for flexible learning communities for all children;

- supporting and building on culturally relevant curriculum and instructional practices;
- designing service delivery based on the principle of universal access, whereby curriculum is differentiated for the needs of all students at the design stage (as opposed to being designed to serve a narrow range of learners and retrofitted to accommodate student differences afterwards);
- proactively supporting students who do not otherwise qualify to receive an education that meets their needs;
- requiring teachers and staff to share knowledge and expertise with each other and their students; and
- providing students who are bilingual with services from neighborhood peers or with a school of choice (In other words, not requiring students who are bilingual to go some place else in the district or in the school to get services).

COLLABORATIVE PRACTICES THAT PROMOTE INCLUSIVE SERVICE DELIVERY FOR BILINGUAL STUDENTS

Having established the contrast between programmatic and integrated approaches to service delivery, we turn to explore in greater detail how collaborative practices, including but not limited to team teaching, promote educational excellence for bilingual students. Brisk's (2006) conceptual framework for quality schooling provides a useful lens for identifying these. Building from the premise that bilingualism is an asset, Brisk identified three responsibilities of school communities for effectively educating bilingual students: (a) cultivating language proficiency to academic grade level, (b) ensuring access to high quality curriculum within effective teaching and learning environments, and (c) promoting the sociocultural integration of all students. We weave together these three dimensions, discussing the requisite knowledge, skills, and dispositions of teachers, and how these are supported by collaborative practices.

Cultivating Language Proficiency

Schools are responsible for cultivating language proficiency. An integrated and comprehensive approach to service delivery frames this responsibility as shared by the faculty and staff at large, not merely the responsibility of bilingual specialists. While some language support models (e.g., developmental bilingual and dual language) promote bilingualism, all language support models attempt to cultivate proficiency in English. Comparing and contrasting these approaches is beyond the scope of this chapter; here we focus on cultivating English language proficiency.

Most fundamentally, to support bilingual students in their dual tasks of developing both language and content, all teachers need to recognize their role as language teachers (de Jong & Harper, 2008; Wong Fillmore & Snow, 2000). In other words, when teaching math, science, art, or other subjects, one is also teaching language. Effectively teaching language requires specific knowledge and skills. To begin, teachers need an understanding of the basic units of language (e.g., phonemes, morphemes, words, and sentences) and component parts of words (e.g., root, suffix, and prefix).

Teachers also need to understand that language learning is not a linear process, but instead is developed in a range of situational contexts and requires support across the curriculum (Gibbons, 2002). Developing proficiency involves learning new registers of text. Different registers are comprised of particular topics, the relationship between speaker and listener (or reader and writer), and the channels of communication. Generally speaking, developing English proficiency involves mastering both a conversational register and an academic English register. Students from linguistically diverse homes often develop fluency in conversational English relatively quickly (within 2 years), as opposed to academic English, which takes longer (5 to 7 years) (American Educational Research Association, 2004).

Scarcella (2003) described academic English as a register associated with the disciplines and involving specific tasks including "reading abstracts, getting down the key ideas from lectures, and writing critiques, summaries, annotated bibliographies, reports, case studies, research projects, expository essays" (p. 9). By designating specific class time to English language development and developmentally tailoring this to the specific students, teachers promote academic English (Genesee, Lindholm-Leary, Saunders, & Christian, 2006). The related skills include teaching vocabulary in context and providing opportunities to practice and receive feedback on new vocabulary and teaching reading comprehension strategies.

Collaborative practices help teachers cultivate language proficiency in general, and academic English in particular. Since academic English needs to develop in the content areas, general education teachers must play a central role in fostering this. However, these teachers benefit from consultative and coteaching arrangements with colleagues who may have more extensive expertise in bilingual and bicultural education. Instead of simplifying tasks or reducing the curriculum, such arrangements can help classroom teachers scaffold students as they develop language proficiency

(Gibbons, 2002). Such collaborative practices are essential so that students develop language proficiency within linguistically heterogeneous settings. As Wong Fillmore and Snow (2000) asserted, to develop academic English, students "must interact directly and frequently with people who know the language well enough to reveal how it works and how it can be used" (p. 24). In addition to directly supporting English language proficiency, this collaboration, when possible, should simultaneously support native language fluency, since research shows that native language literacy promotes the development of English language proficiency (Goldenberg, 2008; Slavin & Cheung, 2005; United Nations Educational Scientific and Cultural Organization, 1953).

Ensuring Access to Quality Teaching and Learning Environments

Hand in hand with promoting language proficiency, schools are responsible for providing bilingual students access to quality teaching and learning environments (Brisk, 2006). As we have discussed, students from linguistically diverse backgrounds have the dual task of gaining proficiency in a new language while also learning content matter. In the same way that they work together to support language proficiency, classroom teachers (who enjoy more expertise in content knowledge) benefit from working alongside bilingual-bicultural colleagues (who enjoy more expertise in methodologies to make these content accessible).

Structuring language supports in manners that allow bilingual students—working alongside their monolingual classmates—to remain in the general education setting helps ensure that they receive ample educational opportunities in terms of the core curriculum, optimal instruction, and appropriate assessment. This is critically important, as evidence shows that these students are disproportionately denied access to the highest quality teachers, educational facilities, and curricular, instructional and assessment resources (Gandara, Rumberger, Maxwell-Jolly, & Callahan, 2003).

Access starts, but does not end, with physical inclusion in the classroom. Instead, instruction needs to be organized in a manner that ensures that bilingual students receive comprehensible input—namely, that the content matter is presented in a manner that they can understand. Specific strategies for organizing instruction, such as the Sheltered Instruction Observation Protocol (SIOP) framework (Echevarria & Graves, 2011; Echevarria & Hasbrouck, 2009; Himmel & Short, 2009), allow teachers to make content accessible to students who are at various levels of English proficiency. Equally important are the expectations that teachers hold for the learning. As Rothenberg and Fisher (2007) stated, "Far too often, teachers hold their English language learners to lower standards, accept inferior work, and make excuses for students' proficiency levels and achievement" (p. 12).

Sociocultural Integration

Sociocultural integration is a final dimension to quality schooling for bilingual students (Brisk, 2006). Sociocultural factors create a context in which students live and influence their beliefs, attitudes, behaviors, practices, and resources (Goldenberg, Rueda, & August, 2008). When schools take these factors into consideration, they can promote student engagement and participation.

In addition, theoretical and practical dimensions of differentiating instruction and providing culturally responsive teaching are complimentary (Santamaria, 2009). This complimentarity points to the overlap in strategies that teachers employ to reach the diversity of learners in their classrooms. Moreover, language is inextricably connected to the social contexts and situations in which we learn and grow (Gibbons, 2002). By respecting and integrating the vernacular varieties of English (different registers) as well as the plurality of languages spoken by children, their families, and their communities, schools approach language as an asset (Wong Fillmore, & Snow, 2000).

ICS for Bilingual Students: An Illustrative Vignette

We began this chapter with the premises that language is an asset, and that the supports for culturally and linguistically diverse students need to be provided through integrated and comprehensive service (ICS) delivery methods. We then described how collaborative practices meet bilingual students' linguistic, academic, and sociocultural needs. In this final section, we turn to present data from a case study illustrating ICS for bilingual students.

Since the implementation of ICS as a result of the Stoughton Area School District's Strategic Plan, a multiyear process has been underway to shift from *programs* to *services* (Stoughton Area School District, 2011). This delivery model resulted in a service delivery overhaul, moving from a situation in which nearly 95% of services were being delivered in self-contained, segregated, pullout classrooms, to one in which support services are fully delivered in the general education classroom through a collaborative model between *learning strategy teachers* (who have bilingual/bicultural and/or English as a second language training) and classroom teachers. The outcomes of this overhaul have transformed service delivery profoundly:

- All students have access to the general education research-based curriculum.
- Bilingual students are taught by most highly trained teachers.
- Classrooms are heterogeneous across multiple dimensions of diversity.
- Teachers use a wide range of techniques to optimize student learning, including coteaching, flexible grouping, and data-based decision making.

Based on delivering services in a more integrated and comprehensive manner, student learning outcomes have significantly improved. For instance, 3 years ago the proficiency levels in Stoughton averaged 45%. These have grown to 73%, a net increase of 28%. Further disaggregating the data between elementary and secondary levels, elementary averages have increased from 65% to 78% while secondary averages have increased from 30% to 66%. Bilingual students have benefited in multiple ways. Not only do they have better access to the content that is assessed through state-mandated standardized testing requirements, but further, they have greatly increased opportunities to interact with the content language with their peers in social and academic situations. This results in consistent, naturally-provided formative feedback that is necessary for mastery.

In addition to language acquisition, it is important to support the mastery of subject matter content. Working collaboratively with classroom teachers, learning strategy teachers assist classroom teachers with planning thoughtful and meaningful differentiated lessons whereby unique strategies are integrated into lesson plans. The additional adult support that is provided to a classroom on a particular day is based upon the data-driven needs of the students and the particulars of the lesson. This flexible scheduling results in support staff being deployed to work in classrooms based upon the individual needs of students, not based upon predetermined and inflexible schedules that are often developed at the onset of a school year or the beginning of a semester break. Such scheduling also forces staff to decide thoughtfully on a daily basis the varying coteaching model that is needed based upon the lesson (Friend & Burusck, 2009) and the needs of the students, rather than implementing a team teaching approach to each and every classroom and lesson every day. It has also lead to greater ownership by classroom teachers for all students, ending the *my* and *your* student references, to now being statements of *our* students.

Finally, for students to increase language acquisition and content knowledge, they need to be treated holistically. One way to do this is to provide ample first language support. Additional first language support is helpful if successfully integrated into service delivery models. In Stoughton, this allows students—particularly those entering schools and classrooms in the middle of development years—to have smoother transitions and reduce classroom anxieties. Having staff that speak native languages also assists parents with engagement through verbal and written translations. Treating students holistically, particularly providing first language support that increases parent engagement, promotes improved student achievement.

CONCLUSION

In this chapter we have argued that students from culturally and linguistically diverse backgrounds are integral members of school communities. They can be well served when their linguistic heritages are affirmed as assets and when the support services they need are delivered in integrated and comprehensive manners. Effectively educating bilingual students includes cultivating their language proficiency to academic grade level, ensuring their access to high quality curriculum within effective teaching and learning environments, and promoting their sociocultural integration. Collaborative strategies are central to this. Collaboration occurs within schools amongst teachers, staff, and administrators, and also extends beyond schools to networks of supports with families and community agencies.

REFERENCES

Adesope, O. O., Lavin, T., Thompson, T., & Ungerleider, C. (2010). A systematic review and meta-analysis of the cognitive correlates of bilingualism. *Review of Educational Research, 80*, 207-245.

American Educational Research Association. (2004). English language learner: Boosting academic achievement. *AERA Research Points, 2*(1), 1-4.

Brisk, M. E. (2006). *Bilingual education: From compensatory to quality schooling*. Mahwah, NJ: Earlbaum.

Capper, C. A., & Frattura, E. (2009). *Meeting the needs of students of all abilities: How leaders go beyond inclusion* (2nd ed.). Thousand Oaks, CA: Corwin Press.

de Jong, E. J., & Harper, C. (2008). ESL is good teaching "plus." In M. E. Brisk (Ed.), *Language, culture, and community in teacher education* (pp. 127-148). Mahwah, NJ: Erlbaum.

Echevarria, J., & Graves, A. (2011). *Sheltered content instruction: Teaching English learners with diverse abilities*. Boston, MA: Pearson.

Echevarria, J., & Hasbrouck, J. (2009). *Response to Intervention and English learners*. Washington, DC: Center for Research on the Educational Achievement and Teaching of English Language Learners.

Frattura, E., & Capper, C. (2006). Segregated programs versus integrated comprehensive service delivery for all learners: Underlying principles and implications for school leaders. *Remedial and Special Education, 27*, 355-364.

Frattura, E., & Topinka, C. (2006). Theoretical underpinnings of separate educational programs the social justice challenge continues. *Education and Urban Society, 38*, 327-344.

Friend, M., & Burusck, W. (2009). *Including children with special needs: A practical guide for teachers* (5th ed.). Boston, MA: Allyn & Bacon.

Gandara, P., Rumberger, R., Maxwell-Jolly, J., & Callahan, R. (2003). English learners in California schools: Unequal resources, unequal outcomes. *Educational Policy Analysis Archives, 11*(36), 1-54.

Genesee, F., Lindholm-Leary, K., Saunders, W., & Christian, D. (Eds.). (2006). *Educating English language learners: A synthesis of research*. New York, NY: Cambridge University Press.

Gibbons, P. (2002). *Scaffolding language, scaffolding learning: Teaching second language learners in the mainstream classroom*. Portsmouth, NH: Heinemann.

Goldenberg, C. (2008, Summer). Teaching English language learners: What the research does—and does not—say. *American Educator,* 8-23, 42-44.

Goldenberg, C., Rueda, R., & August, D. (2008). Sociocultural contexts and literacy development. In D. August & T. Shanahan (Eds.), *Developing reading and writing in second-language learners: Lessons from the report of the National Literacy Panel on language-minority children and youth* (pp. 95-129). New York, NY: Routledge.

Himmel, J., & Short, D. (2009). *Using the SIOP model to improve middle school science instruction*. Washington, DC: Center for Research on the Educational Acievement and Teaching of English Language Learners.

Rothenberg, C., & Fisher, D. (2007). *Teaching English language learners: A differentiated approach*. Upper Saddle River, NJ: Pearson.

Santamaria, L. (2009). Culturally responsive differentiated instruction: narrowing gaps between best pedagogical practices benefiting all learners. *Teachers College Record, 111*, 214-247.

Scarcella, R. (2003). *Academic English: A conceptual framework* (Technical Report No. 2003-1). Irvine, CA: University of California Linguistic Minority Research Institute.

Slavin, R. E., & Cheung, A. (2005). A synthesis of research on language of reading instruction for English language learners. *Review of Educational Research, 75*, 247-284.

Stoughton Area School District. (2011). *Strategic planning*. Retrieved from http://www.stoughton.k12.wi.us/our.cfm?subpage=917567

Thurlow, M. L., Elliott, J. L., & Ysseldyke, J. E. (1998). *Testing students with disabilities: Practical strategies for complying with district and state requirements*. Thousand Oaks, CA: Corwin Press.

United Nations Educational Scientific and Cultural Organization. (1953). *The use of vernacular languages in education*. Paris, France: Author.

U.S. Department of Education. (2000). *To assure the free public education of all children with disabilities*. Twenty-second annual report to Congress on the implementation of the Individuals with Disabilities Education Act. Washington, DC: Author.

Volonino, V., & Zigmond, N. (2007). Promoting research-based practices through inclusion? *Theory into Practice, 46*, 291-300.

Wong Fillmore, L., & Snow, C. (2000). *What teachers need to know about language*. Washington, DC: ERIC Clearinghouse on Languages and Linguistics.

Ysseldyke, J. (2001). Reflections on a career: 25 years of research on assessment and instruction decision making. *Exceptional Children, 67*, 295-309.

Zhang, D., & Katsiyannis, A. (2002). Minority representation in special education: A persistent challenge. *Remedial and Special Education, 21*, 180-187.

CHAPTER 2

MAINSTREAM AND ELL TEACHER PARTNERSHIPS

A Model of Collaboration

Angela B. Bell and Anne B. Walker

Across the United States, many English language learner (ELL) teachers serve their students in the mainstream classroom through a pull-out, push-in, or coteaching model. However, an essential element is often missing in these models: effective collaboration between the mainstream and ELL teacher. The research literature suggests collaboration between mainstream and ELL teachers is vital to the academic achievement of ELLs (Dove & Honigsfeld, 2010; Gottlieb, 2006; Walker, Shafer, & Iiams, 2004). In such collaboration, the ELL teacher contributes knowledge of second language acquisition and teaching strategies for language and academic content, whereas the mainstream teacher contributes knowledge of grade-level curriculum and standards. This combined knowledge allows for strategic planning and instruction.

THE CHALLENGE OF COLLABORATION

Collaboration can be challenging to establish or to sustain, as it is a dynamic and complex process heavily dependent on situational context

---

Coteaching and Other Collaborative Practices in the EFL/ESL Classroom:
Rationale, Research, Reflections, and Recommendations, pp. 15–25
Copyright © 2012 by Information Age Publishing
All rights of reproduction in any form reserved.

and participants (Friend & Cook, 2010; John-Steiner & Mahn, 1996). Collaboration will be particularly difficult to achieve, for example, if a general education teacher believes the ELL teacher should have the main responsibility for ELLs rather than embracing a shared responsibility. Collaboration depends upon factors such as the role of the participants (voluntary or involuntary) and the extent to which participants have shared goals and objectives (John-Steiner & Mahn, 1996).

Friend and Cook (2010) also emphasized the need for (a) personal commitment, (b) effective communication and problem solving skills, and (c) logistical considerations such as scheduling and planning time for collaboration. Further, Bean (2009) found administrator support to be also essential. Barriers that can prevent effective teacher collaboration from occurring include:

1. A lack of effort and an attitude that collaboration is not worthwhile (Davidson, 2006);
2. Personality clashes between teachers (Friend & Cook);
3. Different philosophies of teaching (Arkoudis, 2006);
4. Power struggles among teachers (Creese, 2005; Friend & Cook; McClure & Cahnmann-Taylor, 2010); and
5. Negative attitudes toward having to teach ELLs in the mainstream classroom (Walker, Shafer, & Iiams, 2004).

Can meaningful collaboration take place given the previously identified challenges? The purpose of this chapter is to illuminate findings from a grounded theory study which answers this question.

THE STUDY

We examined ELL and mainstream teacher collaboration at three urban elementary schools in one school district in the eastern United States. The schools were chosen because of their reputation among area principals for promoting collaboration. Each school utilized a professional learning community (PLC) framework in which teams of educators met on a regular basis to define, create, and discuss goals for student achievement in a systematic, structured format (DuFour & Eaker, 1998). Although the three schools did not share identical demographics (see Table 2.1), this did not appear to be a factor in the results of the study.

Participants included five mainstream teachers, three ELL teachers, and three administrators. In the study, teachers were observed for a period of 6 months during teaching, planning, and meeting times in

Table 2.1. Demographics of Schools Participating in Study

	Blue Creek School	Red Oak School	Green Leaf School
Total K-6 enrollment	919	986	673
Total K-6 ELLs	87	466	318
ELL % of total enrollment	9.47%	47.26%	47.25%
Ethnicity			
Asian/Pacific Islander	23.50%	13.18%	22.00%
Black	2.83%	5.68%	8.02%
Hispanic	8.81%	48.88%	50.97%
White	58.11%	25.46%	14.26%
Other	6.75%	6.80%	4.61%
Free and reduced lunch rate	13.49%	55.82%	64.19%
Percentage of ELLs passing English	97%	86%	91%
Percentage of ELLs passing mathematics	93%	77%	84%

order to document the collaborative practices that occurred. Additionally, interviews and a brainstorming session were conducted with the teachers, the school principals, and a district administrator.

A Model of Collaboration

As a result of this research, we propose a model for effective ELL/mainstream teacher collaboration (see Figure 2.1) that can be used by teachers, administrators, or policy makers interested in implementing or improving such collaboration by better understanding the contextual factors and processes in operation. The model consists of six components:

1. The rationale for collaborating;
2. The core phenomenon or the participants' shared definition of collaboration;
3. The collaborative practices that occurred between the ELL and mainstream teacher;
4. The contextual factors that made collaboration possible;
5. The barriers that existed; and
6. The outcomes made possible by the combination of factors and processes at work.

Rationale
Standards
Assessment
Meeting ELLs' needs
Curriculum
Administrations' expectations
Accountability
Goals
"Two heads are better than one"

Core Phenomenon
Mainstream and ELL Teacher Collaboration

What is collaboration?
Common goals and purpose
Planning to meet students' needs
Supporting each other
Sharing ideas/resources/responsibility
Assessing
Working together; Communicating

Contextual Conditions
Strategic placement of ELLs
Service delivery models
Teacher personalities
Teacher buy-in
Enabling teacher leaders
# of classes for ELL teacher
ELL teacher classroom placement
ELL teacher part of planning team
Common standards;
Common routines
Shared goals
Scheduled time for meetings
Administrative support
Culture of collaboration
Experience

Practices
Formal/ Informal Continuum
Discussing/Planning for students' needs
Email, Sticky notes
Before/After school, In the hallways
Teams, Committees
Grade-level planning meetings, PLCs
Common language
Learning from each other
Different strengths
Setting goals
Monday afternoon planning
Bringing in community/culture
Sharing, Give and take
Problem solving
Not territorial
Supporting each other, Scaffolding
Curriculum mapping

Barriers
Time
Scheduling
Logistics
Personalities

Outcomes
Making cross-curricular connections
Community
Inspiration
Enhancing instruction
Student achievement
More purposeful/meaningful work
Interactive notebook; shared drive; calendar
Helping students & each other
Not mine or yours, but "our" students
Professional growth

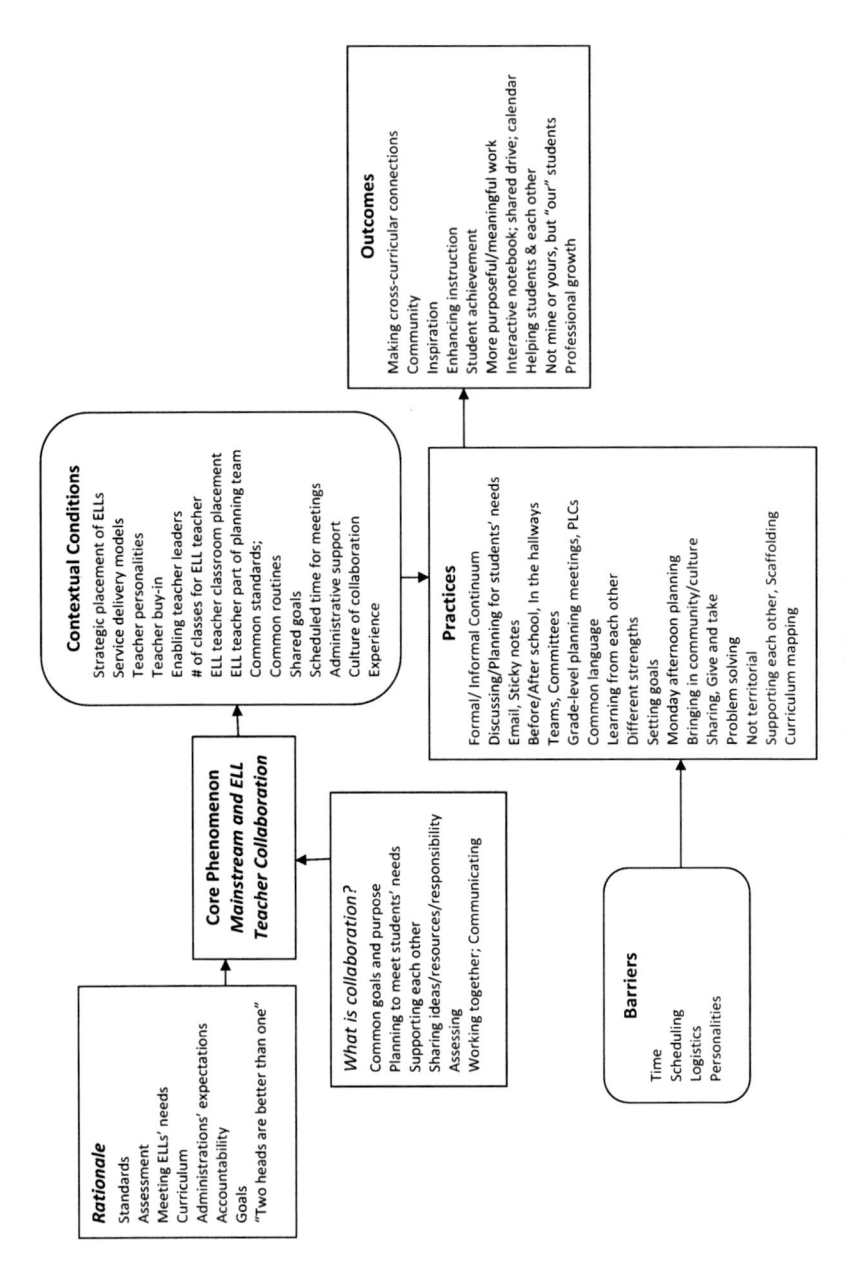

Figure 2.1. Model of mainstream and ELL teacher collaboration.

Findings from this study—as depicted in Figure 2.1—demonstrated that effective collaboration between mainstream and ELL teachers can exist if conditions support it. The following section describes each of the model's components in detail.

Rationale

Teachers are more likely to collaborate if they see a genuine need for it. Like in most U.S. schools, teachers and administrators in the study were concerned with accountability and meeting the needs of ELLs. There was an emphasis on using grade-level standards to teach and to assess students in the district, which led educators to teach language through content, and as a result, teachers needed to understand what was going on in each other's classroom.

Though there was a districtwide plan to implement PLCs, teachers in the study also realized the benefits of collaborating outside the PLC framework. Several teachers commented that they collaborated "because two heads are better than one." One teacher explained that working with more than one person meant "we can share the load" and "play to each others' strengths." With the given accountability measures, teachers found benefits in working together to strategize how to meet students' needs.

Core Phenomenon

The core phenomenon being investigated was collaboration between mainstream and ELL teachers. Participants across school sites shared common ideas of what it meant to collaborate, including (a) having common goals, (b) sharing a purpose, and (c) planning to meet students' needs. Frequently teachers mentioned they worked together and communicated with each other; shared ideas, resources, and responsibilities; and overall, offered support to each other. Participants also indicated that collaboration consisted of mutually assessing students and using the data to respond to their students' needs.

Contextual Conditions

Even though different in size, diversity, number of ELLs, and percentage of students receiving free or reduced lunch, the three schools shared many common contextual conditions. First, all participating administrators genuinely supported their teachers. During summer planning, many factors were taken into consideration to optimize collaboration, including: strategic placement of ELLs, service delivery models, teacher personalities, teacher buy-in, and logistics (classroom location and ELL teacher caseload).

At Blue Creek Elementary, the principal met with the ELL teachers and teams to ensure strategic student placement. Together, they contemplated the ELL service model when assigning ELLs to mainstream classrooms. For example, after attending a summer literacy workshop, the ELL teacher and a third grade mainstream teacher voluntarily decided to work together as a team to implement the instructional practices they had just acquired. The teachers asked the administrators to schedule third grade ELLs into the mainstream teacher's class, and to schedule the ELL teacher into the language arts period, so they could coteach.

When determining student placement, teacher personalities and teaching styles were also considered to ensure a sound relationship could be established between the ELL and mainstream teacher. Scheduling and routines were deliberated, so ELLs would not miss crucial content instruction in a pull-out model, and so teachers could push in to classes during specific instructional times. Logistics—such as the proximity of the ELL teacher's classroom to the mainstream classrooms and how many classes the ELL teacher would be responsible for—were also carefully planned.

Administrators maintained high expectations for accountability and were active participants in the school's PLCs. Meeting times were structured and included an agenda, a note-taker, and a facilitator. There were also norms to follow; for example, at Red Oak School, teachers met at the beginning of the school year to establish team norms and decided on the following rules:

- Appreciate one another's expertise.
- Engage fully in all learning experiences.
- Invest in your own learning.
- Open your mind to new ways of thinking.
- Unite in purpose to improve student learning.

These norms were posted at the top of the PLC agenda. In addition, there was a schedule they adhered to during the current meeting, a list of actions from the previous meeting, and a list for future discussions. At Green Leaf School, the note-taker maintained a professional learning communities team learning log, which included team discussions in response to the following four questions (DuFour, DuFour, Eaker, & Many, 2006):

1. What do we want our students to know?
2. How will we know if and when they have learned it?
3. How will we respond when they don't?
4. How will we meet the needs of those who "already know?" (p. 91)

During PLC meetings, held on a regularly scheduled basis, the ELL teacher and mainstream teacher(s) were part of a planning team.

Together, teachers planned long- and short-term goals for their students by analyzing assessment data. The principal of Red Oak said collaboration at his school "should be figuring out for an individual student what they need regardless of who's working with them." He added that his teachers should be "keeping track of how students are doing and using the time that they are together as a team to share strategies, think through and better understand the curriculum, and brainstorming, troubleshooting with certain students."

In each of the schools, teachers noted the emergence of a *culture of collaboration*. Administrators and educators credited each other for the trust and camaraderie which helped create a positive work environment. One administrator compared collaboration to a dance. She stated, "It might not be your time to move; it's got to be a give and take; it's got to be a very nice dance between the two of you." A teacher described the culture of her school remarking, "You can learn from each other. There is no territory. There's no this is *my* classroom—this is *our* classroom ... so there's this inclusiveness ... we're going to treat each other respectfully."

Camaraderie between ELL and mainstream teachers was also evident during observations. Teachers were seen engaged in discussions before and after school, in the halls, and during planning. During PLCs, the conversations were serious and focused; after school, however, ELL and mainstream teachers were observed laughing and planning for social events together.

Experience with collaboration was also a factor contributing to success. Some participants were in their first year of teaching, whereas others had over 30 years of experience. Teachers new to collaboration were supported by other teachers with more experience. However, teachers with more experience also learned from the more novice teachers. One ELL teacher with over 15 years of experience revealed she enjoyed learning new techniques a first year teacher brought with her from her university experiences. What was more important than how many years teachers had been in education was how long the teachers had collaborated together. For example, one ELL teacher said she and another teacher, who have been working together for a number of years, created a calendar on the school's shared drive where they could manage what was happening in the mainstream teacher's class. The teachers, regardless of years of experience, welcomed collaboration, and those who had collaborated for a longer time, found it became easier.

Barriers

The teachers in the study mentioned barriers to collaboration that have also been frequently documented in collaborative research, most critically, a lack of time to collaborate. Despite all of the effort the participants invested in planning time, scheduling, and logistics, challenges still existed. Teachers had so many responsibilities that it was often difficult for them to find time to meet to discuss students' needs. Scheduling remained a hardship in some instances. For example, one teacher did not have common planning time with another teacher and found it difficult to collaborate with him.

Logistics proved to be yet another barrier. For instance, one ELL teacher's classroom was on the first floor, and the first grade teachers were on another level. She was less likely to communicate with the first grade teachers than she was with the third grade teacher, whose classroom was a few doors down the hall. Finally, although personalities did not appear to be an issue among the teachers in this study, one participant indicated if the teachers did not get along as well as they did, collaboration would be difficult.

Practices

Both barriers and contextual conditions affected the collaborative practices, the actions and interactions between the teachers, as demonstrated by the arrows in the model. At the three participating schools, informal and formal collaboration practices were perceived on a continuum. Informal collaboration often occurred *on the fly* in order to address immediate concerns. Teachers would typically inform the ELL teacher of schedule changes or ask questions about students before or after school or during transition times. As one ELL teacher described her strategy for on-the-fly collaboration, "I carry Post-It notes with me all the time," and then "confirm things over email." Formal collaboration included planned, scheduled events such as PLCs (DuFour & Eaker, 1998) and other meetings where teachers systematically designed instruction together using curriculum maps and assessment data to identify language and content objectives. Additional planning teams and committees, not as formal as PLCs, also met to discuss events such as field trips.

Outcomes

Teachers and administrators in the study identified many positive outcomes of collaboration. The following is a list of the benefits described at the three schools:

- A sense of community: The *give and take* of collaboration helped create a sense of belonging at the schools. One teacher stated, "I feel like I am a part of something bigger than myself."
- Creative cross-curricular teaching: Because teachers from different content and specialty areas collaborated, they had opportunities to bring innovative ideas to support common goals in their classes.

- Purposeful, meaningful work for teachers and students: The mutual goals teachers set and worked together to achieve helped teachers and students relate to what was happening each day.
- Professional growth for teachers: Teachers developed a *common language* representing terminology and ideology from each other's respective content areas. Teachers also learned strategies and practices from each other that they implemented in different settings. For example, the ELL teacher increased her repertoire of reading strategies as a result of working with a language arts teacher. The math teacher began posting language objectives alongside content objectives after observing the ELL teacher daily repeat that practice. Teachers at Blue Creek also benefitted from discussions during PLCs when they read and reflected upon current scholarly articles related to their practice.
- Enhanced lessons promoting academic achievement for ELLs: By sharing expertise, teachers improved their lessons, which led to increased student achievement. All schools made adequate yearly progress in the year of this study.
- Mutual *ownership* of ELLs: Teachers worked together on common goals for *their* students and assumed joint responsibility for their success.

IMPLICATIONS FOR PRACTICE

Results from this study indicate that collaboration between mainstream and ELL teachers can be successful if the following factors are considered:

1. There must be a compelling rationale for teachers to voluntarily collaborate; it could be based on need (expectations for meeting adequate yearly progress, integration of content and language standards in the curriculum), school philosophy or structure (PLC, shared goals, administrators' expectations), or desire to better their practice (information sharing to improve instruction for ELLs).
2. Teachers and administrators must share a common understanding of the core phenomenon: What does it mean to collaborate? What are the goals and purpose of collaborating?
3. As many of the contextual conditions that foster collaboration must be in place as possible. There are many factors listed on the model that should be addressed before implementing a collaborative approach to teaching between mainstream and ELL teachers.

Consideration must be made in regards to the ELL teacher's caseload, schedule, and service delivery model, as well as to collaborating teachers' personalities and attitudes. Teachers must be afforded time and opportunities to meet, and there should be expectations for what occurs during those meetings. There has to be administrative support in order for effective collaboration to occur. Contextual factors which are not addressed can become barriers to collaboration.

4. Some barriers will remain regardless of sincere attempts to eliminate them. Time is the most difficult barrier to overcome; it requires administrators' support and careful planning to alleviate its negative effects on collaboration.
5. Collaboration practices are impacted by the contextual conditions and barriers at a school. For instance, teachers who have a common planning time may be able to share ideas and support each other's language and content goals during instruction more than teachers who do not have a common planning time.
6. If teachers perceive collaboration to be beneficial, share a common understanding of what it means to collaborate, and have the contextual structures in place to support their actions and interactions among other teachers, the outcome can be successful, effective collaboration.

CONCLUSION

We did not write this chapter to say collaboration is easy. In fact, the model presented (see Figure 2.1) should demonstrate the complexity of the components that promote or prohibit collaborative efforts. By illuminating the issues surrounding collaboration, educators and administrators can address conditions to initiate, sustain, and/or improve collaboration between mainstream and ELL teachers. Attention *must* be given to contextual conditions, barriers and practices in schools; simply saying educators should or must collaborate is not enough to create a successful partnership.

REFERENCES

Arkoudis, S. (2006). Negotiating the rough ground between ESL and mainstream teachers. *The International Journal of Bilingual Education and Bilingualism, 9,* 415-433.

Bean, R. (2009). *The reading specialist: Leadership for the classroom, school, and community* (2nd ed.). New York, NY: The Guilford Press.

Creese, A. (2005). *Teacher collaboration and talk in multilingual classrooms*. Clevedon, England: Multilingual Matters.

Davidson, C. (2006). Collaboration between ESL and content area teachers: How do we know when we are doing it right? *The International Journal of Bilingual Education and Bilingualism, 9*, 454-475.

Dove, M., & Honigsfeld, A. (2010). ESL coteaching and collaboration: Opportunities to develop teacher leadership and enhance student learning. *TESOL Journal, 1*(1), 3-22.

DuFour, R., DuFour, R., Eaker, R., & Many, T. (2006). *Learning by doing: A handbook for professional learning communities at work*. Bloomington, IN: Solution Tree.

DuFour, R., & Eaker, R. (1998). *Professional learning communities at work: Best practices for enhancing student achievement*. Bloomington, IN: Solution Tree.

Friend, M., & Cook, L. (2010). *Interactions: Collaboration skills for school professionals* (6th ed.). Boston, MA: Pearson.

Gottlieb, M. (2006). *Assessing English language learners: Bridges from language proficiency to academic achievement*. Thousand Oaks, CA: Corwin Press.

John-Steiner, V., & Mahn, H. (1996). Sociocultural approaches to learning and development: A Vygotskian framework. *Educational Psychologist, 31*, 191-206.

McClure, G., & Cahnmann-Taylor, M. (2010). Pushing back against push-in: ESOL teacher resistance and the complexities of coteaching. *TESOL Journal, 1*(1), 101-129.

Walker, A., Shafer, J., & Iiams, M. (2004). "Not in my classroom:" Teacher attitudes towards English Language Learners in the mainstream classroom. *NABE Journal of Research and Practice, 2*, 130-160.

CHAPTER 3

INCLUSION OR INTRUSION?

Reculturing Schools for Collaborative ESL Instruction

Clara Lee Brown and Andrea J. Stairs

Before the era of No Child Left Behind (NCLB), English language learners' (ELLs) academic achievement was barely mentioned in the national discourse. Despite federal Title III funding for English as a second language (ESL) programs and mandates arising from *Lau v. Nichols* (1974), schools were not held accountable for ELLs' academic performance. NCLB changed the national education landscape by emphasizing accountability for ELLs' academic progress as a subgroup for the first time, and ELLs' achievement became part of the national discourse (Wiley & Wright, 2004).

With steep sanctions attached to accountability, however, NCLB backfired because it placed immense pressure on mainstream teachers (MTs) to produce learning outcomes without the infrastructure necessary for meeting such demands (Scruggs, Mastropieri, & McDuffie, 2007). For instance, if collaboration between MTs and English as a second language teachers (ETs) is going to occur, all teachers need to be supported with time to coplan and professional development as to how to work together. Schools' lack of capacity forced MTs to feel solely responsible for ELLs. In addition, some MTs view ELLs through a deficit lens, thinking ELLs cannot gain content knowledge while their English is limited (Dove & Honigsfeld, 2010).

Perhaps dynamic relationships between MTs and ETs are rather complicated since ETs are professionally marginalized. Often, they are perceived as supporting ELLs to learn English more so than content and are not considered to have the same authority as the MTs, who teach content-area curricula (Arkoudis, 2006). In addition, many ETs feel isolated within the school building (Dove & Honigsfeld, 2010) and some are unsure how to support MTs (Brown, 2003).

At the same time, mainstream teachers across the country are being evaluated on professional performance based on standardized test scores, including the scores of ELLs. These are high-stakes assessments for students, who may not graduate without passing the state tests, and for teachers, who may not receive a pay increase, or worse, may not be renewed in their teaching positions due to test results. Such existing conditions make collaboration between MTs and ETs even more complex. We recognize these complexities and play on them with the title of this chapter. Do MTs and ETs view their collaborations as inclusive or intrusive? How can schools be recultured so that inclusion is the norm?

In this chapter, we first share our definition of true collaboration among teachers based upon our research and professional experience, and we illustrate how K-12 school cultures are often not conducive to collaboration. Then, we discuss ways to remove roadblocks and strategies for MTs and ETs to achieve true collaboration. We conclude by sharing a consultation model for MTs and ETs that provides pedagogical support to MTs while raising the professional status of ETs and leads to long standing, successful partnerships.

SCHOOL CULTURE AND COLLABORATION

Many definitions exist regarding what collaboration is among teachers. We conceptualize *true collaboration* in schools as believing in a collective purpose and working together to achieve a common goal while recognizing factors that may promote goal achievement (e.g., individual teachers' talents) and addressing factors that could inhibit goal achievement (e.g. power dynamics). True collaboration involves creating a symbiotic relationship among partners and viewing success as dependent upon shared values, commitments, and activities.

As straightforward as our definition may sound, competing paradigms about how to best educate ELLs pose challenges even in identifying a common goal for all teachers involved. Some may believe that the primary goal is to have all ELLs meet the grade-level state content standards as measured by standardized assessments no matter what the investment, and others may assume that the primary goal is for ELLs to learn conversational English as quickly as possible. Some may believe the best way to attain either goal is for ELLs to have intensive, pull-out ESL classes while others may argue that sheltered content instruction is most effective. Complicating identification of a goal, however, is that the English proficiency and background knowledge of ELLs can vary dramatically depending on the school context. Such philosophical disagreements in goal-setting and goal-achieving make true collaboration rather difficult.

Schools have long faced the challenge of developing collaborative cultures. Teaching has frequently been viewed as an individual endeavor, where teachers close their doors and spends their days working with their students in the classroom. When teachers want to collaborate with their colleagues, school schedules and the intensification of teachers' work can get in the way. Additional factors that make collaboration difficult in schools include "competing priorities, limited resources, and lack of professional development" (Walther-Thomas, Korinek, & McLaughlin, 1999, p. 2). Particularly guilty of having less than collaborative school cultures are urban schools, which typically enroll the highest concentrations of ELLs. Research has shown that the working conditions of urban schools are one of the main reasons for teacher attrition (Ingersoll, 2004). This is to teachers' detriment as Hargreaves and Fullan (1998) explained:

> Cultures of collaboration strengthen teachers' sense of common purpose and enable them to interact assertively with external pressures for change—adopting changes that they value, selectively incorporating aspects of them that fit their own purposes, and rejecting ones that are seen as educationally unsound or irrelevant. (p. 4)

RECULTURING OF SCHOOLS FOR TRUE COLLABORATION

In order to create the culture of coteaching and collaboration, reculturing of the school context and discourse is a must. That is, roadblocks to achieving trustworthy collaboration have to be eliminated, yet reculturing the school cannot be achieved without addressing the ways in which MTs perceive their role in collaborating with ETs.

In our work with MTs, we often hear their desire to learn more about teaching ELLs effectively. They also express their frustration since they are responsible for ELLs' learning without being properly supported. Research has shown that collaboration has been looked at as either extra work or additional responsibility (Reeve, 2006; Teemant, Bernhardt, & Rodriguez-Munoz, 1996). MTs, at times, seem resentful toward ELLs and

ETs when they perceive that working with ELLs means providing accommodations they do not know how to implement and feeling little support is available to them. Most teachers with these perceptions feel frustrated and stressed. When teachers are unhappy, they are more likely to do the minimum: teaching to the middle while leaving low and high achieving students behind. It does not mean that this practice is acceptable; unfortunately, that is how teachers' perceptions often affect reality in some classrooms.

Teachers who feel overworked may not have any emotional motivation to enhance instruction for students whom they feel they should not be solely responsible for teaching. To this end, we first advocate supporting MTs emotionally as MTs' emotional involvement can influence the outcome of collaboration with ETs. If MTs join in the reform efforts more willingly because they believe that collaboration is their solution for positive change, meaningful and authentic collaboration can occur. In addition, when MTs are emotionally supported, technical and pedagogical supports become the natural next step, which completes the process of reculturing schools. We present this concept through the illustration in Figure 3.1.

The wooden bucket figure represents the concept of dynamic relationships among key factors in achieving school reculturation. In order for the bucket to hold its content to a maximum capacity, no panels can be

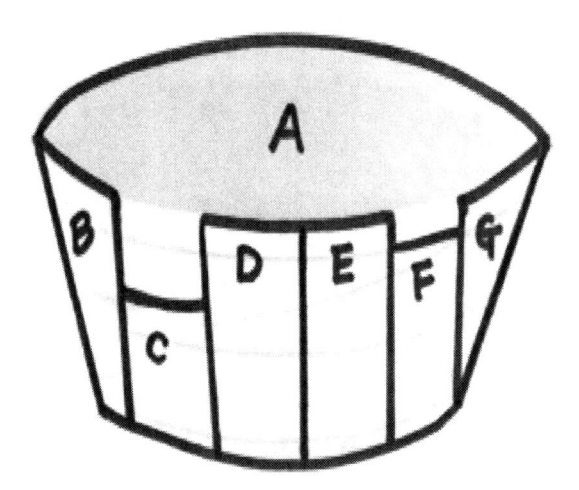

Note: A: reculturing of school, B: mentoring, C: emotional needs of teachers, D: pedagogical support, E: technical support, F: resources, G: professional development.

Figure 3.1. ELL Inclusion through school reculturing.

shorter than the other full length panels. The figure points out that, for instance, school reculturing cannot be fulfilled if there is a lack of resources (F) and emotional support (C) for teachers despite that the fact that sound mentoring (B), pedagogical support (D), technical support (E), and professional development (G) are in place.

Prerequisites

First, roadblocks to collaboration must be addressed if ETs want MTs to share the responsibility of educating ELLs. We, thus, suggest that certain prerequisites be in place for reculturing schools. Some of the prerequisites that we suggest may be viewed as generic in nature and quite obvious to teachers. For example, it is commonly acknowledged that providing MTs with professional development opportunities is critical and that meaningful professional development cannot be achieved through one-time inservice workshops that are prevalent in public schools. Mentoring between novice and veteran teachers has been identified as a way to increase collaboration while ensuring collegiality since novice teachers often do not have to feel insecure about their needs for additional support.

There are other prerequisites for reculturing schools that may be less transparent to all stakeholders. Below, we list six such prerequisites for consideration:

1. *Engage in Honest Dialogue.* Supporting MTs emotionally should start with open conversation, which can take any form of open communication. Having dialogue among stakeholders accomplishes the most fundamental prerequisite for initiating reforms. In so doing, MTs may recognize that their opinions matter and their voices are valued in the process. Administrators need to create opportunities so that MTs can talk about any challenges associated with accommodating ELLs in class for the sake of genuine dialogue. ETs may sit down with the MTs by grade levels or instructional units to ensure intimacy of the forum. Lau vs. Nichols (1974) clearly stated that MTs are responsible for making the curriculum accessible to ELLs; yet some MTs may view this as a burden. Mandating what teachers must do does not translate into how MTs follow the law. ETs and administrators in particular have to acknowledge the pressure that some MTs may feel. After an open dialogue, proper support for MTs can be identified.
2. *Address MTs' Needs.* Identifying individual MTs' needs in-depth is critical in achieving the goal of instructional collaboration at the building level. According to Fullan (2003) and Sparks (2003),

teaching variance within schools represent a greater concern than teaching variance between schools. When individual MTs' needs are addressed, it is more likely that MTs will implement reformative instructional practices.

3. *Provide Time to Practice.* Conducting a needs assessment is crucial, and such efforts have to be on-going. Through sustained practice, innovative approaches to teaching become reality. It takes time for individual teachers to translate knowledge into practice. They need to be supported throughout the entire process to become proficient in collaborating.

4. *Identify Obstacles.* Administrators may anonymously survey MTs and ETs as to their perceived challenges and barriers regarding full collaboration between MTs and ETs. Anonymity can ensure teachers' candid comments without having to worry about power dynamics or retribution. Administrators can compile the list of barriers to effective collaboration among teachers and discuss openly in inservice days through group discussion. During discussion, MTs can zero in on personalized questions but through the third-person point of view. This would help teachers focus on the issues, not on *who said what*, which can easily digress into a personal domain. Discussions at this stage among MTs, ETs, and administrators could center around crystallizing the set of specific problems to be tackled as all stakeholders. Such efforts, thus, have to be followed by the next step since a surface-level discussion only serves as rhetoric and has minimal impact.

5. *Examine Teacher Workload.* In collaboration with both MTs and ETs, administrators should devise an action plan that targets reducing teachers' unnecessary workload. When teachers spend a great amount of time engaging in paperwork, it takes away opportunities for collaboration from teachers who need time with their colleagues. Most critically, overworked teachers may become emotionally burdened and less collaborative. The school culture must support teachers as instructional leaders, not as paper pushers.

6. *Offer Time for Collaboration.* Contact time should be created for coplanning during school hours so that teachers can actually be *collaborating*. There is really no valid substitution for common planning time during school hours. A school conveys what it values when time to collaborate is built into the school day. The act of creating *during school-time coplanning* should be considered as one of the factors that makes true collaboration achievable.

Some of the above suggestions address the technical aspects of supporting teachers achieved through structural and systemic reforms at the district or school level. For example, building common planning time into the school schedule is a part of technical support. Other supports not mentioned above include having resources available in the library media center, such as journals and DVDs related to differentiating instruction and accommodating ELLs. Another provision could be a handbook related to ESL strategies all teachers have in their classrooms so that they can have a ready-to-use resource at their finger tips. Along with addressing MTs' emotional needs, providing technical supports is important in creating a positive environment for effective collaboration to occur.

PEDAGOGICAL SUPPORT FOR MAINSTREAM TEACHERS

When the barriers and roadblocks to collaboration are eliminated or reduced, then reculturing the school will take root because working conditions have become more conducive for collaboration. As a result, teachers will be ready to collectively work to achieve the common goals. Yet, they still need one last leg of support: MTs need the pedagogical know-how of ESL strategies and what better way for approaches for teaching ELLs to be addressed but through MT-ET collaboration.

Although there are various collaboration models (Cook & Friend, 1995; Dove & Honigsfeld, 2010; Vaughn, Schumm, & Arguelles, 1997), we approach MT-ET collaboration slightly differently and offer a *consultation model* (Brown, 2005). We believe that ETs' expertise is under-utilized within the school despite the informal exchanges of opinions/concerns over ELLs that do happen between MTs and ETs. Most important, however, MTs do not seem to take advantage of ETs who have a wealth of knowledge in second language acquisition, ESL strategies, differentiated instruction, assessment modifications, and cross-cultural communication.

The purpose of the consultation model is for ETs to provide expertise to MTs based on individually identified needs. ETs as *consultants* assist MTs with instructional and curricular adaptation strategies to accommodate ELLs. Under the consultation model, the service is delivered to MTs in two ways, directly or indirectly, depending on ETs' involvement with the students. If ETs provide consultation to MTs through instructional planning only, that is indirect consultation, as opposed to direct consultation, which means MTs and ETs teach side by side in the classroom after planning together. In direct consultation, ETs are involved in teaching as well as planning where some MTs need more intensive support from ETs than others. Thus, the delivery model of consultation is decided by factors such as the degree and intensity of the needs for assistance, the number of

ELLs in class, and the level of MTs' working knowledge on accommodating ELLs.

Due to mistaken notions of ESL being considered remedial education, ETs' status is considerably low. As a result, there exists a lack of equal footing for ETs when working with MTs, which is a persistent roadblock for collaboration. One of the major advantages of implementing the consultation model is that the authority imbalance between the two stakeholders is inherently addressed. More important, they become true partners whose shared goal is to accommodate ELLs to the highest degree, as well as to elevate the professional status of ETs.

CONCLUSION

In recent years, much professional discourse has focused on the benefits of teacher collaboration especially in providing inclusion for English language learners. Although it is a step into the right direction, we have to be aware that the discourse of reform can easily fall into symbolic rhetoric if collaborative efforts are carried out haphazardly. Without unwavering convictions from all stakeholders, mainstream teachers may well feel that their space is being infringed upon while ESL teachers may believe that they have become unwanted intruders. As a result, the teachers may revert back to the traditional school culture where each teacher lives in his or her own bubble. We, however, recognize that full inclusion based on true collaboration is a great undertaking that requires changes in behavior and thinking from all teachers and entails multilayer processes. Changing beliefs and behavior are no small matter, but at the same time, we strongly believe that we can achieve a true form of MT-ET collaboration to transform the nature of instruction for ELLs. When such inclusive practices are sustained, everybody wins: Mainstream teachers will feel that they are supported in helping ELLs achieve academic success, and ESL teachers will feel that they are making differences in their students' learning. Most importantly, English language learners will feel that their needs are being addressed and met by both mainstream teachers and ESL teachers.

REFERENCES

Arkoudis, S. (2006). Negotiating the rough ground between ESL and mainstream teachers. *The International Journal of Bilingual Education and Bilingualism, 9*, 415-433.

Brown, C. L. (2003). Who is responsible for English-language learners? A case study from a third-grade classroom [Electronic version]. *Academic Exchange Extra.* Retrieved from http://www.unco.edu/AE-Extra/2003/2/index.html

Brown, C. L. (2005). Ways to help ELLs: ESL teachers as consultants. *Academic Exchange Quarterly, 9,* 255-260.

Cook, L., & Friend, M. (1995). Co-teaching: Guidelines for creating effective practices. *Focus on Exceptional Children, 28*(3), 1-16.

Dove, M., & Honigsfeld, A. (2010). ESL coteaching and collaboration: Opportunities to develop teacher leadership and enhance student learning. *TESOL Journal, 1*(1), 3-22.

Fullan, M. (2003). *The moral imperative of school leadership.* Thousand Oaks, CA: Corwin Press.

Hargreaves, A., & Fullan, M. (1998). *What's worth fighting for out there?* New York, NY: Teachers College Press.

Ingersoll, R. (2004). *Why do high-poverty schools have difficulty staffing their classrooms with qualified teachers?* Washington, DC: Center for American Progress and the Institute for America's Future.

Lau v. Nichols, 414 U.S. 563 (1974).

Reeve, J. (2006). Secondary teacher attitudes toward including English-language learners in mainstream classrooms. *The Journal of Educational Research, 99,* 131-141.

Scruggs, T. E., Mastropieri, M. A., & McDuffie, K. A. (2007). Co-teaching in inclusive classrooms: A metasynthesis of qualitative research. *Exceptional Children, 73,* 392-416.

Teemant, A., Bernhardt, E., & Rodriguez-Munoz, M. (1996). Collaborating with content area teachers: What we need to share. *TESOL Journal, 4*(4), 16-20.

Sparks, D. (2003). Change agent. *Journal of Staff Development, 24*(1), 55-58.

Vaughn, S., Schumm, J. S., & Arguelles, M. E. (1997). The ABCDEs of co-teaching. *Teaching Exceptional Children, 30,* 4-10.

Walther-Thomas, C. S., Korinek, L., & McLaughlin, V. L. (1999). Collaboration to support students' success. *Focus on Exceptional Children, 32*(3), 1-20.

Wiley, T. G., & Wright, W. (2004). Against the undertow: Language-minority education and politics in the age of accountability. *Educational Policy, 18*(1), 142-168.

CHAPTER 4

FIXING THE IMPLEMENTATION GAP

Creating Sustainable Learning Spaces for Successful Coteaching and Collaboration

Anne Dahlman and Patricia Hoffman

LARGE SCALE IMPLEMENTATION OF COTEACHING

In this chapter, we will outline how to implement a large-scale adoption of coteaching practices through a systematic and organic change process. Despite tremendous effort, it continues to be a genuine challenge for educators to implement changes—such as coteaching—in meaningful and sustainable ways. The need to consider the local context, along with the unique needs, strengths, and obstacles, provides an uncommon opportunity for those interested in moving beyond occasional coteaching by isolated pairs of teachers toward systematic implementation of coteaching across a larger group of teachers. Developing the beliefs and structures that create an expectation for collaborative work systemwide is the focus of the ecological, multidimensional framework outlined in this chapter. It employs a top-down, bottom-up approach based on work by Bronfenbrenner (1979) and further informed by research in organizational and educational change (Buckingham & Clifton, 2001; Buckingham &

Coteaching and Other Collaborative Practices in the EFL/ESL Classroom:
Rationale, Research, Reflections, and Recommendations, pp. 37–47
Copyright © 2012 by Information Age Publishing
All rights of reproduction in any form reserved.

Coffman, 1999; Fullan, 2001, 2010) as well as through the authors' extensive staff development work and program evaluations with large, small, rural, and urban school districts.

Research shows that isolated pockets of individuals generally cannot support long-term change; rather, it takes 80% of educators implementing an instructional approach to make a perceivable difference in the learning outcomes of students (Reeves, 2008, 2010). Such a change requires both top-down leadership and bottom-up capacity building. Collective capacity building calls for resolute leaders who can envision the big picture and focus of reform while creating collective ownership of the new initiative among stakeholders (Fullan, 2010).

CHANGING THE MIND-SET

A key component in wide-scale adoption of coteaching is developing the understanding and expectation that it cannot be implemented through a one-shot in-service but rather requires a continuous process and long-term commitment to staff development and collaboration (National Association of Secondary School Principals, 2004). A successful implementation process is nonlinear; but rather a continuous cycle of growth and improvement that initially can be quite chaotic and messy (Zmuda, Kuklis, & Kline, 2004).

DATA AS A STARTING POINT

Coteaching is often explored because educators have examined English learner (EL) student achievement and reached the conclusion that a pull-out model is not adequately addressing students' needs (Fu, Howser, & Huang, 2007). However, effective coteaching models can be the result of other changes that make coteaching the next logical step. As an example, when a district adopted differentiated instruction as a teaching model, coteaching better supported the implementation of this teaching philosophy. Yet, in another district, coteaching was not well received in a school that was already in the midst of 21 other initiatives that had been adopted with little attention to strategic planning or investment by teachers.

Administrators frequently try to enact change in a linear fashion (see Figure 4.1). Student achievement data are gathered and examined to identify weaknesses. Then, strategic goals are identified to address or improve these weaknesses (i.e., ELs' achievement to be improved via coteaching). In this kind of linear model, data are collected throughout the implementation period and then analyzed to see the impact of the inter-

```
Data  >  Problem  >  Intervention  >  Data  >
```

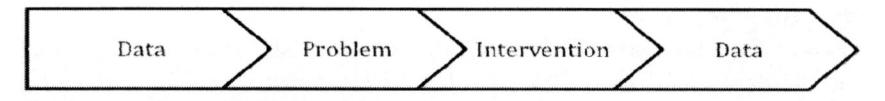

Figure 4.1. A traditional, linear process of change.

vention. The strengths of this process are that data are used to make decisions and to focus on student achievement. The weakness is a lack of understanding of how *multiple* variables affect student achievement and how *any* change will immediately alter the existing conditions. Any new initiative must be considered within the overall staff development plan of a district. Additionally ongoing modifications to the plan (or fine-tuning) should occur at every step of the way (Schmoker, 1996).

Common Pitfalls in Implementing Initiatives

Many educators utilizing a traditional, data-driven decision-making process become frustrated, disillusioned or cynical when they do not see the progress they had envisioned. Sometimes such frustration stems from other educators' resistance or from institutional barriers, such as scheduling, lack of resources or inflexible procedures that have not been uncovered through a careful examination of the context. Early adopters are enthusiastic and able to enact the practice individually but cannot transmit this understanding to others because of a noncollaborative environment. Therefore, when conditions change, the practice is no longer sustainable. Below are some common pitfalls with the traditional linear model of improvement.

The Human Factor
We often hear, "if everyone would just do their part we would be able to move forward." This human factor contributes significantly to the chaotic messiness of the change process. Great leaders capitalize on the fact that everyone is motivated differently, with his or her own vision, beliefs, way of thinking, and unique communication style. Rather than seeing such differences as liabilities, they tap into teachers' diverse, creative perspectives and actively engage and empower all stakeholders through the decision-making *process* (Buckingham & Coffman, 1999). Every decision is ultimately human-dependent, thus time spent creating ownership is essential.

Deficit Thinking

Another weakness of the traditional, linear model is its singular focus on the problem. The deficit mindset is pervasive. In reality, however, much energy spent on remediating weaknesses is ineffective. For example, Gallup researchers who created the Strength Finder self-assessment tool have established that, by focusing on strengths instead of weaknesses, exponential growth can occur because teachers are using and improving students' natural strengths (Buckingham & Clifton, 2001).

Not Recognizing Complexity

A third major weakness of the linear model occurs when each step is viewed as separate and nonconcurrent. A linear model fails to respond to the multifaceted, interrelated, and multilayered factors that affect student learning. To better examine the complex instructional setting of a classroom, both a telescopic and microscopic lens is needed to simultaneously consider the myriad of individual as well as institutional variables affecting instruction and, to generate context-specific structures and solutions that fit the particular classroom (Gleick, 1987).

Reactive Rather Than Proactive

Perhaps the greatest problem with a linear model is its reactive nature. Unless coteaching is seen as part of a bigger picture—of effective instruction—it will not be sustainable. By understanding past successes and failures of other initiatives, leaders can capitalize on the existing strengths within the system and strategically identify key areas to improve and strengthen. This means creating a *culture of continuous improvement* in which coteaching is part of systemwide school reform. This second kind of system is organic and complex. It will be fed through collaboration, communication, and creativity and will evolve continuously (Zmuda et al., 2004).

STRATEGIES FOR SUCCESS

The above examples help illustrate that an inflexible linear model of implementation is only poorly able to facilitate the highly contextual and stakeholder-driven process of change. In the next section, the authors outline an organic model of change, which focuses on creating the conditions for success that result in sustainable improvement. Figure 4.2 shows how each of the components relates to collaboration and coteaching. Questions for self-exploration and decision-making are also included.

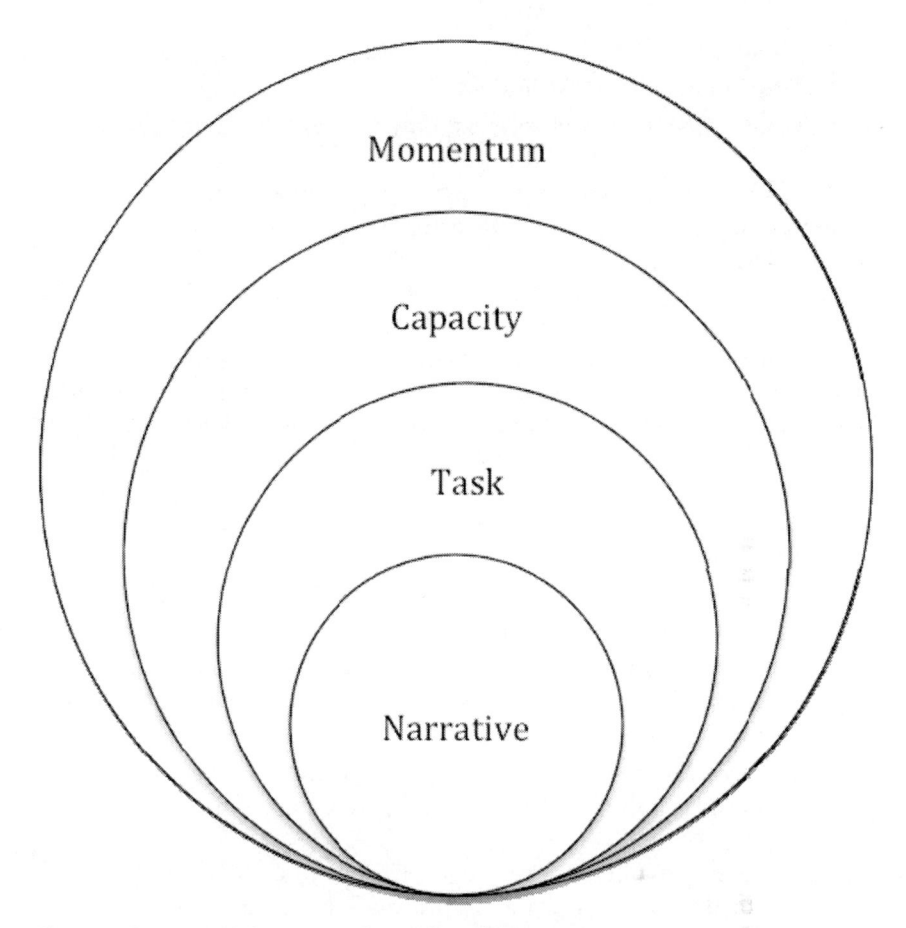

Figure 4.2. A nested process of growth and improvement.

The Narrative: Understanding the Uniqueness of Each Collaboration and Context

The first critical contextual factor is determining the underlying narrative of a place consisting of its vision, identity, purpose, and culture. Undertaking any new initiative independent from considering how this change interfaces with the system's underlying narrative will result in failure. Educators must consider the unique essence of their system by asking inclusive questions such as:

- Who are we?
- What do we believe in and value as a system?

- What is our history?
- Who are our new stakeholders?
- What expertise, as well as questions, do they bring to the table?

It is *not* what is on paper or in a strategic plan that is the essence of an organization, but rather what is believed, stated, and enacted by various stakeholders (Brisk, Burgos, & Hamerla, 2004; Schein, 1992).

The narrative of a system is also the microcosm of individuals' stories and interactions within that system. What values, beliefs, hopes, and dreams are shared? Who works together? Who collaborates? Who provides energy? Who sabotages new initiatives? There must be conversations with various stakeholders to complete the following kinds of statements:

- The way coteaching and collaboration fit the wider vision and mission of our context is ...
- Practices that are already in place that directly and/or indirectly relate to coteaching and collaboration include ...
- If we could name only one core value that nearly all of us subscribe to, it would be.... Coteaching and collaboration support this core value in the following ways ...
- The greatest strengths of our system (school, district, etc.) are ... Coteaching and collaboration can build on these strengths by ...

Stakeholders should be encouraged to generate their *own* prompts, which will further reveal individual's priorities and increase buy-in.

It is important that coteaching is not viewed as just as another instructional approach. For it to yield lasting effects, coteaching must be integrated into a school's philosophy and become part of the organization's culture and practice through genuine connections to existing practices. The challenge—and opportunity—lies in the process of crafting an all-inclusive narrative that reflects the hopes, dreams, and realities of *all* stakeholders, yet is flexible, sustainable, resilient, and ever-evolving. Coteaching may not be the next best step. Yet, by understanding the narrative, it allows participants to become mutually supportive and allow coteaching to be addressed as part of an overall philosophy of inclusive education. When schools take time to consider their core values, such as the belief that all students should have appropriate instruction, coteaching often emerges as part of a system that also includes differentiated instruction, culturally responsive teaching, academic language instruction, or content-based literacy.

The Task: Creating a Culture of Collaboration

When implementing coteaching, some educators treat it as an individual outcome or product rather than a multilevel process of collaboration. A multilevel, process-focused coteaching approach considers connections that exist between several levels within an educational system, beyond the classroom level. As an example, if coteaching is already occurring in special education, how can schedules be modified to capitalize on this existing structure? What lessons can be learned from other coteaching practice taking place in the same context? Successful coteaching necessitates an exploratory stance, where a critical part of implementation of coteaching is investigating and reflecting on the process of the implementation to identify strengths and weaknesses of the process in reflection to that *particular* education context. This is important as we often observe failed attempts of coteaching in contexts where teachers are *doing* coteaching (we call this product-oriented coteaching) rather than integrating coteaching into one's existing context with modifications and frequent reflective interactions with colleagues (process-oriented coteaching). Table 4.1 provides examples and describes the differences between product-oriented and process-oriented coteaching.

The distinction between product-oriented (doing) and process-oriented (being) coteaching refers to different mind-sets in implementation. On one end of the spectrum are efforts where coteaching is implemented mainly through inserting external structures into the existing procedures. These changes in structure involve changes in schedules, assignments, etc. The *product* (the coteaching model) has been designed beforehand and is being implemented without regard to the unique features of the local context, its people, strengths and weaknesses. On the other hand, the process-oriented model of coteaching has *process* in its core; the process of learning, experimenting, reflecting, discussing, revising and sharing about experiences. Coteaching develops as a part of the process and will intimately reflect the school's context.

The various components of this cyclical framework, such as narrative and task are intrinsically related to each other. The *task* (what we do and how we do it) is directly dependent on who we are as a system. In Table 4.1, steps related to task are tightly embedded within the context. Task is both goal setting (the *what*) and action planning (the *who* and *how*). Every action step and goal is articulated with contextual references (names of individuals, places, practices and resources) as the successful completion of these action steps directly depends upon this clarity and accountability.

Decisions educators make regarding the *what*, *who*, and *how* must carefully consider the overall culture and history of their organization as well as the knowledge, skills, beliefs and strengths of the individuals involved.

Table 4.1. Examples of Product- Versus Process-Oriented Coteaching

Product-Oriented Focus on Task: "Doing"	Process-Oriented Focus on Task: "Being/Becoming"
• Externally determined coteaching teams.	• Intentional investment in identifying high functioning teams that emerge organically.
• Engagement in activities focused on the new approach: collaborative lesson planning, cocreating assignments, establishing coteaching roles, etc.	• Engagement in conversations and existing practice. • Conversations about trust, beliefs, strengths/weaknesses, hopes and dreams • Self-assessments, frequent reflection on the connections between new task and one's self (responses, reactions) • Focus on existing practice to explore what already *is*; then proactively integrating new components into existing practice.
• Goals consist of long-term goals and predetermined action steps to bridge the current state of affairs and those goals.	• Long-term goal/s established. • Action steps/subgoals leading up to those ultimate goals are created on *an ongoing basis* (not just at the outset of the project) • Steps adjusted as the system moves forward organically. • Goals articulated showing connections between old and new, including measures of one's own response to change.
• Limited collaboration beyond scheduled meeting times.	• Collaboration an integral part of how the system works beyond the implementation of this instructional practice.

Namely, each pair of coteachers will have their unique way of implementing coteaching. As an example, an ESL teacher may collaborate with five or more classroom teachers and, therefore, must modify his/her coteaching strategies accordingly. Thus, concerted effort must be devoted to developing shared understanding and building trusting relationships so that coteachers are able to communicate openly. There *will* be differences in expectations, curriculum, or teaching styles, which must be discussed nonjudgmentally.

Building Capacity: The Fuel Enabling Meaningful Action

Capacity building requires long-term commitment. Narrative and task directly relate to the capacity of the system; namely, intentional decisions regarding allotment of resources (people, time, materials) are directly linked to the narrative (who we are as a system) and the task (where we want to go). For example, when making decisions about pairing teachers for coteaching, questions should be explored such as:

- What are we already doing that is successful and can be used as a strategy/resource for this new implementation?
- Who can model success?
- What is the best way to decide how teams are formed? How do we know if a team is successful? How will we measure their effectiveness?

The administrators in our partner schools emphasize that people are their greatest resource. They say, "Give me the right people and we can do anything!" In the same breath, however, we hear, "If I didn't have to deal with those people we could really make progress!" It is exactly this paradoxical effect that humans have on any process that makes organizational change so challenging. We have observed that a critical factor in lessening frustration with people is intentionally focusing on individuals' strengths rather than deficits.

Momentum: Tracking and Feeding Progress

Momentum is the fourth and final component of this framework. Even if educators have explored their system's narrative, carefully created meaningful tasks, assessed and increased the system's capacity to capitalize on people's strengths, coteaching will fail if there is no systemic support to monitor progress and refine practice.

Intentional Tracking of Progress
Schools create momentum by building structures and procedures that intentionally use data to monitor progress, identify what is working for *them* and what needs to change (based on our narrative and task), and assure maximal use of resources (capacity). This function of momentum is tracking progress.

Feeding Progress
Many schools fail by underestimating the importance of *feeding* the progress. A basic principle of learning is that when something is working well we are more likely to continue behaviors that have (in the past) produced positive results and abandon or modify strategies that have produced negative effects. As people accumulate positive results, they become more self-confident about being able to reproduce those results in the future. These two simple concepts of learning—positive reinforce-

ment (positive feedback) and self-efficacy (I know I can)—play a critical role in assuring the longevity and sustainability of coteaching.

Naming Progress

Naming achievements in a public way reinforces the efforts that accomplished change and provides visible, positive evidence for coteaching. Grounds for continued practice adds to the self-efficacy of the participants resulting in additional progress and development. One way to publicize and celebrate progress is by providing regular updates on the latest successes, highlighting concrete examples of where you were (the *before*) and how far you have come (the *after*), and what your next targets will be. Sharing stories of success is essential in creating and maintaining self-confidence and a positive work atmosphere.

SUMMARY AND CONCLUSION

The authors liken a successful coteaching system to a spider web, the strands of which are not randomly generated, but rather form a masterful connection of parts to the whole, each strategically linked and essential. A spider begins with a core structure and continuously expands outward to create its web. So too, with coteaching, a small, committed core of coteachers can work to systematically and strategically bring others into their web of influence. The change process we have described in this chapter, narrative, task, capacity and momentum, serve as the building blocks in this masterful system. They constitute the nodes in this interconnected, synchronous ecosystem.

We leave you with the following questions about what to consider in *your* system's web of narrative, task, capacity, and momentum toward collaborative coteaching:

- How resilient is your system? What holds it together?
- What are the meaningful connections that form the Narrative web of your system? Should coteaching be the next step or are there other steps to consider prior to embarking on coteaching?
- When building into your system a new initiative like coteaching, what occurs to assure that this new component fits with the existing web, expanding on its structure rather than merely adding a burdensome weight to it?
- If it does not seamlessly fit, how will it be integrated into the existing structure, or *should* it be?

Create a metaphor for your system, whether a spider web as suggested here, or a sailboat or even a bus (having the right people on the bus). Allow the time and the space for conversations about the uniqueness of your school and its teachers. While coteaching itself is a wonderful strategy, its true value is the collaborative spirit and creativity it inspires.

REFERENCES

Brisk, M. E., Burgos, A., & Hamerla, S. R. (2004). *Situational context of education: A window into the world of bilingual learners.* Mahwah, NJ: Erlbaum.

Bronfenbrenner, U. (1979). *The ecology of human development.* Cambridge, MA: Harvard University Press.

Buckingham, M., & Clifton, D. O. (2001). *Now, discover your strengths.* New York, NY: Free Press.

Buckingham, M., & Coffman, C. (1999). *First, break all the rules: What the world's greatest managers do differently.* New York, NY: Simon & Schuster.

Fu, D., Houser, R., & Huang, A. (2007). A collaboration between ESL and regular classroom teachers for ELL students' literacy development. *Changing English, 14,* 325-342.

Fullan, M. (2001). *Leading in a culture of change.* San Francisco, CA: Jossey-Bass.

Fullan, M. (2010). *All systems go: The change imperative for whole system reform.* Thousand Oaks, CA: Corwin Press.

Gleick, J. (1987). *Chaos.* New York, NY: Penguin Books.

National Association of Secondary School Principals. (2004). *Breaking ranks II: Strategies for leading high school reform.* Reston, VA: Author.

Reeves, D. B. (2008). *Reframing teacher leadership to improve your schools.* Alexandria, VA: Association for Supervision and Curriculum Development.

Reeves, D. B. (2010). *Transforming professional development into student results.* Alexandria, VA: Association for Supervision and Curriculum Development.

Schein, E. H. (1992). *Organizational culture and leadership* (2nd ed). San Francisco, CA: Jossey-Bass.

Schmoker, M. (1996). *Results: The key to continuous school improvement.* Alexandria, VA: Association for Supervision and Curriculum Development.

Zmuda, A., Kuklis, R., & Kline, E. (2004). *Transforming schools: Creating a culture of continuous improvement.* Alexandria, VA: Association for Supervision and Curriculum Development.

CHAPTER 5

COLLABORATIVE INTERDISCIPLINARY TEAM TEACHING

A Model for Good Practice

Andrew Gladman

Miyazaki International College (MIC), in Kyushu, Japan, offers a distinctive educational programme that attracts faculty members from many countries. Using English as its primary medium of instruction, the college implements an unusual team teaching approach. The faculty body of MIC is broadly composed of two large subgroups of roughly equal proportions. One subgroup comprises English language teaching faculty, whereas the other comprises faculty from a variety of different academic disciplines representing the contents of a typical liberal arts curriculum. Individuals from each subgroup are paired together in sustained collaborative teaching partnerships. Dubbed "collaborative interdisciplinary team teaching" (CITT), this instructional practice was originally derived from adjunct models of team teaching (Stewart, Sagliano, & Sagliano, 2002) and principles of content-based language instruction (CBLI) for second language learners (Brinton, Snow, & Mesche, 1989; Sagliano & Greenfield, 1998).

THE COLLABORATIVE INTERDISCIPLINARY TEAM TEACHING APPROACH

In the CITT partnership, the specialist in the academic discipline of the class (for example, psychology, history, or economics) is referred to as the content teacher (CT), while the specialist in English for speakers of other languages (ESOL) is referred to as the language teacher (LT). The two specialists team teach both ESOL and the academic discipline together in the same course, engaging the principles of CBLI for meeting parallel learning goals in both disciplines. They are expected to team teach each course jointly as equal partners, being present in the classroom at all lesson times and sharing responsibility for classroom management, lesson planning, materials development, student assessment, and course evaluation. The CITT approach is applied across the curriculum for virtually all first- and second-year courses, and there is no time limit for how long CITT practitioners may continue to team teach together in established partnerships.

RESEARCH ON COLLABORATIVE INTERDISCIPLINARY TEAM TEACHING

Over the course of 2.5 years, this author conducted three consecutive research studies to explore CITT at MIC from the points of view of its participants (Gladman, 2009). In the initial study, focus group methodology was used to identify themes of importance to small groups of content teachers and language teachers engaged in CITT. A second study was then developed to expand and enhance the findings of the first study, using a questionnaire to survey a larger and more representative group of respondent teachers. A third study was then conducted, also using survey methodology but focusing on the views of students in the CITT classroom, in order to compare and contrast with the teachers' responses. Data emerging from all of these studies were content-analyzed for common themes and insights.

Students' Perspectives

Respondents from the student-focused study largely emphasized the beneficial outcomes of CITT. Negative perceptions that were expressed tended to be limited to criticisms of teachers perceived to be implementing team teaching incorrectly, rather than criticisms of team teaching per se.

Some of the insights emerging from the study were that respondents believed team teaching to improve the students' understanding of class content and increase their willingness to ask questions in class. In fact, respondents expressed a common belief that the active participation of the students was a major influence on the effectiveness of CITT. Students were perceived to constitute as much of a contributing factor to the success or failure of a team-taught class as their teachers. However, though suggesting that the role of students as cocontributors to the effectiveness of team teaching should not be overlooked, respondents also deemed the relationship between the teaching partners to be of key importance. They identified a need for team teachers to establish a mutually cooperative partnership, respecting each other's roles and authority within the relationship. In addition, respondents observed that the presence of cooperating teaching partners in a classroom allowed greater scope for the beneficial modelling to students of diverse viewpoints related to course content.

Teachers' Perspectives

By comparison, respondents of the teacher-focused studies also emphasized the crucial nature of the relationship between teaching partners, and most of their open-ended responses were concerned with the aspects of that relationship.

Of the range of aspects identified by respondents as important to effective team teaching, respect and trust between teaching partners emerged as the most critical, and these aspects were perceived to underlie many other aspects of a working partnership. Also perceived as crucial was the need for team teachers to engage each other in open and regular communications, as well as the flexibility to adapt their behaviour to meet new or unexpected situations. Other important points identified by respondents included the need for partners to reach mutual agreement of their roles in the relationship, and to avoid the critical danger of one partner arrogating power over the other.

One further aspect that teachers considered crucial was the need for partners to avoid presenting their students with conflicting instruction. Similarly, strong emphasis was placed on the importance of one partner supporting the other in front of students, while resolving any conflicts in private. However, respondents also acknowledged the usefulness of partners expressing differences of opinion in the team-taught classroom in order to encourage critical thinking, and identified students' exposure to diverse viewpoints as one of the main benefits of team teaching.

From these responses, a key distinction was made between instruction (what students need to do) and information (what students need to learn), with a consensus emerging that for partners to correct each other's errors and express differences of opinion in the classroom was acceptable only with reference to classroom information, while such behaviour became unacceptable when instructions were being issued. These types of insights prompted the suggestion that the development of guidelines for team teachers would be of benefit in helping them to recognise model distinctions between behavioral modes, as recommended by CITT participants.

THE THREE-MODE MODEL

Using the major findings of the three studies in this research series, a model was developed with the intention of representing the basic processes of what participants believe to be effective CITT practice. The model was designed primarily for application by team teachers, since they are the initiators of the collaborative process. Yet it was intended also to integrate the participation of team-taught students, who appear to perceive themselves as cocontributors to the process. In this sense, the model might be considered an idealization of good practice to help provide the best conditions for effective team teaching to occur, in a way that meets the needs of both students and teachers.

The point of departure for the model is the need for CITT practitioners to make a clear distinction between information and instruction for students. Since these two types of discourse require two distinct sets of behaviour from the team teachers, they are represented in the model as separate interactional modes, which have been labelled the information mode and the instruction mode. In addition to these modes, a third mode is required to represent the team teachers' interactions outside the classroom, where preparations and negotiations can take place that are not considered appropriate for student involvement. This third mode has been labelled the management mode. Taken together, the three modes constitute what has been dubbed CITT's *three-mode model*.

See Figure 5.1 for a visual representation of the interactions of participants in the three modes. The two team teachers are represented by the two central squares, while the students are represented by the outer circle (where applicable). The communicative interactions of the participants are represented by lines and arrows, with double-headed arrows representing two-way cooperative interactions and single-headed arrows representing one-way interactions with communication passing from giver to receiver. A solid line between teachers signifies their unanimity of action

Collaborative Interdisciplinary Team Teaching 53

Information Mode	Instruction Mode	Management Mode
• Teachers provide students with information for learning	• Teachers provide students with instructions for what they are expected to do	• Open communications between partners
• Teachers/students can share differing viewpoints	• Teachers present "united front" of mutual agreement	• Preterm negotiation of teachers' roles and responsibilities
• Teachers are free to exercise adaptive skills, allowing flexible changes in classroom events	• Teachers' instruction is coordinated through advance planning of "management mode"	• Establishing and maintaining mutual trust and respect to extend to all modes of the partnership
• Students become active cocontributors with teachers of "team lesson"	• More traditional classroom role for students as receivers of instruction	• Conflict resolution: "Reflect and repair" function for other modes
• All participants have opportunities to ask questions		• Lesson planning and assessments
		• Class evaluations

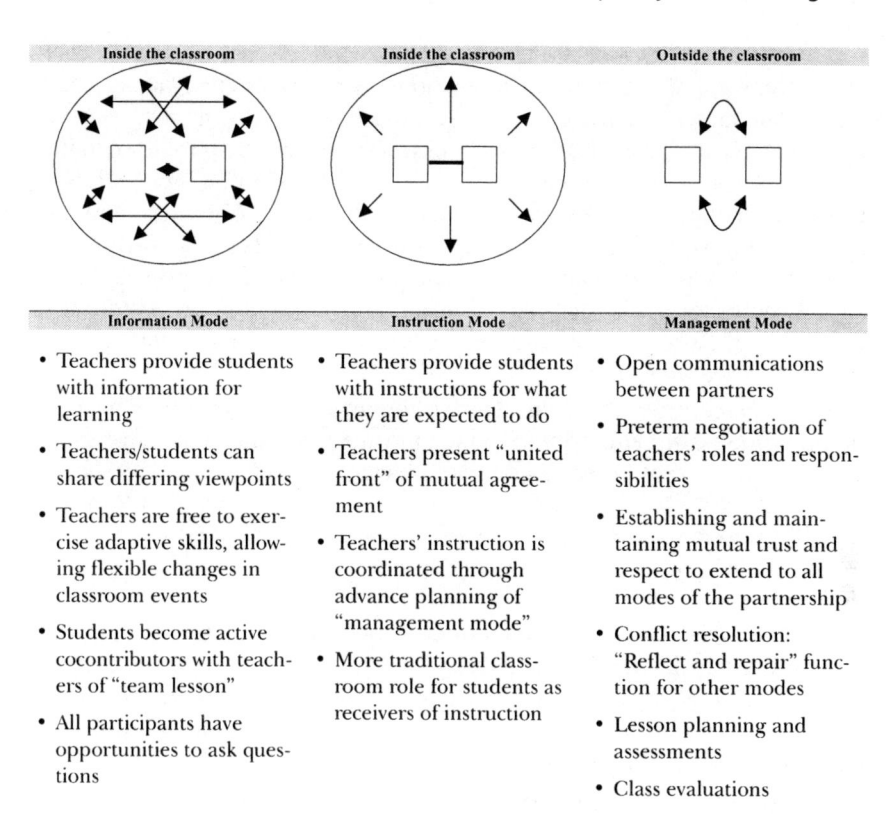

Figure 5.1. The three-mode CITT model.

through a shared purpose. Figure 5.1 includes a summary of key points for each mode.

Information Mode

The information mode is a commonly applied mode of behaviour inside the CITT classroom. In this mode, the classroom participants share information for learning. Teachers and students are free to offer and discuss differing viewpoints and can benefit from the potential learning opportunities that arise. In this mode, the team teachers' adaptive skills are likely to be most beneficial, since the discourse may progress in unexpected directions, and spontaneous shifts in classroom events can occur. Teachers need to be flexible to handle the unpredictability of interactions in this mode.

In information mode, students become cocontributors with their teachers in the implementation of the lesson. The students are encouraged to participate actively in the classroom, asking questions as much as possible and challenging claims when they believe it is appropriate to do so. Thus, the teacher-student distinction is reduced to a minimum, since all classroom participants are behaving in fairly similar ways. Any classroom participant may voice his or her disagreement (or agreement) with claims expressed by any other classroom participant if deemed appropriate to do so. All participants interact in an environment where they are encouraged to support their arguments and think critically about the information with which they are presented.

While teaching partners are free to disagree with each other in information mode, they should not engage in professional conflicts in front of the students, nor attempt to arrogate power over each other. The behaviour of the team teachers in information mode must be guided by a relationship based on mutual trust and respect, as developed through the management mode of the model. Criticism should be constructive, not disparaging.

As the more qualified and experienced participants in the classroom in terms of curricular requirements, the teachers are most likely to facilitate and guide classroom interactions, addressing students both collectively and individually, and using classroom discourse to access and explore the different aspects and arguments of any given issue. Yet the teacher-talk to students should not be prescriptive.

Instruction Mode

The instruction mode is another mode of behaviour for participants inside the CITT classroom. In this mode, the two team teachers provide students with instructions for what they need to do to meet class requirements (for example, completing a class activity, participating in a group project, or doing a homework task). Teachers adopt a more traditional role in relation to their students in this mode, since the interaction is primarily one-way, from teacher to student. In this case, the teachers constitute the authority figures with regard to the messages being conveyed, while the students constitute the receivers of those messages. Typically, the students would not challenge the teachers' instructions.

The instruction mode requires both teaching partners to achieve consistent instruction. In other words, teaching partners must be coordinated with each other in terms of the messages they pass to their students. This coordination requires advance negotiation and planning between the partners as conducted through the management mode. In contrast with the information mode, the two team teachers should not disagree with each other, but should present a united front in providing students with nonconflicting instructions. In this way, students should not become confused by mismatched messages that emerge from the different expectations of the teaching partners.

It is not necessary that both teachers provide students with the instructions together, but it is crucial that the instructional messages issued by either teacher at any time be consistent with what was agreed between them. If instruction-giving is implemented effectively, the students should perceive both team teachers as interchangeable in this regard.

Management Mode

The management mode encompasses the professional interactions between the two teaching partners, typically in an office meeting situation, or through virtual channels.

In this mode, the teaching partners communicate with each other to take care of all the business of their shared course that needs to be handled outside the classroom. It is particularly important in allowing for advance planning of the instructions to be issued to students in instruction mode, since the coordination necessary for partners to agree on the instructions should occur outside the classroom.

However, management mode constitutes more than just lesson planning meetings, since it is a suitable forum for partners to negotiate differences and resolve any conflicts that may impede the partners' effective coordination inside the classroom. It serves a useful reflect and repair function, by allowing the partners to forestall or to resolve any problems that might arise in the other modes of team teaching implementation. Research suggests that partnerships are more likely to fail if the partners do not maintain open channels of communication with each other in one form or another, for the duration of their collaboration (Gladman, 2009; Gottlieb, 1994; Perry & Stewart, 2005). Therefore, it is vital that partners use these communications in management mode to initiate and develop a professional relationship based on mutual trust and respect, which can then extend to all interactions of their partnership.

If team teachers feel that they have a forum for speaking openly to their partners with a view to negotiating differences and reaching mutually acceptable agreements, it will prove easier for partners to provide support for each other when in the classroom. Teaching partners should also use the management mode to engage in preterm negotiation of their respective roles and responsibilities within the partnership, reaching an agreement that is acceptable to both partners before classes begin. The stability of this agreement is represented by the symmetrical visual aspect of management mode shown in Figure 5.1.

APPLICATIONS OF THE THREE-MODE MODEL

The applicability of the three-mode model to a range of different types of team teaching is evident in the universality of its themes. Many of the responses from the research participants touched upon fundamental aspects of social relationships between people in collaborative associations, rather than any details of institutional roles or logistical rules for how these associations ought to be formalized. In fact, prominent themes emerging from these studies, such as respect, trust, and flexibility, are so basic to the essential properties of close social relationships between individuals that they invite comparisons with marital relationships (a common analogy for describing team teaching partnerships; see Perry & Stewart 2005; Shannon & Meath-Lang, 1992).

Thus, as an idealized representation of the most common types of interactions in team teaching, the three-mode model was not designed for prescriptive application in the classroom. Certainly, it is not a comprehensive depiction of all possible communicative interactions between classroom participants. It is easy to imagine interactions occurring that are not well represented by this model. For example, students could ask clarification questions of their teachers during instruction mode (or challenge the instruction if they think it is unacceptable); or teachers may present a 'united front' of agreement during information mode; or one teaching partner may be required to issue instructions to a student outside the classroom.

It is worth noting that the model is of limited value if teaching partners cannot negotiate mutually acceptable agreements in management mode and reach an impasse. In such a case, the services of a third-party mediator (such as a senior teacher) are likely to prove necessary to solve the problem, transcending the limits of what the model offers.

Instead, the purpose of the model is to give team teachers a guide for helping them to avoid the conflicts that can arise from misunderstandings of each other's assumptions or behaviour across modes. For example, teaching partners might experience conflict if one partner tries to problematize what the other is saying in the classroom while the other is trying to issue nonconflicting instructions to students. The teachers can make reference to the model to clarify their differences and correct this misunderstanding. Another example might be that if one teaching partner tries to resolve conflicts with his or her partner inside the classroom, the latter can refer to the model to justify the claim that such interactions are best applied in management mode, away from the students.

It is also important to note that the modes are not intended to represent equal periods of shared time between teaching partners. For example, team teachers may be engaged in information mode for most of a lesson, and change to instruction mode only for the final few minutes before the participants depart. It is, of course, possible for participants to shift back and forth between information and instruction modes over a short space of time, as required.

One can also imagine a situation where the two teaching partners are in different modes inside the classroom at any given time. For example, one teacher may be assisting a group of students to think through a problem-solving task (information mode) while the other is providing clarification for another student who experienced difficulty in understanding previously issued instructions (instruction mode). Such a situation does not transgress the guidelines of the model if the teachers' actions are agreeable to both partners, and if both partners are united with regard to the instruction being issued by the latter (since it was previously negotiated by both teachers in management mode). Of course, team teachers are free to adapt and apply the guidelines of the model to the degree that will suit the requirements of their own classrooms, as long as the key distinctions between the behavioral modes are recognized.

As an ideal model of good practice, the three-mode model can usefully be integrated into training activities for new team teachers. For example, simulated demonstrations of poorly implemented team teaching might be explained to trainees in terms of contraventions of the principles made explicit through the model. It may also be employed as a reference guide for practising team teachers seeking to sustain effective partnerships and avoid potential conflicts. Since team teachers may be called upon to collaborate with a range of different partners at different times, and engage in a highly varied range of social interactions, a conceptual model of good practice can provide a consistent framework for applying those interactions most effectively, without limiting partners to a one-size-fits-all set of rules that can all too easily become irrelevant to their own particular collaboration.

CONCLUSION

In conclusion, the three-mode model was intended to serve as a guide for good practice in team teaching situations. Although it was derived from research findings investigating the perspectives of participants in one particular interdisciplinary form of college teaching collaboration, the universality of its themes suggests that it might be usefully applied across a wide range of different team teaching contexts. By recognizing and respecting the distinctions between the three interactional modes of behaviour represented in the model, and applying the principles of these sets of behaviour, it is hoped that team teachers can work together more effectively with their students and forge satisfying and mutually beneficial partnerships in the process.

REFERENCES

Brinton, D. M., Snow, M. A., & Wesche, M. B. (1989). *Content-based second language instruction*. Boston, MA: Heinle & Heinle.

Gladman, A. (2009). *Collaborative interdisciplinary team teaching in Japan: A study of practitioner and student perspectives* (Unpublished doctoral thesis). Macquarie University, Sydney, Australia.

Gottlieb, N. (1994). Team teaching Japanese language in Australian universities. In M. Wada & A. Cominos (Eds.), *Studies in team teaching* (pp. 186-200). Tokyo, Japan: Kenkyusha.

Perry, B., & Stewart, T. (2005). Insights into effective partnership in interdisciplinary team teaching. *System, 33*, 563-573.

Sagliano, M., & Greenfield, K. (1998). A collaborative model of content-based EFL instruction in the liberal arts. *TESOL Journal, 7*(3), 23-28.

Shannon, N. B., & Meath-Lang, B. (1992). Collaborative language teaching: A co-investigation. In D. Nunan (Ed.), *Collaborative language learning and teaching* (pp. 120-140). Cambridge, MA: Cambridge University Press.

Stewart, T., Sagliano, M., & Sagliano, J. (2002). Merging expertise: developing partnerships between language and content specialists. In J. Crandall & D. Kaufman (Eds.), *Content-based instruction in higher education settings* (pp. 29-44). Alexandria, VA: TESOL.

CHAPTER 6

COTEACHING FOR ENGLISH LANGUAGE LEARNERS

Recommendations for Administrators

Jocelyn Santana, Jennifer E. Scully, and Shaniquia L. Dixon

The following are the voices of an administrator, a teacher, and a student in the midst of coteaching situations for English learners:

> I am a new principal in an elementary school in NYC. I am assessing the English as a second language (ESL) delivery program I inherited. My teacher calls himself a "push-in ESL teacher." He teams with five different teachers each school day. He also teaches two classes of beginners in a pull-out setting. Because of his workload, he is unable to plan lessons with his coteachers.
>
> When this ESL teacher goes into some classrooms, the teacher turns the students over to him and uses the time as a prep period. In some others, he is helping a few English language learners (ELLs) at the back of the room while the classroom teacher works with the rest of the students. In another, he serves as an aide, roving around the room to help students who do not understand the instruction. I am not an expert in second language instruction, but I know that this is collaborative teaching at its worst. (Mrs. K, elementary school principal)

I had been teaching ESL for 10 years when I was hired as a substitute at a large urban elementary school with a predominantly pull-out ESL program. When my principal announced at the faculty meeting the day before school began that all ESL programs would now be comprised completely of push-in instruction, I was surprised. Following the meeting, I attended a workshop where a district representative delivered a 2-hour presentation on choosing, defining, and reinforcing "juicy vocabulary" in a push-in setting. I began my program the following day.

I had little experience with ESL coteaching, and I felt unprepared. Some of my coteachers monopolized instruction, relegating me to the role of an aide; others asked me to teach so they could use the bathroom or grade papers. I was coteaching content area lessons without understanding the material or skills being presented .Some colleagues even said they did not want me to push in, but my principal told me to be tough and stand up for myself. The final straw came when one of my coteachers screamed at me in front of my students that I should learn to develop my own lessons. I reported this to my principal, who told me I needed to learn to get along with people. The next day I gave 2-weeks' notice. (Ms. R, elementary ESL teacher)

I am sitting in Ms. Williams's fourth grade class, watching the clock. I know that Mr. Reyes, my ESL teacher, should come at 11:05, because today is Tuesday. Sometimes he doesn't come for days or weeks. I don't know why. Today, he comes in, with a red face and saying "Sorry" to Ms. Williams, with his big bag and a cup of coffee. Four students from other fourth grade classes are with him. "What are we doing today?" Ms. Williams tells him "science," and he bends to look at the opened textbook on Ramon's desk. He asks us to come to the carpet with our books. Ms. Williams, our real teacher, calls to him, "Oh, I forgot. Today is gym, so we're leaving 5 minutes early.

My ESL teacher always makes class fun, but sometimes I just don't get it. It helps to do things, instead of just reading about it, like with Ms. William, but it always takes so long to get through the book first.

My science book is in English, but I'll be taking the test in June in Spanish. Sometimes Mr. Reyes tells us the meaning of the words in Spanish. I like that, but Ms. Williams doesn't like it when we talk in Spanish. "This is America. You should learn English," she says in a mad voice. Sometimes she tells Mr. Reyes that we're being too loud. Sometimes it's so loud in the other group that we can't hear Mr. Reyes. (Miguel, a student)

THE COMPLEXITIES OF COTEACHING

Budgetary limitations, space constraints, overloaded student programs, and limited expertise in the complexities of coteaching often leave administrators confused, frustrated, and unsure about how to design, support, and supervise coteaching partnerships. The purpose of this chapter is to provide administrators with a road map to avoid common pitfalls and to ensure the success of the teaching partnership. In our shared years of teaching and administrative experience, we have been a part of or have witnessed too many ineffective coteaching partnerships for English learners. Recently, we decided to collaborate to provide administrators with much needed guidance toward the development of a more effective coteaching English as a Second Language service delivery model. The goal is for students to benefit from having two teachers who function synergistically and are mutually accountable for the success of all students, not just the ELLs.

Fortunately, administrators are moving away from using a pull-out model. The time spent by students away from their regular classrooms, coupled with a lack of collaboration between mainstream teachers and specialists, places English learners at risk for a higher incidence of missed material and poor performance. While the notion of coteaching might have garnered the passing interest of pedagogical luminaries since the days of the *little red schoolhouse* (Honigsfeld & Dove, 2008), it began to take formal shape in 1963 when William Alexander devised a *team-teaching* system for middle schools (Gaytan, 2010). Team-teaching and its modern descendent, English as a Second Language (ESL) coteaching, were historically associated with special education (Abdullah, 2009; Coffee, 2010; Conderman, Bresnahan, & Pedersen, 2009; Dove & Honigsfeld, 2008, 2010; Villa, Thousand, & Nevin, 2008).

In time, the collaborative instructional model was expanded to include English learners; its success in that forum—given sound implementation—has been shown to produce promising results (Theoharis, 2007; Frattura & Capper, 2007). However, the last decade has seen a rise in the number of ELLs that has outpaced the ability of administrators to grant ESL instructors their own classrooms in urban schools. As available classroom space diminished, many specialists were forced to vacate their teaching spaces to make way for new, grade-level classrooms. Administrators often requested that ESL teachers *push-in* and *pull-aside* the English learners in their regular classrooms as a space-saving measure. Without adequate support or time to plan, this new push-in model of ESL instruction was even less desirable than its similarly disruptive pull-out predecessor. In instances like the one described by the instructor at the beginning of the chapter, teachers were pushed into a complex and demanding situation, in spite of a near-complete lack of sufficient training and support.

We have observed that, in most cases, well-intentioned administrators set up coteaching structures with the presumption that their teachers would intuitively work out logistics and improvise methods with which to collaborate and share their work. In a recent multicase study conducted by this chapter's authors, we found that six respondents, all elementary school principals, stated that their ESL teachers were expected to "[push] into the general education classroom to collaborate with the teacher." Three out of six respondents indicated that the two credentialed professionals were anticipated to be "partners in the instruction of the lesson," sharing "equal responsibilities for planning instruction."

Without exception, all of the principals surveyed believed that the coteaching model would result in improved achievement for all due to "lower student-teacher ratios and the availability of differentiated instruction." Interestingly enough, however, only one principal had assured that two periods a week were set aside for common planning and collaboration for all participating teachers. Additionally, only one of the polled principals integrated time for common planning or set aside provisions for ongoing professional development for coteachers. By the middle of the year, five of the surveyed principals reported that coteaching had failed miserably; they seemed to have placed the blame on teachers who exhibited an inability to "make it work."

THE ROLE OF ADMINISTRATORS

Inasmuch as teachers do play a significant role in making coteaching work, the role of administrators as de facto architects of successful implementation models cannot be overlooked. Not unlike any other initiative involving collaboration, coteaching requires careful planning, support, monitoring, and evaluation. Feedback from administrators and teachers who have successfully implemented coteaching as well as a review of the literature have led us to arrive at what we refer to as nonnegotiable recommendations for school leaders to implement a successful coteaching model:

- *Know who the most supportive teachers are:* Seek out volunteer grade-level teachers to be part of the coteaching model and build a cadre of trained partners who can support the expansion of the coteaching model. Do not mandate the coteaching partnership.
- *Introduce the model with an orientation for staff, parents, and students:* Publicly acknowledge the collaboration, time, and effort the ESL teacher and the classroom teachers are putting into the work of creating a successful coteaching ESL model for the students.
- *Support the teacher leaders willing to take on the challenge of coteaching:* Build time into the schedule for joint lesson planning between grade-level and ESL teachers. Set expectations and accountability for the work and conversations such as goal sheets, outlines, and time lines of the strategies being implemented, all the while

remaining mindful of the next steps that document the common planning process. Because coteachers need time and support to develop partnerships with one another, provide the necessary underpinning of professional development to the coteachers. Enlist the support of experts to provide ongoing guidance to both teachers. Provide the time and opportunity for both teachers to participate in conversation sessions that are keenly focused on their mutual goals as well as professional development. Participate in the planning sessions or have a fellow administrator assigned to the process.

- *Schedule classes so that the ESL teacher coteaches in no more than three classrooms:* Group ELLs into fewer classes to decrease the number of classrooms that need to be outfitted to meet the needs of the incoming ESL teacher.
- *Provide ESL teachers with copies of materials*—teachers' guides, state standards, curricula, pacing charts, and grade based goals—and ensure that they are familiar with all manuals and textbooks being used in the classroom.
- *Allocate funding to support this initiative.*
- *Remain an involved and present leader*; teachers need to see that coteaching is a priority for the leadership.
- *Create opportunities for teachers to collect and to access students' assessment data; provide professional development on how to use data in a c*oteaching partnership.
- *Hold both teachers accountable* via the *Co-Teaching Observation Protocol* (see Appendix).

THE COTEACHING OBSERVATION PROTOCOL

One last nonnegotiable recommendation that deserves a deeper analysis is the process of conducting formal observations for both teachers. The Co-Teaching Observation Protocol (Co-TOP) has been used successfully since its inception in 2008 to observe coteachers. A dozen elementary school principals and their teachers have most recently used it in New York City following its initial publication (Santana, 2008). The protocol is most effective when it is integrated into the preobservation conference with both teachers and has the main benefit of establishing what we call *distributive accountability,* or the expectation that coteachers share equal responsibility for the students' academic success.

During a preobservation discussion with both teachers, the administrator reviews the indicators as they pertain to the coteaching partnership and expectations for student learning. It follows that if teachers are expected to proficiently plan and teach together, supervisors should observe and evaluate them as coteachers. The resultant co-observation sends the most powerful message to students, colleagues, and the entire school community that the pair of instructors are regarded, valued, and recognized in the classroom as coteachers who bear equity of power and authority.

If our ultimate aim is to help English learners realize their full potential, then we need to comprehend and implement the requisites of a successful coteaching model. Administrators must create a culture where teachers can voice their concerns and hardships, while working together as professionals to help administrators *live* the practical reality of the ESL service delivery model they implement on a daily basis.

With proper implementation, coteaching can transcend its misconstrued reputation as a hit-and-miss model to become instead an unfailing method that ensures a successful teaching and learning experience for all involved. When leaders create and employ methodologies that forge collaboration among partners, provide time for common planning, encourage trust, and evaluate teachers jointly, the coteaching model will thrive. The coevaluation process eliminates the *your students versus my students* mentality that is all too prevalent in many coteaching situations. Once a leader and her teachers establish coteaching and collaboration as priorities, occupational challenges such as scheduling constraints, scarcity of funding, or contractual/union issues become easier to tackle and to surmount.

CONCLUSIONS

Evidently, sustained administrative support is essential for sustained collaboration and effective coteaching relationships (Davison, 2006; Spraker, 2003). Time apportioned for collaborative planning and formal evaluation of coteaching partnerships can no longer be overlooked. As Davison (2006) suggested, the model requires ongoing, critical analysis. The list of recommendations in this chapter, especially the Co-TOP to observe coteachers, provides administrators with a basic yet tested guideline to support and to assess coteaching relationships. Effective coteaching starts with administrators who understand the process, provide authentic support to teachers, and expect mutual accountability for students' learning.

ACKNOWLEDGMENT

The authors acknowledge the contributions of the NYU ELL Think Tank for their insights.

APPENDIX: CO-TEACHING OBSERVATION PROTOCOL, CO-TOP

Co-TOP Indicators	Strongly Disagree	Disagree	Neutral	Agree	Strongly Agree
1. Exhibits evidence of common planning and collaboration.	1	2	3	4	5
2. Exhibits evidence of mutual, collegial, and professional respect.	1	2	3	4	5
3. Exhibits evidence of in-depth familiarity with students' content and language needs.	1	2	3	4	5
4. Exhibits evidence of clear, unambiguous language and content objectives.	1	2	3	4	5
5. Exhibits evidence of appropriate scaffolds.	1	2	3	4	5
6. Exhibits evidence of ELLs advocacy as needed.	1	2	3	4	5
7. Exhibits evidence of authentic student participation and engagement.	1	2	3	4	5
8. Exhibits evidence of differentiation for assessing learning.	1	2	3	4	5
9. Exhibits evidence of learning as demonstrated by the work produced by all students.	1	2	3	4	5
10. Exhibits evidence of planned extension, reinforcement activities to practice material presented during lesson.	1	2	3	4	5

Source: Santana (2008).

REFERENCES

Abdallah, J. (2009). Benefits of co-teaching for ESL classrooms. *Academic Leadership Online Journal, 7*(1). Retrieved from http://www.academicleadership.org/emprical_research/532.shtml

Coffee, H. (n.d.). *Team teaching*. Retrieved from http://www.learnnc.org/lp/pages/4754

Conderman, G. J, Bresnahan, M. V., & Pedersen, T. (2009). *Purposeful co-teaching: Real cases and effective strategies*. Thousand Oaks, CA: Corwin Press.

Cook, L., & Friend, M. (1995). Co-teaching: Guidelines for creating effective practices. *Focus on Exceptional Children, 28*(3), 1-16.

Davison, C. (2006). Collaboration between ESL and content teachers: How do you know when we are doing it right? *International Journal of Bilingual Education and Bilingualism, 9,* 454-475.

Dove, M., & Honigsfeld, A. (2010). ESL co-teaching and collaboration: Opportunities to develop teacher leadership and enhance student learning. *TESOL Journal 1*(1), 3-22.

Frattura, E., & Capper, C. A. (2007). *Leading for social justice: Transforming schools for all learners.* Thousand Oaks, CA: Corwin Press.

Gately, S., & Gately, F. (2006). *Understanding co-teaching components.* Retrieved from http://bsnpta.org/geeklog/public_html//article.php?story=Co-Teaching_Components

Gaytan, J. (2010). Instructional strategies to accommodate a team-teaching approach. *Business Communication Quarterly, 73*(1), 82-87.

Honigsfeld, A., & Dove, M. (2008, Winter). Co-teaching in the ESL classroom. *The Delta Kappa Gamma Bulletin, 74*(2), 8-14.

Honigsfeld, A., & Dove, M. (2010). Co-teaching 201: How to support ELLs. *New Teacher Advocate, 17*(3), 4-5.

Huggins, M., Huyghe, J., & Iljkoski, E. (n.d.). *Co-teaching 101: Lessons from the trenches.* Retrieved from http://www.cec.sped.org/AM/Template.cfm?Section=Home&CONTENTID=11473&TEMPLATE=/CM/ContentDisplay.cfm

Santana, J. (2008). Making co-teaching effective for ELLs and assessing the indicators of a successful partnership. *Idiom, 38*(4), 4.

Spraker, J. (2003). *Teacher teaming in relation to student performance: Findings from the literature.* Portland, OR: Northwest Regional Educational Laboratory.

Theoharis, G. (2007). Social justice educational leaders and resistance: Toward a theory of social justice leadership. *Educational Administration Quarterly, 42,* 221-258.

Villa, R., Thousand, J., & Nevin, A. (2008). *A guide to co-teaching: Practical tips for facilitating student learning* (2nd ed.). Thousand Oaks, CA: Corwin Press.

York-Barr, J., Ghere, G., & Sommerness, J. (2007). Collaborative teaching to increase ELL student learning: A three-year urban elementary case study. *Journal of Education for Students Placed At Risk, 12,* 301-335.

PART II

DOCUMENTARY ACCOUNTS OF COLLABORATIVE INSTRUCTIONAL AND LEADERSHIP PRACTICES

CHAPTER 7

COLLABORATIVE CONVERSATIONS

Cynthia Lundgren, Ann Mabbott, and Deirdre Bird Kramer

> At their June faculty meeting, Jefferson School staff expressed frustration about the academic performance of their English Language Learners (ELLs). Many students continued to lag on standardized tests despite the fact that the teachers had been paying special attention to ELLs. After much discussion, the teachers concluded that coordination between the English as a Second Language (ESL) and mainstream teachers would be helpful. As the meeting ended, two teachers discuss the decision by asking, "What does it mean for us to collaborate?" and "What do we do?"

Conversations similar to the one above are taking place in schools across the country. With the pressures of No Child Left Behind (2001) sanctions for a lack of adequate progress by ELLs, many districts are expecting all their teachers to learn sheltered instruction practices for working with language minority students (Echevarria, Vogt, & Short, 2008; Herrera & Murry, 2005; Hill & Flynn, 2006). Sheltered instruction is a variety of practices that make learning content accessible for ELLs while simultaneously developing their English language skills.

Professional development in the area of sheltered instruction has undoubtedly been helpful in educating teachers about the needs of ELLs (Echevarria, Short, & Powers, 2006; Short & Echevarria, 1999). However, the authors' extensive observations in K–12 schools indicate that most general education teachers still struggle to meet the language development needs of these students. Teachers are often puzzled by the expectation to include language development objectives in all instruction and claim that they are not language experts and do not have the background in applied linguistics that they would ideally need to work with ELLs. They are unsure about what language development objectives are, how they relate to academic text purpose, and how they can be crafted to support their curricular goals.

ESL teachers, who are second-language-learning experts, are often called upon to take leadership roles to collaborate with colleagues to implement sheltered instruction. This chapter focuses on conversations about improving instruction for ELLs, particularly in regards to language development. It includes a series of exercises and questions to facilitate collaborative discussion.

The approach presented in this chapter—based on the authors' own work in professional development and related current research (August & Shanahan, 2006; Goldenberg, 2008)—requires that all teachers embrace the responsibility for language development of ELLs. Building on what mainstream teachers know about content standards and instructional design (Wiggins & McTighe, 2004) and what ESL teachers know about second language acquisition, language structure (Zwiers, 2008), text purpose (Derewianka, 1990; Schleppegrell, 2004), and academic language functions (O'Malley & Pierce, 1996), a collaborating team can work toward developing academic English across the curriculum. To this end, the authors present three essential concepts for working with ELLs. First, how access to content must be created; second, the ways explicit language instruction must be provided; and third, by what methods interaction with content concepts and language must be facilitated.

ACCESSIBLE INSTRUCTION

Accessible instruction minimizes the barriers that language and culture can pose while maintaining content standards. Consider the problem in Table 7.1 presented to students from a math teacher. Are there any obstacles to accessible instruction for ELLs?

This problem is intended to give students practice with multidigit multiplication in a practical application. Students are expected to multiply $5,200 by 12 and get $62,400 as Bob's annual salary. The math teacher explained that she had taught multidigit multiplication to her class of ELLs, but when they attempted this problem, her ELLs got the wrong answer. Assuming that they did not understand the math, she retaught the concept. It was not until the math teacher had a conversation with the ESL teacher that she realized there were language and cultural issues

**Table 7.1. Access Through Awareness
of Language and Culture**

Bob earns $5,200 a month. What is his annual salary?

interfering with students' ability to calculate the problem. In addition to not knowing what *salary* meant, many of the students were immigrants and refugees who had no experience with people earning a reliable, monthly income. Students understood the math concept; it was the language and cultural context they did not understand.

A salary is a cultural phenomenon; yet understanding this concept was crucial in its application to the math problem. Despite popular myth, math is not a universal language. In many cultures, commas are used where Americans place decimal points, and vice versa. If math teachers are not aware of these discrepant conventions, they may not check for understanding of basic concepts, and students will remain confused.

Formative Assessment

Part of creating accessible instruction is making no assumptions about what students know. Due to the spiraling nature of curricula, teachers often make assumptions about knowledge students bring to the classroom. However, ELLs come with varied schooling experiences. With this in mind, the ESL teacher can assist the classroom teacher to better understand students' background knowledge, previous education, and the academic challenges they face. In addition, ESL teachers can help create diagnostic activities to provide information about what students know. In this way, students' personal knowledge can support the process of building essential background for academic learning.

Formative assessments should evaluate language skills as well as content knowledge. Backward-style planning (Wiggins & McTighe, 2004), a strategy that centers on assessment first and instructional activities last, provides the teachers with greater clarity about what students already know and what they need to learn. With this knowledge, teacher can plan how students will be expected to demonstrate skills. With formative assessment, not only do linguistic requirements become clear, but so too does the essential vocabulary students need to succeed academically.

The Conversation Begins

Teachers engaging in collaborative conversations need to discuss the purpose of instruction and how students demonstrate understanding. Once the content objectives are clear, conversations turn to how to remove language barriers and scaffold instruction by focusing on language development. Collaborative conversations between ESL and mainstream teachers can include the following type of questions:

1. What is the purpose of the text (Derewianka, 1990) that students must read?
2. How might we scaffold instruction to present a historical narrative, explain a phenomenon, or provide information about a class of objects?
3. What language (structures and vocabulary) is necessary for students to demonstrate they have met the content objectives?
4. What linguistic and/or culturally specific knowledge is required to build background?
5. How can we use realia (real objects, visuals, and manipulatives) to support instruction?

An Integrated Approach

Collaborative instruction is an approach to teaching ELLs in the mainstream classroom to develop grade-level content-area knowledge, academic skills, and increased English proficiency. To illustrate how ESL and mainstream teachers can implement instruction collaboratively, first review a common teaching scenario illustrated in Table 7.2.

Although the teachers in the scenario work collaboratively, the ESL teacher appears only to assist the instruction of the classroom teacher. A better approach to the one described above would be for the ESL teacher

Table 7.2. Access Through Preteaching

A fourth-grade class in a suburban school is reading *Sarah, Plain and Tall* (Maclachlan, 1987). Two Mexican-born ELLs in the class, Luis and Lupe, who have been in this U.S. school for 2 years speak quite a bit of English. However, both students find the book extremely challenging. The classroom teacher conducts a whole-class lesson on the novel. During this time, Luis puts his head down on his desk, and Lupe appears distracted and plays with her hair. At the end of lesson, the classroom teacher asks the ESL teacher to complete a worksheet with the ELLs, as they are not able to do it by themselves.

to prepare the ELLs by preteaching the story before the whole-group reading lesson. The two teachers also could have planned to provide scaffolding in the form of teacher notes for a section of the book, identifying key vocabulary, or explaining frontier life, one of the book's settings, for support before or during the reading lesson. By understanding the purpose of instruction and key aspects of the story ahead of time, Luis and Lupe would have had a better chance of engagement and access to the mainstream teacher's instruction. To enhance instruction and further collaborative practices, a follow-up conversation between the ESL and mainstream teachers using student performance data could guide the planning of subsequent stages of the instructional cycle.

EXPLICIT LANGUAGE INSTRUCTION

Explicit language instruction requires text analysis. To that end, the conversation between ESL and content teachers should focus on how language is used in academic texts (Derewianka, 1990; O'Malley & Pierce, 1994), grammatical structures (Zwiers, 2008), and the vocabulary (Beck, McKeown, & Kucan, 2002) that will support learning. While the mainstream teacher identifies the content objectives, the ESL teacher can point out the specific ways language functions and determine which language features need to be taught (Echevarria et al., 2008).

The Importance of Language Objectives

In order to meet content objectives, students must first understand how language is being used and its purpose or function. For example, comparing and contrasting are common language functions in social studies texts, and students are likely to encounter words that signal similarity or difference, such as *like, but, in contrast, however, similarly, both, however,* and *even though*. If students do not recognize the meaning of these words, they will not be able to fully comprehend the text. Therefore, teaching the functions of key vocabulary and grammatical structures support students meeting the objectives set for content learning.

After examining an excerpt from a sample fourth grade achievement test (see Table 7.3) (Minnesota Department of Education, n.d.), a conversation between ESL and mainstream teachers was noted in response to the following question: *What essential vocabulary words do ELLs need to know in order to comprehend this passage?*

Initial responses include nouns, verbs, and adjectives such as *feathers, mammals, wings, fly, actual,* and *sunset*. However, after some discussion,

Table 7.3. A Sample Reading Comprehension Task

Even though they fly, bats do not have feathers. Instead they have fur like many other mammals. Bats do not have actual wings, either.... Most bats come out only at night, although some may fly at sunset.

teachers began to recognize that *even though*, *instead*, and *although* were more difficult for students to understand than *mammal* and that they were also essential to understanding the passage. *Even though*, *instead*, and *although* are not easily defined. In the above passage, they are used to differentiate bats from other creatures that fly. Through this discussion about prerequisite vocabulary, teachers began to understand that such words are not easily visualized and that they are best taught through student interaction with multiple examples of their use.

Understanding Vocabulary Instruction

The metaphorical terms *bricks* and *mortar* (Dutro & Moran, 2003) can extend the vocabulary conversation among teachers. *Bricks* are the nouns, verbs, adverbs, and adjectives that are relatively easy to explain to ELLs. Teachers can show pictures or demonstrate actions that illustrate them, and these types of words are the most easily learned. However, comprehension of a text also requires mastery of the *mortar*, the language that holds the bricks together and conveys the text's meaning and purpose.

Identifying the *bricks* and *mortar* is essential for extracting language development objectives that support content objectives. Language development objectives as we define them include three aspects: vocabulary (Beck et al., 2002), language structure (Zwiers, 2008), and text purpose (Derewianka, 1990; O'Malley & Pierce 1996; Schleppegrell, 2004). Using the sample reading comprehension task about bats, Table 7.4 illustrates how a *bricks* and *mortar* text analysis can further the conversation about how language development and content work together.

Choosing the right vocabulary is an intentional process. Teachers can employ the following questions to discuss their vocabulary selection decisions:

1. What vocabulary do students need to comprehend to meet the content objectives (*bricks*)?
2. What *mortar* do students need in order to make sense of the function of the text?

Table 7.4. Components of a Language Objective Using the Text About Bats

Text Purpose	Mortar	Bricks
• compare • contrast • differentiate	• even though • instead • although	• feathers • mammals • wings • fly

Tiering Vocabulary

To make vocabulary instruction efficient, teachers need to discuss how to make calculated decisions about what to teach. Beck et al. (2002) advocated focusing on Tier 2 words—academic vocabulary that can be meaningful across content areas. Examples from the elementary curriculum would include *even though, line, principle*, and *reciprocal*.

Basic nouns or verbs (Tier 1 words such as *man, house,* and *school*), are more likely in place for most learners. However, these primary words are essential for beginning-level ELLs to know and understand. Content-specific vocabulary limited to specific subject matter and situations (Tier 3 words such as *photosynthesis, carpetbagger,* or *onomatopoeia*), do not often transfer to other disciplines. Most crucial to vocabulary instruction, Tier 2 word selection should be dynamic and based on criteria such as age, task, instructional purpose, and linguistic proficiency. Since students do not retain vocabulary in isolation, teachers must create multiple, meaningful opportunities for practice and application embedded into daily activities.

INCREASING INTERACTION WITH LANGUAGE AND CONTENT

For decades, student–student interaction and student–content interaction have been promoted through cooperative learning activities (Gillies, 2007), which support students' engagement, leading to more robust discussions around content and extending ideas beyond the current task (Nagel, 2001; Tompkins, 2006). Interaction can be as simple as a quick turn to one's partner in a *think–pair–share* exercise or can include cooperative groups with complex assignments. Regardless of the form interaction takes, the additional step of verbalizing knowledge and engaging in the communicative process provides critical support for students who are learning language and content simultaneously.

Promoting Cooperative Strategies

There are two ways ESL and mainstream teachers can collaborate on increasing the amount of interaction in the classroom—through planning and by cofacilitating and managing student groups. Carefully planning varied group configurations is equally important when the class is a mix of native and nonnative English speakers or a sheltered-content class for ELLs. Questions to guide the teacher conversations include:

1. What is the purpose of student grouping for this instructional unit?
2. Where does grouping fall in the instructional cycle?
3. If the purpose of grouping is to activate prior knowledge, is the use of native language possible?
4. If grouping is to deepen the learning process, how can native and nonnative English speakers be combined?

- Are there cultural considerations?
- How can the task product be differentiated for language proficiencies?
- What language must be explicitly taught in order for students to demonstrate knowledge pertaining to the task?
- How do the thinking tasks relate back to the academic language functions?
- Are turn-taking strategies and expectations clear to all group members?
- What kind of accountability exists for participation?

In addition to coplanning, the ESL teacher can provide instructional collaboration, working side by side the mainstream teacher in the same classroom. Together, these teachers can foster interaction that can teach oral academic discourse. Effective group work is a learned skill for students, and until cooperative procedures are a natural part of classroom expectations and student behavior, the ESL teacher can help provide management as well as language support. To that end, instruction might focus on strategies students need for presenting information, seeking clarification, paraphrasing and restating, asking questions, and disagreeing in group discussions.

TEACHER ROLES IN COLLABORATION

ELLs' success is dependent on the degree to which they can access the curriculum. These students require content-embedded, explicit language instruction to acquire academic English and to learn the content simultaneously. ELLs' learning needs call on teachers to rethink their instruction and to draw on the expertise of both partners. ESL teachers are typically well-versed in linguistic and cultural issues that ELLs face, whereas mainstream teachers are content experts; it is in the intersection of these two academic domains (language and content) where the success of ELLs lies.

As teachers begin the deeper discussion of language and content, both are stretched to learn new ways of thinking about accessible instruction. The cocreation of new understanding also encourages changes in teacher behaviors, beliefs, and roles. Collaboration is more than working together; it is working together to create a new way of teaching that reaches all ELLs.

REFERENCES

August, D., & Shanahan, T. (Eds.). (2006). *Developing literacy in second language learners: Report of the National Literacy Panel on language minority children and youth*. Mahwah, NJ: Erlbaum.

Beck, I. L., McKeown, M. G., & Kucan, L. (2002). *Bringing words to life: Robust vocabulary instruction*. New York, NY: Guilford Press.

Derewianka, B. (1990). *Exploring how texts work*. Newtown, Australia: Primary English Teaching Association.

Dutro, S., & Moran, C. (2003). Rethinking English language instruction: An architectural approach. In G. Garcia (Ed.), *English learners reaching the highest level of literacy* (pp. 227-258). Newark, DE: International Reading Association.

Echevarria, J., Short, D., & Powers, K. (2006). School reform and standards-based education: A model for English-language learners. *Journal of Educational Research, 99*, 195-211.

Echevarria, J., Vogt, M. E., & Short, D. (2008). *Making content comprehensible for English learners: The SIOP model* (3rd ed.). Boston, MA: Pearson/Allyn & Bacon.

Gillies, R. M. (2007). *Cooperative learning: Integrating theory and practice*. Los Angeles, CA: SAGE.

Goldenberg, C. (2008, Summer). Teaching English language learners: What the research does—and does not—say. *American Educator*, 8-23, 42-44.

Herrera, S., & Murry, K. G. (2005). *Mastering ESL and bilingual methods: Differentiated instruction for culturally and linguistically diverse (CLD) students*. Boston, MA: Pearson/Allyn & Bacon.

Hill, J. D., & Flynn, K. M. (2006). *Classroom instruction that works with English language learners*. Alexandria, VA: Association for Supervision and Curriculum Development.

MacLachlan, P. (1987). *Sarah plain and tall*. New York, NY: Harper & Row.

Minnesota Department of Education. (n. d.). *Minnesota comprehensive assessments—Series II: Reading item sampler, Grade 4*. Retrieved from http://www.stma.k12.mn.us/curriculum/testing/_document/Grade4ReadingItemSampler.pdf

Nagel, G. (2001). *Effective grouping for literacy instruction.* Boston, MA: Allyn & Bacon.

O'Malley, J. M., & Pierce, L. V. (1996) *Authentic assessment for English language learners: Practical approaches for teachers.* Reading, MA: Addison-Wesley.

Schleppegrell, M. J. (2004). The language of schooling: A functional linguistics perspective. Mahwah, NJ: Erlbaum.

Short, D., & Echevarria, J. (1999). *The sheltered instruction observation protocol: A tool for teacher-researcher collaboration and professional development.* Retrieved from http://www.cal.org/resources/digest/sheltered.html

Tompkins, G. E. (2006). *Literacy for the 21st century: A balanced approach* (4th ed.). Upper Saddle River, NJ: Merrill Prentice Hall.

Wiggins, G., & McTighe, J. (2004). *Understanding by design: Professional development workbook.* Alexandria, VA: Association for Supervision and Curriculum Development.

Zwiers, J. (2007). *Building academic language: Essential practices for content classrooms, Grades 5–12.* San Francisco, CA: Jossey-Bass.

CHAPTER 8

BARN RAISING IN NEW ENGLAND

Working Together on Sheltering Spaces

Patricia Page Aube, Bonnie Baer-Simahk, and Kelly Waples McLinden

BACKGROUND

The landscape shifted for English language learners (ELLs) and their teachers in our district, when the proponents of the English-only movement prevailed, and our state enacted regulations requiring elimination of transitional bilingual education. Required by Massachusetts state regulation, Sheltered English Immersion became the new program model (Massachusetts Department of Elementary and Secondary Education, 2009a), and brought us to a new frontier in teaching ELLs in Fitchburg, MA. A team of concerned and innovative educators has been working collaboratively to improve student outcomes, and their story is told in this chapter by the district's ELL director, curriculum integration specialist, and one of the ESL (English as a second language) teachers involved in the project.

For most of its history, Fitchburg has been a mill town, home to a once flourishing paper industry. Located in North Central Massachusetts, our city has always been attractive to immigrant groups, who have moved here for economic opportunity. Recent years have seen a decline in the paper industry, along with other manufacturing businesses in the surrounding area, as plants have closed leaving many struggling to earn a living.

Fitchburg has a linguistically diverse urban school district in which 30 percent of its students speak a home language other than English. Sixty-six percent of them qualify for free and reduced lunch on the basis of family income. Teachers confront the challenges of economic disparity, student mobility, and limited-English proficiency in their classrooms every day.

Over the years, teachers in our district have tried many ways to address the content-learning needs of ELLs in general education classrooms, but nothing has been as effective as our collaborative teaching project designed to teach the language of mathematics. The ELL director brought together math and ESL teachers to write a content-based ESL curriculum, which was piloted in ESL classes, and guided by the district's curriculum intervention specialist. The ESL teachers in the project were supported with coaching, coteaching, technical assistance, and time to plan together. We created a content-based ESL curriculum and strengthened math teachers' capacity to deliver sheltered-content instruction. Like the New England farmers that came before us—who gathered in community to build each other's barns—we found that the best way to do this work is *together*.

THE CHALLENGE

Our ELLs were struggling in school, especially in math class, reflecting similar difficulties seen across the country. They were not engaged in classroom discourse, academic achievement was below average, and performance on Massachusetts state assessments was low. Teachers expressed a need for support, and the sense of urgency in the district was increasing. Four main goals were identified:

1. Improve academic performance of English language learners in mainstream math classrooms.
2. Improve classroom engagement and academic discourse.
3. Provide job embedded professional development for ESL and math teachers.
4. Design a content-based ESL curriculum with a focus on math.

Service delivery for the district's ELLs needed to change. ESL instruction was essentially disconnected from content instruction, and many of our ELLs were floundering in the regular classrooms. Past practices included middle-school principals assigning ESL teachers to teach math to ELLs. Although ESL teachers were not licensed to do so, the principals thought that the math teachers were less prepared to differentiate for students who could not easily comprehend the language. Local concerns about these decisions and an understanding of state regulations put an end to this practice. Our math teachers were faced with the challenge of making their instruction accessible to the ELLs in their classrooms, but were largely unfamiliar with second-language-teaching methodology. Frustration was growing, and teachers were ready for a change. As it turned out, the most striking change occurred in the teachers themselves.

THE COLLABORATIVE PROJECT

Our district launched a pilot project, which featured the collaborative design of content-based ESL curriculum and coteaching, with an emphasis on the preteaching of mathematical language in the ESL class. This project began in one middle school and then expanded into two elementary schools. Teams of teachers came together—with support from a full-time curriculum integration specialist—to design a curriculum to improve the instruction of ELLs. During this process, teachers continually strengthened their collegial relationships in ways that supported maximum student achievement.

Framing

The initial phase of this project emphasized the development of a middle school ESL curriculum with a focus on the academic language of math. Our ESL teachers, along with the math-certified curriculum integration specialist, came together to write curriculum over the summer. The director secured grant funding to support the project, and an ESL teacher recruited math teachers to become involved. She started by inviting one math teacher, known for her diligence, enthusiasm and work ethic, and before long several similarly inclined had joined in. The team embarked on a comprehensive process of curriculum development, using the Massachusetts Department of Elementary and Secondary Education (2009b) online curriculum guide. Curriculum maps were drafted, but the real work began during the school year when the ESL and math teachers began to write lessons together creating the framework for the project.

Building

Supported by grant funding and facilitated by the curriculum integration specialist, three paired teams of middle-school teachers met to jointly prepare lessons after school. At each grade level (6-8), a math teacher and an ESL teacher formed a partnership. Each team worked together on ESL preteaching lessons that aligned with grade level math content. As a result of these partnerships, the ESL teacher addressed the academic language of a particular standard in math during one weekly ESL class period prior to students being instructed in their regular math class.

Throughout the year, the partners continued to examine each other's content standards and designed new preteaching lessons at monthly meetings consistently incorporating the district math curriculum standards into content-ESL lessons. This collaboration also helped the math teachers to strengthen their capacity to provide sheltered content instruction to ELLs. Sheltered content instruction integrates language and content objectives in each lesson, providing access to grade-level content while promoting English language proficiency. In addition to the informal learning that occurred between the math and ESL teachers, thirty hours of in-service training in sheltered content instruction was provided for math teachers.

The role of our curriculum integration specialist was important. This project called for an on-site overseer to manage the details of the project, to support connecting relationships among participating teachers, to consult with the ELL director regarding progress as well as necessary adjustments, and to take the lead on the documenting the lesson development. Her duties included:

- supporting the collaboration of teaching teams in all aspects of this project;
- scheduling and facilitating the conversations between and among teams of teachers;
- documenting the work of the teaching teams;
- researching resources and materials that were used in the lessons;
- working with the teachers to develop the common lesson plan template based on the components of a SIOP lesson plan (Echevarria, Vogt, & Short, 2007); and
- listening to the concerns, helping teams trouble shoot, and celebrating each student success.

Coaching and technical assistance had always been envisioned as key aspects of the role of the curriculum intervention specialist. She coached math teachers in sheltered content methodology and helped ESL teachers to consolidate their knowledge of math content in order to present related language in authentic mathematical context. She demonstrated lessons for teachers and conducted debriefing sessions, observed teacher instruction and provided feedback, and conducted observational assessment of students in their math classes. Spending time observing in classrooms, recording data, and documenting student performance was especially important in the early months as teachers wondered if this project would pay off in student outcomes. Fortunately, early assessment data indicated that following the pretaught lessons, the ELLs were more academically engaged in the math class as evidenced by their mathematical discourse. This finding reassured the teachers involved in the project that they were on the right track.

Making Room

It soon became apparent that in order to design and deliver relevant content-based ESL lessons with a focus on math effectively, the ESL teachers needed to spend some time observing and interacting with students in the math classroom. We needed to see if the pretaught lessons were paying off.

What started out as a curriculum initiative began to influence instructional practice in some interesting ways. Coteaching practices began to evolve, and ESL teachers began to spend more time teaching language within the math classroom in addition to their preteach lessons. Although the math teachers had received in-service training in sheltered content instruction provided by an outside consultant, they appeared to learn more from their colleagues in the course of actually working together in the coteaching relationship. This is frequently referred to as embedded professional development (Croft, Coggshall, Dolan, Powers, & Killion, 2010) and it is where we saw the most powerful learning occur: Teachers were learning from one another.

The coteaching had not been part of the original plan, and it needed to be explored carefully. The approved program model in Massachusetts

Table 8.1. The ESL Teacher Reflects

Are our students more engaged in the math class, after having had the preteach lesson? Are they more confident? Are they formulating answers on their own, or are they waiting to see how their classmates are responding? Many questions are arising. I am hoping the answers will become evident through this collaboration.

is known as Sheltered English Immersion (Massachusetts Department of Elementary and Secondary Education, 2009a), and it features two distinct instructional practices. The model requires direct ESL instruction to groups of ELLs by licensed ESL teachers using specialized materials and sheltered content instruction provided by licensed content teachers. In the past, this district was issued a directive from the Massachusetts Department of Elementary and Secondary Education requiring it to discontinue the practice of assigning ESL teachers to work in content classrooms. In some schools, this had devolved into the ESL teacher serving as an instructional assistant in the delivery of content instruction, which is a common complaint among ESL teachers working within content classrooms in other school districts around the country (Baecher & Bell, 2011). For coteaching to be allowed, this project needed to be very clear in its implementation, and instruction had to be delivered according to the state program model. ESL teachers in the math classroom needed to focus on teaching the *language* of math, and clarifying language-based misunderstanding. They had to be teachers, not math helpers, and with that in mind, the coteaching remained in place.

Curriculum development continued, and the curriculum integration specialist worked with the teams in their classrooms and at the monthly meetings. She edited and expanded upon their lesson drafts and refined the formatting, completing a collection of over 80 lessons across three grade levels. In addition to the monthly planning meetings, teachers began to seek each other out informally throughout the days and weeks as needed to refine their planning and scheduling.

In the second year of the project, the curriculum development along with preteaching and coteaching was expanded into two elementary schools. Building on insights offered by participants of the middle school pilot project, coteaching was presented as an opportunity to the elementary teachers, from the beginning of their involvement with the project. However, the focus on curriculum development remained central to the work. From the start, the ELL director knew that one of the most important factors contributing to the success of this collaboration was that initial

Table 8.2. The ESL Teacher Reflects

Finding time to meet is always an issue, as differing teaching schedules make sitting down not always an option. When we can't make time to meet, any spare moment must do. Drive-bys (spare moments in the hallways, lunchroom, parking lot to share vital information about upcoming lessons, student progress, or misunderstanding) have become an integral and essential part of our collaboration repertoire. While those brief meetings do not replace the crucial common planning time, they have filled in the cracks as needed.

curriculum work. These middle school and elementary math and ESL teachers did not originally come together to *collaborate*, they came together to create something. In order for people to develop the good working skills that support strong collaborative practice, they need to have an authentic purpose for working together, and to continue working together, because it is not easy.

We found that collegiality and trust are the foundation of collaborative practices. These fundamental elements do not occur solely because teachers socialize together. While social connections are important, the real key to building strong partnerships and effective working relationships is having a shared focus—a job to do. The process of creating the curriculum together helped teachers to more fully appreciate their shared dedication to their content areas as well as to the students they serve.

Our New England predecessors knew much about the power of collaboration. They would come to each other's homes and work together to build barns for their neighbors. As teachers, we come to each other's classrooms to build better instruction for our students. Teachers report that collaboration has changed the way in which they teach in dramatic ways.

RESULTS

As hoped, our team of ESL teachers, math teachers, and project leaders saw benefits to our work, some expected and some more surprising. We expected to accomplish a good deal of curriculum writing and we did. Seventy-eight content-ESL lessons were created at the middle school and 87 at the elementary school level. We also expected to see an increase in the academic engagement of ELLs in math class and we did. Students were more engaged in their learning. Observational data were collected and the changes noted were that the ELLs:

- communicated the content and language objectives;
- raised their hands to ask and answer questions;
- had academic conversations in both their home language and English;
- focused on the teachers and other students during whole class discussions; and
- participated in small group and partner work.

Students demonstrated academic growth as well. In certain cases, students' content grades have increased two to three letter grades. Some

Table 8.3. The ESL Teacher Reflects

This "experiment" in collaboration was truly a success for this ESL teacher. It had always been a joy to see my ESL students being successful in my own classroom, but seeing them thrive in the mainstream math classroom was fantastic! Not only were they using the language correctly, but confidently. Having self-confidence has done them wonders. An unexpected benefit to this coteaching was the shift in how both ESL teachers and students are viewed. The regular classroom teachers, recognizing that the ESL preteach strategies have worked so successfully, are now interested in using them with the mainstream class. What a morale boost!

Table 8.4. The ESL Teacher Reflects

This lesson has me fairly nervous, although talking it through with my colleagues helped. It amazed all of us how many different meanings there are for flip, slide, and turn before you even start to talk about math. Once we discussed all these possible meanings together it again helped my classroom teacher friends to begin to understand how difficult the acquisition of English can be for these kids. It has helped this ESL teacher to feel more of a part of the students' everyday academic life inside their regular classroom. Both classroom teachers have told me that this preteaching has made their students feel more confident. They are raising their hands more, are relating what we have done together prior to the classroom lesson to their peers, and even explaining concepts. Success!

beginners have scored proficient or advanced on the Massachusetts Comprehensive Assessment System (MCAS) (http://www.doe.mass.edu/mcas/). ELLs were recruited by a math teacher to enroll in eighth grade Algebra class, in spite of their test-based ineligibility. This math teacher believed these students could handle the advanced math content, and that the test scores were a reflection of language proficiency level, not their ability to succeed in his algebra class. This was quite a departure from the days when the ELLs were sent off to the ESL teacher because nobody knew what to do with them!

One of the most promising outcomes has been the change in collegial relationships that has evolved over time. Math and ESL teachers now express a greater understanding and appreciation of each other's work, recognizing the complexity of the instructional objectives for which each group is responsibility. ESL teachers know the math curriculum frameworks, and math teachers know the *Massachusetts English Language Proficiency Benchmarks and Outcomes* (Massachusetts Department of Elementary and Secondary Education, 2003). ESL teachers have noted a growing sense of partnership with their content colleagues, feeling valued as an

Table 8.5. The ESL Teacher Reflects

This collaboration has changed me as a teacher. While I always knew my students had the ability to be successful in them, the preteaching of the math lessons allowed for them to readily display their talents. Looking back it makes sense: teach them what they need before, as that is the key to unlocking their knowledge. I also feel that my students and I are a part of every aspect of our school. The ESL students are no longer seen as mine or as my sole responsibility: we all share in their successes.

---

equal member of the team with important contributions—an observation not unique to staff in our school district (Honigsfeld & Dove, 2010).

RECOMMENDATIONS

There are several elements that have been key to the success of this work in our school district, and these factors have been noted by others in the field (Dunne & Villani, 2007; Honigsfeld & Dove, 2010; Spraker, 2003; Teemant, Wink, & Tyra, 2010):

- Dedicated staff assigned to facilitate the effort—The curriculum integration specialist coached and collaborated with the teams involved in the curriculum work, served as liaison to administrative leadership, presented demonstration lessons and facilitated group work.
- Voluntary participation—Teacher enthusiasm for this work and the commitment they demonstrated were related to the power of choice.
- Administrative support—Grant funding, technical assistance, encouragement and oversight were essential elements, and continue to be required for ongoing implementation.
- Scheduling facilitated—Principals and guidance counselors made every attempt to arrange schedules in a way that allowed for clustering ELLs on one team.
- Curriculum Foundation in place—Curriculum benchmark documents were already in place for mathematics content, serving as a great springboard for our collaborative efforts.

As the numbers of ELLs in our schools increase, our district needs to move forward with instructional and structural changes if we are to help our students succeed. The collaborative efforts of the ESL and math teachers have been a promising step in the right direction. The word has spread from teacher to teacher, and there is growing interest in expanding this model among educators. We believe that in order for this type of collaborative project to succeed, it is important to preserve the voluntary nature of participation, at least initially. Support from the administrators and teachers is essential. Collaborative work takes time and focused effort. Additionally, funding is needed at the beginning in order to start-up the curriculum development and team-building.

For continued program success, teachers need time to meet for planning and coordinating their instruction as well (Teemant, 2011). Finding common planning time in the school schedule is challenging, and although teachers do make the effort to meet, administrators need to identify resources to support this work. Finally, curriculum review needs to be regularly scheduled so that maps, units, and lesson plans are refined.

We have all heard the old sayings about the power of community to get results: "Many hands make light work" and "Two heads are better than one." We know that "all of us are stronger than one of us." And although it might be possible, we know that it generally takes more than one farmer to build the barn.

REFERENCES

Baecher, L., & Bell, A. (2011, March). *Elementary push in/pull out instruction: From coping to collaborating*. Paper presented at the 45th Annual Convention and Exhibit of Teachers of English to Speakers of Other Languages (TESOL), New Orleans, LA.

Croft, A., Coggshall, J. G., Dolan, M., & Powers, E., with Killion, J. (2010). *Job-embedded professional development: What it is, who is responsible, and how to get it done well.* Retrieved from http://www.tqsource.org/publications/JEPD%20Issue%20Brief.pdf

Darling-Hammond, L., & Richardson, N. (2009). Teacher learning: What matters? *Educational Leadership, 66*(5), 46-53.

Dunne, K., & Villani, S. (2007). *Mentoring new teachers through collaborative coaching: Linking teacher and student learning.* San Francisco, CA: WestEd.

Echevarria, J., Vogt, M. E., & Short, D. (2007). *Making content comprehensible for English learners: The SIOP model* (3rd ed.). Boston, MA: Pearson Allyn & Bacon

Honigsfeld, A., & Dove, M. (2010). *Collaboration and co-teaching: Strategies for English learners.* Thousand Oaks, CA: Corwin Press.

Massachusetts Department of Elementary and Secondary Education. (2003). *English language proficiency benchmarks and outcomes for English language learners (ELPBO).* Retrieved from http://www.doe.mass.edu/ell/benchmark.pdf

Massachusetts Department of Elementary and Secondary Education. (2009a). *Guidance on using MEPA results to plan sheltered English immersion (SEI) instruc-*

tion and make reclassification decisions for limited English proficient (LEP) students. Retrieved from http://www.doe.mass.edu/ell/guidance_laws.html

Massachusetts Department of Elementary and Secondary Education. (2009b). *Guide for developing a content-based English as a second language curriculum.* Retrieved from http://www.doe.mass.edu/ell/cdguide/

Spraker, J. (2003). *Teacher teaming in relation to student performance: Findings from the literature.* Portland, OR: Northwest Regional Educational Laboratory.

Teemant, A. (2011, March). *Examining ESL coaching outcomes: Transformation, sustainability and student achievement.* Paper presented at the 45th Annual Convention and Exhibit of Teachers of English to Speakers of Other Languages (TESOL), New Orleans, LA.

Teemant, A., Wink, J., & Tyra, S. (2010). Effects of coaching on teacher use of sociocultural instructional practices. *Teaching and Teacher Education, 27,* 683-693.

CHAPTER 9

DOUBLE-TEAMING

Teaching Academic Language in High School Biology

Rita MacDonald, James Nagle, Theresa Akerley, and Heidi Western

> *Students gathered for the first day of biology class seem unsettled. Two teachers are at the front of the classroom, alternating discussion of expectations and requirements. Why two teachers? What kind of biology class was this?*

These students soon learned that this was a very different science class, one in which two teachers—a biology teacher and an English as a second language (ESL) teacher—collaborated on a biology course that integrated the academic language of science with the content of biology. Educators have long known that sheltered instruction alone is insufficient to close the English language learner (ELL) achievement gap, that explicit instruction in academic English is needed, and that language and content instruction must occur simultaneously (Goldenberg, 2008). Given the increased focus on literacy across the curriculum (Biancarosa & Snow, 2004) and the growing awareness that native English speakers also need explicit instruction in academic language (Zwiers, 2008), the integration of literacy instruction into content classrooms is well supported.

Coteaching and Other Collaborative Practices in the EFL/ESL Classroom:
Rationale, Research, Reflections, and Recommendations, pp. 91–99
Copyright © 2012 by Information Age Publishing
All rights of reproduction in any form reserved.

Yet, most teachers lack the training to provide instruction in academic English (National Council of Teachers of English, 2004). Literacy initiatives fit easily into the elementary school, where teachers' roles already include literacy development. For secondary teachers, however, who define their jobs as teaching content, the pressure to move quickly through a tightly packed curriculum and lack of training in literacy development combine to make the added focus on content literacy beyond the reach of many.

This chapter describes the path taken by a unique double team of coteachers and mentors formed by these authors to address this challenge. First, we outline the theoretical framework of coteaching and the importance of related professional development. Second, we discuss the process of planning, teaching, and assessing student understanding using the coteaching model. Third, we analyze student work and discuss students' growth in content and literacy. Finally, we discuss the benefits of using functional language analysis in coteaching and professional development in secondary schools.

THE THEORETICAL BACKGROUND FOR COTEACHING

Coteaching derives its theoretical roots from Little's (1990) construct of joint work. Studying teachers who worked together, Little defined joint work as shared responsibility for teaching, involving collective conceptions of autonomy, support, and initiative with regard to professional practice. Joint work requires teachers to both collaborate as professionals and investigate their teaching in an honest and forthright manner for the benefit of their students' learning.

Many since Little's (1990) seminal work have found the dual elements of collaboration and inquiry as essential for teacher learning as for student learning. Collaboration among special educators and general education teachers initially defined the coteaching framework (Gately & Gately, 2001), which has been successfully expanded into a variety of models involving ESL and content specialists (Dove & Honigsfeld, 2010; Honigsfeld & Dove, 2008). In this chapter we describe one such model in which two teachers—an ESL teacher and a biology teacher—collaborate to teach biology.

THE STUDENTS, THE TEAM, AND THE PROCESS

The purpose of the cotaught biology course was to increase ELLs' participation in a college-oriented science class, which many had avoided due to its rapid pace and heavy demands for academic reading and writing. The course was structured around a standard biology text, which for many ELLs as well as native English speakers posed a significant challenge, but the less demanding course available did not satisfy college admission requirements. Believing that all students should be prepared for college, the high school teachers committed to teach this challenging course together. The school administration provided valuable coplanning time, and they were further supported by a team of two faculty from a local college whose expertise paralleled that of the teachers: a secondary science professor from the education department and an ESL specialist from the applied linguistics department. After meeting to explore goals and approaches to teaching, the two teams agreed to form a double team of coteachers and mentors.

During the summer, the four team members met for shared study, reading and discussing *The Language of Schooling: A Functional Linguistics Perspective* (Schleppegrell, 2004) and *Reading in Secondary Content Areas: A Language-Based Pedagogy* (Fang & Schleppegrell, 2008). As they grappled with the initially daunting conceptual framework and vocabulary of functional linguistics, their belief that coteaching would lead to shared knowledge and expertise (Dove & Honigsfeld, 2010) gave them confidence to continue.

Merging Roles and Responsibilities

Team members worked separately at first. The biology teacher and secondary education professor developed activities based on critical thinking skills to encourage deep engagement with the content of biology. The ESL specialists added sheltered instruction strategies (Echevarria, Vogt, & Short, 2004) to differentiate instruction across English proficiency levels and analyzed the language of the texts, the higher-order questions, and the cognitive tasks through which students would construct meaning. Knowing that ELLs can often read a passage flawlessly yet be unable to extract its deep meaning, they recognized the need for instruction beyond vocabulary. Students needed to correctly interpret discourse features common to science: the language of cause and effect, comparison, sequence and inference (Zwiers, 2008). To participate meaningfully in the discourse community of science, students needed control of that language. Thus, the ESL specialists planned separate activities to teach the language of science.

Separated initially by comfort and experience into traditional specialty areas, team members soon developed enough shared understanding to move into what Davidson (2006) called creative coconstruction. When teachers developed the shared understanding that the content of biology was expressed, in large part, through the language of biology, the instructional plans changed; biology was taught *through* its language, as compared to earlier lessons that taught biology *and* its language (Fang & Schleppegrell, 2008).

Moving Toward Academic Language

Working on academic language was difficult: new ideas, new vocabulary, and too many abstractions. Team members asked repeatedly, "But what does that look like?" until one of the college faculty suggested a careful examination of the language in an exemplar lab report. Deconstructing that text, team members discovered firsthand how nominalizations enabled the writer to use theme-rheme patterns to deliver information and build a logical chain of evidence concisely. The formerly abstract notion that academic writing is lexically dense suddenly made sense. In addition, they noted the author's finely nuanced portrayal of the study's conclusions, casting doubt on previous research simply by the careful choice of modals.

This analysis of the content of the lab report—the *what* of meaning—accompanied by discourse analysis of the language used—the *how* of meaning—moved the team beyond theory to collaborative practice. The biology teacher remarked, "After we looked together at the actual language in a lab report, I understood why we use the patterns we do in academic writing, and why my students need to learn them;" and "Working together to analyze how meaning was constructed *through language* was like crossing the Rubicon. We had finally arrived!"

The coteachers had been disheartened by students' early lab reports, replete with unsupported inferences and personal pronouns and written in conversational tone. Clearly, even the English-fluent students needed instruction in academic writing. Throughout their school experiences, students had been taught to write personal narratives and persuasive essays, rather than the more formal, objective discourse of science. They had not been taught to use theme-rheme patterns to move the logic of an argument forward concisely, nor had they been taught to use passive verbs to foreground events under consideration while keeping the actor in the background. They had not been taught the gradation of certainty that can be constructed through careful use of qualifiers and modals. With their new and shared understanding of scientific writing, the team set out to develop the resources needed.

Resources Developed

Together, the two teams of coteachers and mentors explored the interplay of cognitive and language functions in the construction of meaning.

Using lab reports and science articles as mentor texts, the high school teachers helped students identify specific language structures used to accomplish the cognitive and linguistic tasks of science. With their students, they developed a series of *language menus*, posted in the room and copied into students' notebooks. Table 9.1 shows examples of language structures and their uses in science. Both teachers provided modeling and instruction in the use of the specific language structures outlined in Table 9.1. Students practiced using them in oral responses and were required to incorporate them in written reports.

Changes in Instruction

The movement of team members beyond their specialty areas was mirrored in the classroom. Like those studied by Dove and Honigsfeld (2010), this team began with one coteaching model but soon moved fluidly among several. Early in the year, the biology teacher introduced the content objectives and the ESL teacher the language objectives; ELLs worked with the ESL teacher and native English speakers with the biology teacher; and the ESL teacher delivered minilessons on language to ELLs in the midst of the biology lesson.

Later observations demonstrated a dramatic change when—for the first time—the biology teacher asked, "How do you know this writer is certain of his conclusions? What specific language identifies that? Let's examine these lab reports to see how scientists express uncertainty and certainty in scientific writing." Following this prompt, both teachers monitored mixed groups of students developing charts of language structures expressing various degrees of certainty. An observer would have had difficulty identifying the biology and ESL teachers; each teacher taught the entire class. Having developed a shared conceptual framework of scientific language, the teachers worked as one.

Writing Like Scientists: Improvement in Academic Language

Critical to *doing science* is students' ability to construct meaning through higher-order cognitive activities of analyzing data and making reasonable inferences. Reporting complex higher-order thinking requires the skillful use of academic language (Zwiers, 2008). Early in the semester, teachers had noted students' superficial data analysis, their inability to describe the data accurately, and their unqualified inferences. Together, they

Table 9.1. Examples of Language Functions and Structures in Biology

Language Functions and Their Relationship to Cognitive Functions	Sample Language Structures
Comparison and Contrast These structures are used in both the process and retelling of data analysis, as students note similarities and differences in data sets or construe meaning from written reports of other scientists. Accurate, concise description of findings is a critical component of scientific writing.	**Comparison** also as well as likewise just as... so Similarly in the same manner The insects *all* responded *the same way.* In *both* situations... **Contrast** on the other hand on the contrary nevertheless even though whereas while yet however by comparison in contrast compared to although unlike instead All subjects *except* one... The increase in size was *greater* for X.
Cause and Effect These discourse structures occur frequently, and are rarely signaled by the well-known conversational marker "because." Recognition of the varied forms are critical to correct construal of meaning.	for this reason due to this resulted from in order to since therefore hence thus if ... (unstated "then") subsequently Rabbits' fur turns white in winter; *due to this,* it is camouflaged from its predators. *Subsequently,* the survival rate of rabbits with this trait is greater, *resulting in* the increase in this trait in the gene pool.
Hypothesis and Degree of Certainty Structures that express varying degrees of certainty are used to describe or to predict a possible model based on given information and data.	appears seems estimate predict suspect that likely or less likely given the evidence lesser chance probably theoretically since we know that ... *If* pine trees grow in sandy soil they will *probably* grow in this area. The unreal or hypothetical uses the subjunctive: (had it not been, were we to have done so) to present alternative, yet unrealized, possibilities. Modal verbs—can, could, should, may, might, must—are used to express degree of certainty.
Process and Sequence Correct and skillful use of these structures allows for the exact portrayal and replication of scientific procedures. Precise description of process and sequence is critical to the correct construal of cause and effect.	**Putting Action in Order:** first, second, third, following, then, next, at this time/point, after that, subsequently **Signaling Other Action:** concurrently, simultaneously, while, meanwhile, previously, since Concluding: finally, summative

Table 9.2. Student Interpretation of Graphs Before and After Instruction

Student	Before Instruction	After Instruction
A	This is a graph showing adults in Great Britain that have lung cancer from smoking. The relationship between lung cancer and smoking is shown in these trends that they go hand in hand. 1948-2005 is the time period for this graph and it shows that more men smoked than women and the percentage has gone down for both genders since 1948.	This graph *illustrates the relationship between* lung cancer and smoking with adults from Great Britain. From looking at the graph, *it appears that* more men smoke than women, but the smoking rates have gone down since 1948. The *graph also indicates* that smoking goes hand in hand with lung cancer and that smoking *may increase* your chance of getting lung cancer.
B (ELL)	Human population and extinctions When human population increases the species extinction also increases. As human population grow they took the species' habitat	*The graph shows* the evidence about human population and extinctions. If the human population decreases, the extinctions *may also* decrease.
C	The taller people were playing baseball. The green shows the average height of Americans and that height increases because more food was being produced and nutrients were being watched.	The growth of the average U.S. person *demonstrates the fact that* nutrition became a bigger part of peoples' lives and they reached full potential. *This further illustrates* how baseball players also increased in height but probably paid *even more* attention to their nutrition *than* the average person.

planned instruction to increase students' skill in data analysis and in the careful development and statement of inference.

Table 9.2 provides transcriptions of students' written interpretations of data depicted on graphs, and shows the effect of instruction on both the process and language of data analysis. Prior to instruction, students did little beyond describing the graph, with limited data interpretation and few supportable inferences. After instruction in the process and language of data interpretation, all students demonstrated increased specificity of descriptions and more careful attention to degree of certainty of stated inferences. Their demonstrated mastery of these aspects of scientific language suggests that they will decode this language correctly in complex scientific text, thus increasing their comprehension of the content of biology.

REFLECTIONS AND IMPLICATIONS FOR PRACTICE

Given the sophisticated content of biology—expressed in the complex academic language of biology—teachers need to plan, instruct, and assess for both scientific literacy and content. Coteaching is an ideal teaching model when the integrated expertise of language and content specialists is needed.

We have described a process of coteaching that incorporates collaborative analysis of the higher-order cognitive demands of biology with functional analysis of the language needed for deep engagement as a tool for analyzing, planning, instructing, and assessing learning in a high school biology class. By merging the process of coteaching with the analytical framework of functional linguistics, we have provided a way for teachers to work together to improve student learning in academic language and content at the secondary level. Having done so, we have three conclusions:

1. Coplanning time is essential. Without time to familiarize each other with the content of biology and the process of functional language analysis, and to analyze text, review student work, and plan lessons together, the participating teachers would not have been able to learn from one another.
2. Coteaching requires shared understanding of the specific content and language expectations for the course. Even though early in the year the two high school teachers thought they shared the same expectations for student learning, it was not until they grappled with the exemplar laboratory report that they developed a shared understanding of what it meant to teach the academic language of biology.
3. Coteaching is an ongoing process. These coteachers continue to analyze text and student work, looking for areas to improve student understanding of academic language—and, therefore, of biology.

It is often said that two heads are better than one. In this case, it took the four heads of this double team of coteachers and mentors to move beyond abstractions about academic language to a shared understanding of how language means what it does. This team now realizes that content and language are not separate; content is realized through language. Coteachers who understand this can apprentice their students into meaning-making in academic language, enabling them to move forward into the opportunities that await them.

REFERENCES

Biancarosa, G., & Snow, C. (2004). *Reading next—A vision for action and research in middle and high school literacy: A report from Carnegie Corporation of New York.* Washington, DC: Alliance for Excellent Education.

Davison, C. (2006). Collaboration between ESL and content teachers: How do we know when we are doing it right? *International Journal of Bilingual Education and Bilingualism, 9*, 454-475.

Dove, M., & Honigsfeld, A. (2010). ESL coteaching and collaboration: Opportunities to develop teacher leadership and enhance student learning. *TESOL Journal, 1*(1), 3-22.

Echevarria, J., Vogt, M., & Short, D. (2004). *Making content comprehensible for English learners: The SIOP model* (2nd ed.). Needham Heights, MA: Allyn & Bacon.

Fang, Z., & Schleppegrell, M. (2008). *Reading in secondary content areas: A language-based pedagogy*. Ann Arbor, MI: University of Michigan Press.

Gately, S., & Gately, F. (2001). Understanding coteaching components. *Teaching Exceptional Children, 33*(4), 40-47.

Goldenberg, C. (2008). Teaching English language learners: What the research does—and does not—say. *American Educator, 32*, 8-23, 42-44.

Honigsfeld, A., & Dove, M. (2008). Co-teaching in the ESL classroom. *Delta Kappa Gamma Bulletin, 74*(2), 8-14.

Little, J. W. (1990). The persistence of privacy: Autonomy and initiative in teachers' professional relations. *Teachers College Record, 91*, 509-536.

National Council of Teachers of English (NCTE). (2004). *A call to action: What we know about adolescent literacy and ways to support teachers in meeting students' needs.* Retrieved from http://www.ncte.org/positions/statements/adolescentliteracy

Schleppegrell, M. (2004). *The language of schooling: A functional linguistics perspective*. Mahwah, NJ: Erlbaum.

Zwiers, J. (2008). *Building academic language: Essential practices for content classrooms, Grades 5-12*. San Francisco, CA: Wiley.

CHAPTER 10

E-COLLABORATION

Connecting ESL Teachers Across Contexts

Lan Ngo, Susan Goldstein, and Lucy Portugal

Using electronic communication to facilitate collaboration among English as a second language (ESL) teachers can improve instructional practices and enhance the learning experiences of English language learners (ELLs). Moreover, a professional circle, cultivated through computer-mediated communication, may provide support and continual training in the field. E-collaboration may defy traditional conceptions of teacher collaboration, but the case study documented in this chapter highlights the benefits of this innovative integration of education and technology.

According to Thousand, Villa, and Nevin (2007), teacher collaborators possess unique and essential expertise as well as share common goals. When these same collaborators also teach ELLs, their goals include accommodating linguistically and culturally diverse students. Although Jorgensen (2006) stated that "a collaborative team must include the right people" (p. 41), in some cases, the right people are in different locales. For this reason, professionals sometimes utilize Internet access engines such as Google to communicate electronically from various locations (Richtel, 2009). Similarly, educators including ESL teachers often seek nontraditional means of collaboration due to inadequate time for in-house collaborative practices within the school day.

Coteaching and Other Collaborative Practices in the EFL/ESL Classroom:
Rationale, Research, Reflections, and Recommendations, pp. 101–110
Copyright © 2012 by Information Age Publishing
All rights of reproduction in any form reserved.

Membership in a collaborative team or strong support network is particularly important for new teachers. Stark statistics reveal that an estimated one third of the country's new teachers leave teaching within 3 years, and in some districts, half of the new teachers quit within 5 years (National Commission on Teaching and America's Future, 2008). According to our observations and personal experiences, challenges related to meeting the diverse needs of students add to the stress already experienced by new teachers. Due to their apparent need for support, novice teachers may seek alternative collaborative venues if they are not provided by their schools. This chapter documents the electronic collaboration practices among three ESL teachers, the authors of this study, who teach at different schools. Our investigations centered on how to overcome obstacles to collaborate and better serve ELLs (Honigsfeld & Dove, 2010). The methods of e-collaboration presented in this chapter and their results demonstrate the potential of communicative technology to enhance teaching and learning across different ESL contexts.

ELECTRONIC COMMUNICATION IN TEACHING AND LEARNING COMMUNITIES

Our collaborative practices were informed by the theory of constructivism, or "inquiry-based, discovery learning" (Hazari, North, & Moreland, 2009, p. 189), in which participants contribute their own prior knowledge and experiences to a shared context for planning and learning. Constructivists position learning as a social rather than an isolated process (Vygotsky, 1962) and promote "socialization in a learning context to create and share knowledge" (Hazari et al., 2009, p. 189), which—as a philosophical ideal—became an integral part of our collaborations.

Electronic communication might be viewed as an instrument of constructivist ideals for its ability to harness the synergy of teamwork. As Kamhi-Stein (2000) observed, the popularity of computer-mediated communication tools, including web-based bulletin-boards (BBs), in the classroom has been increasing. According to observations of various TESOL teacher education programs, BBs seem appealing to a variety of practitioners and are frequently used in teacher preparation courses that embrace collaboration.

In studying the integration of computer-mediated communication into the teaching practicum, Kamhi-Stein (2000) remarked that electronic forms of communication may promote collaboration among teachers in-preparation. The potential of collaborative practices may be attributed to the asynchronous nature of web-based BBs, which impose no geographic or time constraints, enabling participants to become "active contributors and producers of content" (Hazari et al., 2009, p. 195) at their own pace.

Electronic communication is currently utilized in graduate education courses, and an analogous concept may be applied to the teaching environment. Through a virtual professional circle, ESL teachers can "engage in collective thought and shared ideas" (Hazari et al., 2009, p. 188), with the ultimate goal of enhancing instructional practice.

A SCHEMA FOR E-COLLABORATION

In order to take advantage of the benefits of asynchronous electronic communication, we developed a schema for collaboration that utilized the Google Docs application, which allowed us to cooperatively plan instruction in a shared context. Google Docs is a web-based, word-processing document application that mirrors the basic functions of Microsoft Word. Google account holders can create online documents and send email invitations to allow others to view or edit the document as a collaborator. Collaborators can access and edit the most updated version of the online document at any time from any location and changes made are saved automatically for others to view.

Our electronic collaboration plan echoed the stages of exploration, integration, and resolution described in the *Community of Inquiry* approach (Garrison, Anderson, & Archer, 2001). This schema for e-collaboration called for one teacher-collaborator to first share tentative lesson ideas, usually via email, and the others provided feedback. Following the triggering phase of this approach (McLoughlin & Mynard, 2009), a question or task was posed. The lesson idea originator then considered the received feedback and created the initial lesson plan framework on Google Docs.

Once the framework was shared, we each engaged in individual thinking and revised the lesson plan on Google Docs at our own pace while adhering to deadlines. Points of clarification as well as encouraging comments were included in the document as pedagogical *conversations* occurred. In this exploration phase, we as "participants [came] to terms with the initial dilemma and [started] to explore the issue in greater depth" (McLoughlin & Mynard, 2009, p. 150).

During the next stage—the integration phase—we attempted to construct meaning by incorporating ideas we encountered (McLoughlin & Mynard, 2009). The lesson originator incorporated the ideas shared on Google Docs to create a final lesson plan. Often, after lesson implementation, the teacher shared her experience and reflection with the collaborators. These last steps represent the resolution phase, in which the initial issue has been resolved and participants have gained new knowledge (Garrison et al., 2001).

Due to the plethora of teaching responsibilities, time created an obstacle to collaboration. The use of Google Docs capitalized on "found time" (Dove & Honigsfeld, 2010, p. 19), allowing teachers to collaborate when it was convenient. Due to the asynchronous nature of computer-mediated communication, we were given time "to reflect on and process new ideas" (Kamhi-Stein, 2000, p. 448), potentially leading to enhanced instructional practice and student learning.

THE LOCAL EDUCATIONAL CONTEXT

Though we met through a graduate program, we had never taught in the same school, and therefore, we each represented differing teaching contexts. Nonetheless, we were able to apply the above steps to better serve our own ELLs. As a representative example, the local educational context of focus was a class of ELLs at an urban high school serving students predominantly from the Dominican Republic.

Students in this class were at the beginning levels of ESL proficiency, many being considered students with interrupted formal education (SIFE). Social interactions occurred primarily in the students' first language, Spanish, though limited native language literacy skills impeded the transfer of these skills to English. Some students used humor to compensate for what they perceived to be language deficiencies and an inability to succeed academically. Although a positive school environment was established by administrators and teachers, many students communicated ambivalent feelings about school and whether education would benefit their future.

Our collaborative efforts were documented for this class as Shakespeare's *Hamlet* was studied in preparation for the New York State English Regents exam, a statewide, standardized assessment administered annually. Though many students were recent arrivals to the United States, a passing grade on the exam was required for graduation, rendering the English Regents a high-stakes test. The unit of study that will be described addressed the skills needed for Task 4 of the English Regents. This component of the exam includes a *critical lens* essay, in which students must connect a quote to a work of literature, provide a valid interpretation of the quote, and explain whether they agree or disagree with the quote.

OUTCOMES OF E-COLLABORATION

Each of us contributed our unique perspectives, dissecting the challenge of teaching essay-writing to SIFE learners into accessible components. Through e-collaboration, the developed unit plan evolved to include more structured supports, guiding students toward writing the culminating critical lens essays. Students developed essay-writing skills, and most importantly, actively participated in class with confidence. Prior to implementing the enhanced lesson structures throughout the unit, 47% of the students from this class completed the essay assignment. After employing the new strategies, however, 82% of the students produced satisfactory critical lens essays. Additionally, seven specific improvements in unit planning also resulted from the e-collaboration, as described below.

Student Participation and Language Use

According to one initial lesson plan, students were to remain at their desks to take a survey. However, after we jointly edited the lesson plan, students were invited to roam the classroom to survey each other. This activity served as a form of collaborative brainstorming since students used ideas and language components from the survey as a foundation for the critical lens essay. The survey emphasized developing questions, negotiating the meaning of quotes, and asking classmates for their opinions and corresponding reasons. These tasks—which bridged oral language to academic writing—suited the literacy skills of the students, as speaking and listening in a social manner were initially the only ways the students felt comfortable participating. Students may have been more engaged because the essay was introduced through manageable, scaffolded activities that helped develop confidence and the necessary schema to write.

Student Engagement and Language Production

As appropriate, class participation structures were manipulated to strengthen student engagement and to provide increased opportunities for language practice. Rather than independently responding to a quote as originally planned, students worked in pairs to discuss the quote before sharing with the class. Also, students were asked to write paragraphs in pairs, rather than alone, to prepare for future independent writing. As Holt (1993) argued, effective frameworks for working with ELLs include "strategies that link the students in mutually supportive ways" (p. 2).

Efficient Organization

We reconsidered the organization of one lesson, and decided to arrange and post student pairings in advance. This plan adjustment allowed students to begin the lesson activity immediately in cooperative pairs. Due to the language needs of the students, maximal time allocated for planned language practice was imperative.

Prior Knowledge and Personal Connections

One lesson in the *Hamlet* unit originally asked students to discuss the meaning of *conflict*. Through e-collaboration, the lesson evolved to include a preactivity to activate students' prior knowledge: students were presented with three different events—one representing a conflict—from acts of *Hamlet* that they had read. The students were then asked to identify which event represented a conflict before discussing the meaning of the word. Through our collaborations, we also created additional opportunities for students to deepen their understanding of the text by making personal connections to the play, reflecting the notion that we cannot acquire meaning *from* text "unless we can bring meaning *to* it" (Weaver, 1980, p. 21).

Differentiated Instruction

Through our collaborations, varying levels of scaffolds were devised for a writing activity. Cloze paragraphs were developed for beginner students, intermediate students' writing was assisted with word banks, and advanced students were provided guiding questions. Additionally, optional sentence prompts were provided to all students to support the writing process. Demos and Foshay (2009) noted that through differentiated instruction, educators engage in "an ongoing adjustment of content, process and products to meet individual needs" (p. 26). Infusing differentiated instruction into unit planning ensured that students were appropriately supported and challenged.

Comprehensible Input and Focused Language Objectives

Active participation was maintained throughout the unit with the aid of comprehensible input (Krashen & Terrell, 1983). In one initial lesson, students were required to brainstorm a class list of quotes and proverbs. To ensure that the students understood the material, one teacher collaborator made notes in Google Docs suggesting a discussion of the meaning of *quote* and *proverb* before the brainstorming activity. Another lesson was altered to include a warm-up activity to ensure that students comprehended the meaning of selected quotes before evaluating them. Moreover, the language objectives of each lesson were revised to target specific language functions and structures necessary to complete lesson tasks. By engaging in activities targeting the language of the lessons, students were better able to navigate the target content.

Higher-Order Thinking Skills (HOTS)

Our own collaborative efforts were a catalyst for increasing opportunities for the students to develop HOTS, which encompasses "skills such as comprehension, analysis, synthesis, evaluation, and application," (McLoughlin & Mynard, 2009, p. 148) asking students to manipulate rather than simply memorize information. As de Jong and Derrick-Mescua (2003) explained, teachers should ask ELLs questions that simultaneously support language development and cultivate critical thinking. Therefore, it was recommended that HOTS questions be prepared in advance to promote cognitive challenges. Despite the students' beginning levels of language proficiency, it was still possible to promote complex thoughts and engaging discussions.

These seven outcomes may be directly attributed to the layers of collaboration that resulted in the editing of the *Hamlet* unit to create a series of increasingly student-centered lessons. Additionally, the lesson tasks became more accessible to students of different language proficiencies, providing increased opportunities for meaningful interaction. Table 10.1 summarizes the collaborative contributions made to the *Hamlet* unit.

CONCLUSION

Multiple challenges make traditional forms of collaboration difficult, and at times, impossible within schools. Even when teacher collaboration is supported, challenges still exist. Nevertheless, ESL teachers and all their colleagues can use technology to mediate limitations of school structures and time constraints by creating virtual professional circles. Such a support system can foster solidarity and enrich communication among teachers with the goal of enhancing student achievement. For the purpose of this investigation, the collaborative participants utilized Google Docs as a forum for the comfortable and valued exchange of all members' perspectives.

Many school districts offer teachers in-service credits for forming professional circles within their district. Perhaps they should recognize the value of virtual professional circles as well. Some educators may view e-

Table 10.1. Lesson Plan Improvements Resulting From E-Collaboration

Initial Lesson Elements	Revisions Resulting From E-Collaboration	Added Learning Benefits
Whole class survey	Students individually surveyed each other	Increased student participation and language use
Independent activities: • response to a quotation • essay paragraphs	Some independent activities supported or replaced with pair work	Increased comprehension and language production
Pair work	Student pairs devised in advance and listed for all to see	Efficient use of instructional time
Vague language objective asking students to use "connecting" language	Language objective asked students to use language for providing evidence for an argument	Language objective focusing on language structures and functions necessary to complete lesson tasks
Discussion of "conflict"	Warm-up activity inserted before discussion and students asked to make personal connections to text	Activation of prior knowledge and personal connections to academic content
Writing activity	Writing activity supported with cloze paragraphs, word bank, guiding questions, and sentence prompts	Various access points to learning depending on language proficiency
Class list of quotes and proverbs and evaluation of *Hamlet* quotes	Class first discussed new vocabulary words and meaning of quotes	Increased comprehensible input
Activities emphasizing both lower- and higher-order thinking skills	HOTS questions prepared in advance	Additional opportunities for development of HOTS

collaboration as only a temporary solution; one that fills the void in schools lacking collaborative structures, or it may be viewed as a supplement to face-to-face collaboration. Despite its critics, e-collaboration allows teachers and their students to benefit from collaborative structures when traditional, face-to-face conversations are not possible.

While teachers from various schools may not fully understand other contexts, the insight provided from an outsider's perspective may benefit instructional planning. Moreover, because a significant amount of time is needed to develop reflective contributions, asynchronous means of electronic communication may hold its own merits, as it allows for extensive time for participants to reflect on and internalize newly presented ideas and craft thoughtful feedback within their own time frame.

E-collaboration allows teachers to defy boundaries of geography and time to engage in pedagogical dialogues. As a result of our own online dialogues, we have incorporated various perspectives to augment our lesson plans with differentiated instruction and targeted scaffolds. In turn, we have grown significantly as ESL professionals through e-collaboration and contend that our students have grown as well.

REFERENCES

de Jong, E. J., & Derrick-Mescua, M. (2003). Refining preservice teachers' questions for second language learners: Higher order thinking for all levels of language proficiency. *Sunshine State TESOL Journal, 2*(2), 29-37.

Demos, E. S., & Foshay, J. (2009). Differentiated instruction: Using a case study. *The New England Reading Association Journal, 44*(2), 26-30.

Dove, M., & Honigsfeld, A. (2010). ESL coteaching and collaboration: Opportunities to develop teacher leadership and enhance student learning. *TESOL Journal, 1*(1), 3-22. Retrieved from http://www.tesol.org/s_tesol/sec_document.asp?CID=1997&DID=13152

Garrison, D. R., Anderson, T., & Archer, W. (2001). Critical thinking, cognitive presence, and computer conferencing in distance education. *American Journal of Distance Education, 15*(1), 7-23.

Hazari, S., North, A., & Moreland, D. (2009). Investigating pedagogical value of wiki technology. *Journal of Information Systems Education, 20*, 187-198.

Holt, D. H. (Ed.). (1993). *Cooperative learning: A response to linguistic and cultural diversity.* McHenry, IL: Center for Applied Linguistics.

Jorgensen, C. M. (2006). Ten promising practices in inclusive education: The inclusion facilitator's guide for action. In C. M. Jorgensen, M. C. Schuh, & J. Nisbet (Eds.), *The inclusion facilitator's guide* (pp. 25-64). Baltimore, MD: Paul H. Brooks.

Kamhi-Stein, L. D. (2000). Looking to the future of TESOL teacher education: Web-based bulletin board discussions in a methods course. *TESOL Quarterly, 34*, 425-455.

Krashen, S. D., & Terrell, T. D. (1983). *The natural approach: Language acquisition in the classroom.* San Francisco, CA: Alemany Press.

McLoughlin, D., & Mynard, J. (2009). An analysis of higher order thinking in online discussions. *Innovations in Education and Teaching International, 46*, 147-161.

National Commission on Teaching and America's Future. (2008). *Learning teams: Creating what's next.* Retrieved from http://www.nctaf.org/documents/NCTAFLearningTeams408REG2.pdf

Richtel, M. (2009, April 12). Tech recruiting clashes with immigration rules. *The New York Times.* Retrieved from http://www.nytimes.com/2009/04/12/business/12immig.html?_r=1&scp=1&sq=richtel

Thousand, J. S., Villa, R. A., & Nevin, A. I. (2007). *Differentiating instruction: Collaborative planning and teaching for universally designed learning*. Thousand Oaks, CA: Corwin Press.

Vygotsky, L. S. (1962). *Thought and language*. Cambridge, MA: MIT Press.

Weaver, C. (1980). *Psycholinguistics and reading*. New York, NY: Little, Brown, & Company.

CHAPTER 11

COLLABORATION TO TEACH ELEMENTARY ENGLISH LANGUAGE LEARNERS

ESOL and Mainstream Teachers Confronting Challenges Through Shared Tools and Vision

Melinda Martin-Beltrán, Megan Madigan Peercy, and Ali Fuad Selvi

The ubiquitous and pressing need to enhance instruction provided to English language learners (ELLs) in the United States necessitates collaboration between teachers of English to the speakers of other languages (ESOL), and mainstream (or content-area) teachers, to share their expertise. This collaboration can be manifested in a number of ways such as coteaching, parallel teaching, and coplanning. In line with this argument, scholars have recognized ESOL-mainstream teacher collaboration as a powerful support system (Arkoudis, 2006; Creese, 2002, 2006; Davison, 2006; Dove & Honigsfeld, 2010; Gardner, 2006; Rushton, 2008), and have acknowledged the need for a better understanding of the nature and the process of collaboration between teachers. The study described in this chapter builds upon earlier studies that have documented challenges in teacher collaboration (Arkoudis, 2006; Creese, 2006; Davison, 2006;

Coteaching and Other Collaborative Practices in the EFL/ESL Classroom:
Rationale, Research, Reflections, and Recommendations, pp. 111–120
Copyright © 2012 by Information Age Publishing
All rights of reproduction in any form reserved.

Gardner, 2006). It sheds light on how teachers can overcome challenges and find ways to bridge pedagogical gaps by using and creating communicative tools and artifacts for teaching and learning.

CONTEXT

In this chapter we synthesize some of the lessons learned from a research project (Martin-Beltrán & Peercy, 2010; Peercy & Martin-Beltrán, 2009) which grew out of a university–school district partnership for professional development designed to enhance pedagogical practices for ELLs. This professional development series took place over 5 months for 26 teachers across 11 elementary schools. The primary focus was to unpack the benefits and challenges that exist in ESOL-mainstream teacher collaboration.

During the monthly professional development sessions, we observed teacher discussions related to opportunities and obstacles for teacher collaboration, and we identified three focal pairs who were willing to participate in interviews and observations of their coplanning, teaching, and debriefing of their lessons. The first pair (Kathleen and Gina) was working collaboratively at their own initiative. The second pair (Dorothy and Hannah) was collaborating together because their school district had asked them participate in a plug-in pilot project, in which ESOL and mainstream teachers taught ELLs together in the same classroom. *Plug-in* is an instructional model in which "the ESOL teacher instructs the student in the general education classroom, which can include instructing small groups during center time, coteaching, or modeling/guiding instruction with the classroom teacher" (Addison-Scott, 2010, p. 4).

The third pair (Samantha and Tanya) represented a pull-out ESOL model. *Pull-out* is an instructional model in which "the ESOL teacher instructs the student outside of the general education classroom in an ESOL classroom or separate area using the ESOL curriculum as a resource" (Addison-Scott, 2010, p. 4). These three diverse pairs were brought together to collaborate as part of the professional development carried out by the authors of this chapter, along with an ESOL instructional specialist from the school district in which the training occurred.

MEETING CHALLENGES THROUGH COLLABORATIVE TOOLS

From our observations of coteaching, coplanning, and teacher debriefing, we identified several key factors that teachers perceived as challenges or successes, situated in their teaching context. In order to conceptualize relationships as successful collaboration, we referred to Davison's (2006) evaluative framework, which describes more and less successful levels of collaboration between ESOL specialists and classroom teachers. Davison articulates five levels, ranging from Level 1, which is pseudo-compliance or passive resistance on the part of teachers regarding collaboration, to Level 5, in which teachers coconstruct their instructional practices, have a positive attitude about collaboration, and prefer collaborative teaching to working alone. We used Davison's (2006) five levels and compared them with the teachers' own conceptualizations of their collaborative effectiveness. When asked to describe their coteaching experiences, teachers often mentioned collaboration as an ongoing process of working through challenges together.

Because challenges in teacher collaboration are inevitable, it is important to identify tools that teachers can and do use to work through problems, and to develop, support, and sustain collaborative teaching practices. We found that teachers often mentioned the difficulties of collaborative teaching first, but the more interesting finding was how these challenges could become opportunities for teachers to learn together, especially when teachers used tools to enhance their collaboration.

The teachers in our study who worked through difficulties to teach collaboratively did so by creating and using tools that enhanced their collaborative efforts. As a result, they developed stronger collaborative relationships. This finding is visually represented in Figure 1, which illustrates the (a) challenges to teacher collaboration the teachers were experiencing and (b) the tools that they used to successfully meet those challenges. In Figure 11.1, we summarize the major challenges and tools that teachers identified as important in their collaborative teaching practices. We argue that by working through the problems and utilizing these tools for collaboration, teachers were developing and envisioning more successful collaboration together.

CHALLENGES FOR TEACHER COLLABORATION
- Lack of time to communicate with co-teacher
- Misunderstanding about shared teaching/learning goals
- Division of labor/teaching (instructional decisions)
- Division of space/curriculum/students

TOOLS FOR COLLABORATION
- Curriculum framework
- Co-constructed lesson plans
- Shared student assessment tools
- Email communication
- Sharing plans and calendars
- Written notes in student work

→ **SUCCESSFUL COLLABORATION**

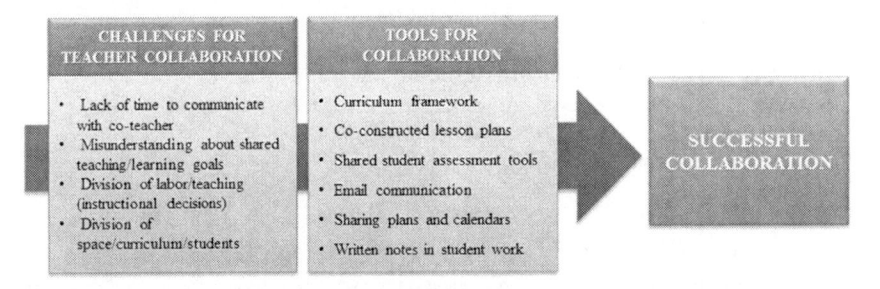

Figure 11.1. Working through challenges using tools for collaboration.

Challenge 1: Lack of Time

When asked about teacher collaboration, both ESOL and mainstream teachers most often mentioned the lack of time (see left box in Figure 11.1) during their workday to communicate with other teachers. This lack of time to communicate resulted in many other challenges such as misunderstanding about teaching and learning goals. Teachers worked to address the time issue by creating new tools or using institutional tools (that already existed at their school or district) more creatively to better serve their purposes for coteaching. For example, several teachers who participated in the professional development series mentioned calendars created by teachers or by their district that outlined lesson foci for each day. These teacher-created calendars were shared monthly via email or biweekly across grade level teams. The teachers used the calendars to compare common topics of study, and teachers explained that this was an efficient way to keep track of how many, different teachers were using the district curriculum. One teacher explained that the calendar was a tool to centralize planning among the mainstream teachers, ESOL teachers, and other school specialists (totaling 10 professionals all working with the same grade level).

Several teachers mentioned that they used email regularly to check in with their teaching partners and to document their coplanning. Dorothy, an ESOL teacher, explained that while she and her mainstream teaching partner (Hannah) coplanned, she took notes, which were easily shared with other teachers—such as the special educator, reading specialist and fellow grade level teachers—to raise awareness of ESOL issues and coteaching practices across the school.

In the following quote, Dorothy described a systematic checklist that she was creating to meet the challenge of communication between ESOL and mainstream teachers at her school.

> I am trying to come up with a checklist that needs to be constructed weekly ... because there are some teachers that we do not catch otherwise ... to have more understanding on the part of the mainstream teachers to understand what things we do. A lot of people say, "they pull the kids out, they come back 45 minutes later with a sticker and we have no idea what is happening in between." ... This is also to alter and improve the communication within the ESOL team because we do not have a lot of chance to discuss the data and help each other ... I'm hoping that it will improve everybody's communication.

An adaptation of Dorothy's checklist is summarized in Table 11.1.

We found the school district's curriculum framework (henceforth CF) was an important institutional tool that facilitated communication

Table 11.1. Weekly Communication Log

Questions for the mainstream teachers
- Are you on the scheduled page in the curriculum? (This assumes all teachers have access to same curriculum framework, which in this case included content and language objectives.)
- What do you see in this week's curriculum that ESOL teachers should focus on with specific students?
- What would you like ESOL teachers to do to support your instruction?

Questions for ESOL teachers
- What are we doing in ESOL this week? (mention assessments, curriculum, supporting objectives, materials)
- How can we work together with classroom teachers this week?

---

between several teachers. The CF was a day-by-day planning guide that gave a detailed description of the daily objectives, skills, and activities that teachers should include in their lessons. ESOL teachers had access to the CF that mainstream teachers were using in their classrooms, and often referred to it independently to determine for what content and language they would provide support in their pull-out and plug-in lessons. While we are not advocating for heavily-scripted curriculum with no room for teachers' professional judgment and expertise, the CF provided an important touchstone for teachers to quickly check in and coordinate instructional efforts.

The CF also provided ESOL teachers with a shorthand way to communicate with mainstream teachers about what they were both teaching. For example, Samantha (ESOL teacher) commented, "I will know what story they should be on by the pacing calendar and usually I will check and say 'Are you on Day 2 of this story or are you behind?' Dorothy (ESOL teacher) concurred, "I can read the curriculum [framework] and I sort of check in with the classroom teacher 'Where are you in the curriculum? What are you doing?'"

Although this institutionally created tool was not designed specifically for the purposes of teacher collaboration, we found the teachers in our study took ownership of the CF when they used it as a tool to connect their own understanding of mainstream and ESOL instruction.

Challenge 2: Lack of Clarity About Shared Teaching and Learning Goals

Another great challenge for collaborating teachers was the lack of clarity around shared teaching and learning goals. As previous research has confirmed (Arkoudis, 2006; Creese, 2002, 2006; Davison, 2006), because ESOL and mainstream teachers often have different teacher preparation and separate planning groups within schools, they are often unaware of the instructional goals of their counterparts.

We found that the CF and shared lesson plans were also important working tools to help teachers mitigate the lack of clarity and to bridge their gaps in understanding about their counterparts' teaching and learning goals. For example, Kathleen stated that the CF was a tool that helped her make sense of the brief interactions during grade level team meetings when curriculum was discussed in the context of other weekly teaching demands. Kathleen also explained that she used the CF as a basis to help guide her planning for the classrooms from which she pulled students out, because she was not regularly coplanning or coteaching with these teachers.

In the following quote, Gina, the mainstream teacher with whom Kathleen cotaught, also described the use of the CF as a mediating tool to link teacher knowledge and to negotiate teaching concepts.

> I think it is also important to be willing to share the curriculum with the ESOL teachers because it is especially when they plug-in, they are not doing their own thing; they are meshing with you.

Clearly, the curriculum framework served as an important tool around which the teachers could build collaborative teaching efforts. However, it was not without its constraints and contradictions (see Martin-Beltrán & Peercy, 2010; Peercy & Martin-Beltrán, 2009). While it was evident that the CF was helpful to establish a common starting point to discuss what students needed to learn, teachers sometimes had differing viewpoints regarding how to use the CF. This dissonance about how to approach the curriculum framework did not lessen its value as a tool for collaboration; in fact, it could lead to fruitful discussions that could enhance teacher learning. When teachers did discuss their disagreements, they found that working through challenges together led to greater teacher collaboration.

In practice, working through challenges meant that teachers needed to recognize and address conflicts about teaching. Kathleen explained that she could admit to her coteaching partner when her instructional practices were not working well in the classroom, which led to a re-analysis of her teaching and further opportunities for learning and collaboration. In contrast, Dorothy admitted that she and Hannah were still "learning to work with each other." The fact that they did not feel comfortable addressing any underlying disagreements about their teaching philosophy greatly hindered Dorothy and Hannah's cooperation (see Peercy & Martin-Beltrán, in press). In contrast to Kathleen and Gina's relationship, which allowed them to take risks and tackle disagreements, Dorothy and Hannah did not seize the opportunity to work through disagreements in order to develop more successful collaboration.

Challenge 3: Issues of Ownership, Division of Space, Labor, and Responsibility for Students

The final category of challenges we identified in our data analysis centered on issues of ownership and the division of space, labor and responsibility for students. We found that the act of sharing space and teaching practices was often a delicate dance between teaching partners as they attempted to implement instruction without stepping on each other's toes. Teachers explained that they needed to establish norms to agree upon how their physical environment would be divided and when these norms were not discussed explicitly, teachers confronted further obstacles.

Kathleen and Gina needed to talk through classroom management and organization issues—such as keeping materials in the same place, placing small groups in the classroom, and taking care not to talk too loudly—in order to resolve problems that would otherwise take away from their collaborative teaching. They noted that their friendship enabled them to confront these kinds of difficulties, which could have created friction and misunderstanding had they not shared mutual trust.

Kathleen and Gina, arguably the most collaborative—according to Davison's (2006) descriptive framework—made use of several innovative tools in their practice which allowed them to interface smoothly when coteaching. One of these was a system of using sticky notes when conferencing with students about their writing during Writing Workshop to indicate what the teacher had talked about with the student, and what areas the student needed to focus on for improvement. This sticky note was saved in the student's writing folder until the next writing assignment, which allowed either teacher to reference what had been talked about before with the student. These written notes were a tool for communication, not only with the student but also between teachers. This allowed for consistency in their feedback to students, regardless of which teacher was meeting with the student and created an opportunity for coconstructed teaching that was focused on their common goal of student learning.

We found that shared assessment tools, like the informal teacher assessment described above, allowed teachers to confront the challenge of sharing responsibility for student learning. Another instance in which teachers re-created a tool that supported teacher collaboration was their use of a language proficiency continuum (Hill, 2001), which was used by the school district to help teachers assess student progress in English and share that progress with parents. Samantha explained that discussing where students were on the continuum provided an opportunity for her to interact with mainstream teachers about the progress of the ELLs whom they shared. She explained that she sat down with her mainstream teacher counterparts and asked about each student's progress in terms of listening, speaking, reading, and writing on the continuum. Samantha noted that this tool required much time on the part of both teachers to talk individually about each student; however, the continuum created an opportunity for communication between teachers that otherwise might not have existed. Gina also noted that the language proficiency continuum was useful because it provided a way for her and Kathleen, her ESOL counterpart, to share similar feedback with parents of ELLs about how their child was doing in school.

Another set of tools that Kathleen and Gina used were shared rubrics to assess student performance on assignments. Gina explained that creating common rubrics was an activity that required negotiation on both teachers' parts, as she had to incorporate Kathleen's practice of detailed rubrics that were not as common in her own teaching. However, Gina indicated that she had learned from this process, and this tool facilitated common communication about teaching and learning practices.

Each of the pairs we observed demonstrated differing degrees of collaboration, supported by a variety of tools. Working through challenges together often allowed pairs to envision their work as collaborative. Below we outline elements of successful teacher collaboration.

ENVISIONING SUCCESSFUL COLLABORATION

We found that the way that teachers envisioned their relationship and their approach to teaching was critical to their successful collaboration (Peercy & Martin-Beltrán, 2010). We use the term *envision* to describe the teachers' shared construction of teaching as an *ongoing process* that was built through the development of common goals and the willingness to discuss disagreements and recognize each other's expertise while continuously learning from one another (Peercy & Martin-Beltrán, 2011).

The teachers in this study with the most collaborative teaching relationship, Kathleen and Gina, explained that they had developed common goals for teaching and learning. This was evident in their talk about teaching and their shared teaching practices. Both Kathleen and Gina thought it was important to make their expectations and thinking transparent to students and devised shared rubrics for evaluating students. The teachers sought out opportunities to work together and approached their principal on their own, requesting to coteach together.

The second pair (Dorothy and Hannah), who struggled the most to work together collaboratively, had not yet developed a common vision as they articulated dissonance regarding their goals for teaching. Dorothy explained that it was challenging to lead a classroom together because they each had a different vision for the classroom; however, she never discussed this explicitly with Hannah.

Although the third pair (Samantha and Tanya) did not teach together in the same classroom, they were beginning to develop common goals for teaching and learning as they planned a lesson together and discussed ways they could build upon each other's practices. In their de-briefing, the teachers explained how the students benefited from their collaboration on their lesson planning, and they acknowledged important advantages to developing common goals in their teaching of ELLs.

IMPLICATIONS AND OUTCOMES FROM COLLABORATIVE TEACHING

As collaborating teachers worked through challenges and developed common teaching and learning goals, they were able to learn together and showed great potential to increase student learning as a result. Teacher learning emerged during their interactions around the tools discussed above, which were used to help them communicate about and develop their teaching and learning goals. In sum, this chapter acknowledges that challenges to coteaching are inevitable, given the everyday realities of teachers' professional lives. The chapter suggests the utilization of shared tools as a way for teachers to confront such challenges, maintain successful coteaching practices, and engage in the lifelong process of learning together.

REFERENCES

Addison-Scott, K. L. (2010). *Implementation evaluation of the English for speakers of other languages (ESOL) program in elementary schools*. Retrieved from http://sharedaccountability.mcpsmd.org/reports/list.php?selection=872

Arkoudis, S. (2006). Negotiating the rough ground between ESL and mainstream teachers. *The International Journal of Bilingual Education and Bilingualism, 9*, 415-433.

Creese, A. (2002). The discursive construction of power in teacher partnerships: Language and subject specialists in mainstream schools. *TESOL Quarterly, 36*, 597-616.

Creese, A. (2006). Supporting talk? Partnership teachers in classroom interaction. *International Journal of Bilingual Education and Bilingualism, 9*, 434-453.

Davison, C. (2006). Collaboration between ESL and content teachers: How do we know when we are doing it right? *The International Journal of Bilingual Education and Bilingualism, 9*, 454-475.

Dove, M., & Honigsfeld, A. (2010). ESL co-teaching and collaboration: Opportunities to develop teacher leadership and enhance student learning. *TESOL Journal, 1*, 3-22.

Gardner, S. (2006). Centre-stage in the instructional register: Partnership talk in primary EAL. *International Journal of Bilingual Education and Bilingualism, 9*, 476-494.

Hill, B. C. (2001). *Developmental continuums: A framework for literacy instruction and assessment K-8.* Norwood, MA: Christopher Gordon.

Martin-Beltrán, M., & Peercy, M. M. (2010). *Using semiotic tools to find mediational spaces for teacher collaboration and teacher learning.* Paper presented at the annual meeting of Teachers of English to Speakers of Other Languages Convention, Boston, MA.

Peercy, M. M., & Martin-Beltrán, M. (2009, April). *Networks of co-constructive collaboration to teach elementary ELLs.* Paper presented at the annual meeting of the American Educational Research Association. San Diego, CA.

Peercy, M. M., & Martin-Beltrán, M. (2011). Envisioning collaboration: Including ESOL students and teachers in the mainstream classroom. *International Journal of Inclusive Education.* doi: 0.1080/13603116.2010.495791

Rushton, K. (2008). Cooperative planning and teaching for ESL students in the mainstream classroom. *TESOL in Context, 18*, 21-28.

CHAPTER 12

SHARING VOCABULARY AND CONTENT ACROSS THE DISCIPLINES

L. Jeanie Faulkner and Carol J. Kinney

Administrators, teachers, researchers, English language learners (ELLs), and their parents all strive to optimize the achievement of ELLs. The challenges are multiple, with a number of student, teacher, and administrative factors affecting the mastery of academic content.

For many ELLs, academic achievement requires significantly more than learning a new language. United States social and cultural contexts pervade standard educational materials but are unknown to immigrant students. Additionally, the age and education level of immigrant children often do not align with U.S. school system requirements, and many students are placed several grades beyond their academic training. In New York City, for example, a child aged 14 must enroll in high school, no matter what educational level was previously achieved. In our ninth-grade class of newcomers, only a small percentage of students could divide a greater number by a lesser number (math), knew the six basic food groups (science/health), were aware of historical events outside their home country (social studies), or had read an entire book—

Coteaching and Other Collaborative Practices in the EFL/ESL Classroom:
Rationale, Research, Reflections, and Recommendations, pp. 121–130
Copyright © 2012 by Information Age Publishing
All rights of reproduction in any form reserved.

even a children's picture book (English language arts). Thus, educators need to address three key hurdles that block ELLs' path to academic success:

1. un- or underdeveloped capability in academic and social English;
2. incomplete foundational training in content area studies; and
3. limited exposure to the U.S. cultural context underlying school curricula and assessments.

While English as a second language (ESL) classes address the first factor, the other two factors pose equal or greater barriers.

In New York City, federal Title III funding has been allocated to address education gaps for students with interrupted formal education (SIFE) (Advocates for Children of New York, 2010). Frequently, however, the funding supports after school programs that help with current homework. The students are not taught the foundational academic concepts they lack.

RESEARCH ON COLLABORATION

Research has repeatedly demonstrated that collaboration and consultation among colleagues improve work quality, and several studies have reported the value of teacher collaboration in a variety of settings. Goddard, Goddard, and Tschannen-Moran (2007) reported that teacher collaboration enhanced student performance in mathematics and reading in a large Midwestern urban school district. Herman et al. (2008) included teacher collaboration among approaches used to improve instruction in 35 low performing schools that "achieved substantial gains in student achievement within 3 years" (p. 5).

Yet, the perceived investment of time and effort required, as well as the constraints of school programming, have been reported to limit collaboration activities. Leonard and Leonard (2003) concluded that "the realization and maintenance of schools as so-called 'professional learning communities' seems to remain, in many instances, little more than an elusive aspiration" (p. 6). Teachers in the study suggested the need for (a) training about how to collaborate, (b) opportunities to collaborate with other schools, (c) extra pay for time invested in collaboration work, and (d) schedules supporting regular collaboration. Additionally, Dillon (1999) reported that, at a school serving mostly ELLs, scheduled meeting times, curriculum integration, and shared goals were all essential for effective collaboration. The literature also demonstrated the importance of administrative involvement to enable successful teacher collaboration. Herman et al. (2008) noted a need for administrators to foster collaboration through structural supports, such as scheduling common planning periods.

SOLUTIONS FROM THE FIELD

The concept of *sheltered instruction* identifies the need for broad-based strategies to directly support ELL learning of academic content, including the pivotal strategy of scaffolding, which calls upon teachers to create varied classroom experiences that provide contextual bases on which to build new learning (Gibbons, 2002). Gibbons stressed teaching a second language through the content classes in order to provide important context (scaffolds) for creating meaning and facilitating comprehensible output.

The well-known Sheltered Instruction Observation Protocol (SIOP)—developed by Echevarria, Vogt, and Short (2003)—describes an effective teacher collaboration model to scaffold ELL learning. In this sheltered instruction model, content area and ESL teachers create collaborative learning modules in which the theme, key concepts, and vocabulary are driven by content area objectives, complemented and supported through language objectives. The SIOP protocol calls for extensive teacher preparation time to develop collaborative units of instruction.

A COLLABORATIVE APPROACH TO EXPAND CONTEXTUAL SCAFFOLDING

An alternative approach to collaborative practices requires minimal investment in cooperative planning, yet allows students to experience common vocabulary, concepts, and related tasks in two or more content classes and their ESL class, thus developing a rich context for learning. This approach can be implemented with significantly less time and effort because the resulting products are individual, complementary curricula, rather than a single, unified module. After teachers initially exchange information, there is minimal need to find time and space to work jointly.

Complementary, rather than unified curriculum development also enables teachers of *multiple* disciplines to participate in one collaborative effort, aligning with Gibbons' (2002) paradigm for scaffolding learning through diverse, context-rich approaches. This approach to teacher collaboration across several disciplines acts as a mini-immersion program that can deepen student understanding of content components and improve performance outcomes in both content subject matter and language skills.

Integral to the success of a SIOP-derived collaboration is the flexibility inherent in ESL instructional goals to utilize nearly unlimited subject matter—that is, content from any discipline easily can be developed as exemplars for ESL instruction. The mini-immersion approach recognizes that math and ELA teachers also can achieve their content objectives through a diverse range of subject matter. Recognition of this broad flexibility provides a multidisciplinary base for teacher collaboration that allows contextualized learning across multiple content area classes.

Our pedagogical strategy is to build students' contextual knowledge of a central topic through diverse, multidisciplinary approaches that incorporate focal concepts and vocabulary. The goal is to accelerate language and content acquisition through simultaneous exposure to the same or closely related concepts in the partnering classrooms. Thus, teacher collaboration provides our shared students a common vocabulary and context for meeting the instructional goals of each participating teacher.

Implementation Structure and Process

The authors of this chapter—a math teacher and an ESL/ELA teacher—collaborated with colleagues teaching the same ninth-grade ELLs in an urban high school. The collaborating teachers selected science and social studies as the focal content areas to provide topics and vocabulary for the three supporting disciplines of math, ESL, and ELA.

Collaborative instructional practices included joint planning, curriculum alignment, codevelopment of instructional materials, and parallel teaching of content (Honigsfeld & Dove, 2010). To begin, the four collaborators met to share instructional objectives and coursework time lines. The science and social studies teachers reviewed important topics and their lesson timing in the upcoming semester. The math, ELA and ESL teachers brainstormed projects to determine which topics could best accommodate the multiple learning objectives and allow parallel timing. Our collaborative teacher group selected two topics (one science and one social studies).

After the focal content teachers shared texts and supplementary materials, each teacher worked independently. Each supporting teacher developed a project aligned with state standards for his or her own discipline that exposed students to the vocabulary, academic language, and concepts from the focal content course (see Appendix for project summaries). As in the SIOP model, the ESL curriculum was directly aligned with the focal content area curriculum, but extended the contextual scaffolding by addressing content goals for the ELA unit as well (see Table 12.1). The math and ELA teachers incorporated the focal area vocabulary and concepts to explicate their core instructional objectives. The focal area teach-

Table 12.1. Multidisciplinary Collaborations Scaffold Contextual Knowledge

Science/Math/ELA/ESL
- Living environment (focal topic)—Students study predators, prey and their habitats and prepare a PowerPoint presentation on a selected biome.
- Math—Students learn statistical analysis with a simulation that tracks predator and prey populations over time.
- ELA—Using predators and prey as characters and their habitats as setting, students study literary elements and techniques in reading, analyzing and creating poetry and dramatic dialogue.
- ESL—Students learn about adverbs and adjectives and the use of analytical tools (Venn diagrams) in comparing and contrasting predators, prey, and habitats.

Science/Math/ESL
- Health (focal topic)—Students complete a unit on the food pyramid.
- Math—Students learn to map data by tracking their own sleep and exercise hours and junk food intake.
- ESL—Students work on reading comprehension skills with supplemental materials on nutrition and develop expository writing skills in preparing correspondence to advise friends on healthy habits.

Social Studies/Math/ESL/ELA
- Global history (focal topic)—Students study a unit on medieval history with a focus on social class differences in power and lifestyles.
- Math—Students work on scale and proportion by constructing scale models of castles and develop contextual background through word problems on medieval topics that address math concepts including rate of change, slope and percentages.
- ELA—Students study the genre of drama, focusing on (1) characterization and (2) dramatic conflict. Students prepare character analyses on members of medieval society and write dramatic interpretations of conflicts within and between medieval social groups.
- ESL—Students hone research and bibliography skills by collecting and compiling data on medieval social roles, and strengthen their language skills by refining and performing their ELA vignettes.

ers supported ESL and ELA goals by including research and communications skills among their instructional objectives.

Collaborators shared draft curricula through written comments dropped in mailboxes, hallway conversations, and email. Implementation followed established school methods, including student group work in class and on projects. At times, groups were maintained across classes; at other times they were remixed as teachers matched students with different skill levels.

During the semester, feedback across classes came through student commentary and teacher conversations. Students were encouraged to discuss activities in other classes to develop academic language for speaking about learning. Additionally, collaborating teachers were invited to attend student presentations and performances in each class.

Outcomes

The synergies in our mini-immersion approach expanded and accelerated content learning and language acquisition in all classes. Semester-end portfolio assessments demonstrated increased mastery of the subject matter in the focal content areas. For example, beginner ELLs described biomes and predator-prey interactions with greater facility than other topics. In the supporting classes, portfolio assessments showed greater than expected gains in student comprehension and knowledge retention. Most easily observed were language advances, especially enhanced listening and speaking skill development for newcomer ELLs.

Math and ELA teachers also noted enhanced content acquisition. As a result of the improved understanding of the focal topic and vocabulary achieved through the mini-immersion, the math instructional topic of *simulation* was free of situational vocabulary interference and was less abstract. Grounded in a *known* context—such as predator-prey scenarios occasionally demonstrated by a boisterous acting out of hawks swooping down on rabbits or lions attacking an antelope—students were more likely to successfully complete the data collection and graphing than before. The simulation results surprised many students and helped cement an essential science concept by clearly illustrating how predator-prey populations maintain a balanced ratio over time. Because students had a clear vision of the substance behind the simulation, the math concepts in graphing as representation were more easily grasped and validated, thus building a base of general knowledge and academic skills useful in future coursework.

In the ELA class, the shared vocabulary and concepts provided a scaffold on which students could build an understanding of poetic structure and literary elements in a poem about the Southwestern desert. In creating their own poetry and discussing each other's work, students produced comprehensible academic output on ELA instructional goals. The ESL class provided another context for utilizing their focal content knowledge, and students were able to move quickly to more advanced exercises in language structure. In all classes, students exhibited greater confidence in demonstrating their understanding of the material, taking pride in their finished products through PowerPoint slide presentations, poems, dramatic creations, tables and graphs, and model castles. They enthusiastically invited other teachers to view their creations.

The collaboration also provided professional development for the teachers through sharing language and content goals across disciplines. Student discussions in class supplemented teacher knowledge acquired during the initial information exchange. Additionally, observation of posters and other project materials on display in the classrooms provided resources for teachers to make overt connections with the other instructional contexts, further enhancing scaffolding.

Additionally, we observed a positive schoolwide team-building effect. Focal topic teachers acknowledged their colleagues for helping teach the complex vocabulary and concepts. At staff meetings, administrators recognized participating teachers for the breadth of the collaborative activities and the positive results for student learning and enjoyment. All teachers were encouraged to develop more interdisciplinary projects.

RECOMMENDATIONS: DEVELOPING MULTIDISCIPLINARY COLLABORATIONS

The authors' high school has 50% ELLs and strong administrative support for ESL practices, including a project-based curriculum. However, teachers in other settings can start by implementing vocabulary sharing activities. Most projects are easily divided into independent activities, offering flexibility for teachers in schools where collaborating is more difficult to arrange. Starting small can produce positive results that generate demand for more.

Sometimes finding willing collaborators is the biggest hurdle. ESL teachers often have the greatest connection with different content areas, and may be able to catalyze a movement toward collaboration. Reaching out to one content area teacher and proposing collaboration through a few overlapping assignments is one cooperative strategy. Simply incorporating vocabulary and key concepts for a single topic into a few ESL assignments can measurably improve students' performance in the content area and start building enthusiasm and support on a broader basis.

When there is resistance or disinterest, the ESL teacher can take on the first creative task fully. Start by merely asking a content area colleague to share some instructional goals and materials in order to develop an ESL lesson/unit. Be sure to solicit that teacher's feedback on the draft ESL plan in order to stimulate recognition of the potential benefits. After implementation, try to generate a discussion of the students' performance in both classes. This will help the content area teacher recognize progress made by the ESL students, which often can be obscured when contrasted with mainstream classmates. Improved performance will produce buy-in for expansion—first to more topics and later to a wider set of collaborators.

Most important, take time to enjoy the excitement of your students as their learning accelerates and deepens through the sharing of vocabulary and concepts in multiple classes. By reducing the often frustrating barrage of new vocabulary that can block ELLs' access to new concepts, these mini-immersion experiences enable students to progress simultaneously on multiple fronts, enhancing their academic achievement and building their confidence for the next unit/assignment.

ACKNOWLEDGMENT

Thank you to David Meek, Yolanda Olsen, Darce Osler, and Alicia Sandager for being terrific colleagues and collaborators, as well as extremely skillful educators.

APPENDIX: SAMPLE PROJECT—PREDATORS, PREY, AND THEIR BIOMES

Each collaborating teacher created a project that related to the Living Environment unit on environmental diversity and biomes (the focal content). The Living Environment project (a PowerPoint presentation) requires students to consolidate the core content for the unit, but includes performance goals related to academic skills (research methods and referencing sources) and language skills (creating presentation slides and delivering oral presentations).

Projects in the three supporting classes incorporate a framework of focal vocabulary and concepts to exemplify each course's core content. Each teacher decides how extensively to incorporate the focal material in classroom lessons. For example, in learning poetic styles and structure, the ELA students study a poem in class about the desert and its inhabitants and complete project assignments about biomes, predators and prey. In Math class students conduct a predator and prey simulation, creating a data table and a graph, within a unit focused on graphing, patterns and exponential growth and decay. Although reference to the biome exemplar is frequent, students also apply the mathematical concepts to many other situations.

All projects align with the standards and include multiple exercises in support of the shared instructional objectives. As seen in the project descriptions, each supporting class scaffolds the primary content in multiple ways by providing opportunities:

1. to utilize the vocabulary in speaking, listening, reading, and writing exercises; and
2. to apply the focal concepts in different contextual settings.

Students progress more rapidly with the instructional objectives of the three supporting classes because their exemplars and practical applications incorporate vocabulary and concepts they are learning in science class and reinforcing in all the other classes.

PROJECT DESCRIPTION SUMMARIES: PREDATORS, PREY AND THEIR BIOMES

- *Living Environment—Biome PowerPoint Presentation.* In this project each student will research a different aspect of a terrestrial biome and prepare a portion of your group's PowerPoint presentation. All presentations will address the environmental aspects: abiotic (temperature/rainfall), biotic (animals/plants), climax community, food web, and human impact.
- *Math—Growth and Decline of Predator and Prey Populations.* In this project, you will answer, "How are changes in the population sizes of predator and prey organisms related?" You will demonstrate skills of data gathering and analysis and data organization, and the use of tools of data display and measurement. You will demonstrate the use of mathematic tools both graphically and through clearly written English. You will present data using standard data comparison tables, graphs, and charts.
- *ELA—Predators and Prey in Literature.* This project addresses the literary elements of setting and characterization and the literary genres of drama and poetry. You will use knowledge from your science unit on predators, prey and their biomes to author a poem and a dramatic dialogue in which you demonstrate the use of descriptive language to create setting and characterization.
- *ESL—Learning About Predators and Prey.* This project focuses on developing strategies to analyze and compare related ideas and things, and on communicating about academic topics. You will develop vocabulary and learn to use Venn diagrams as a tool for analysis, and you will practice communicating your findings in both oral presentations and written reports.

REFERENCES

Advocates for Children of New York. (2010). *Students with interrupted formal education: A challenge for the New York City public schools.* Retrieved from http://www.advocatesforchildren.org/SIFE%20paper%20final.pdf

Dillon, P. (1999). *Processes and perceptions of collaboration: Two teams at the International High School. ERIC Digest.* Retrieved from ERIC database. (ED447074)

Echevarria, J., Vogt, M., & Short, D. (2003). *Making content comprehensible for English language learners: The SIOP model* (2nd ed.). Boston, MA: Pearson Allyn and Bacon.

Gibbons, P. (2002). *Scaffolding language, scaffolding learning: Teaching second language learners in the mainstream classroom.* Portsmouth, NH: Heinemann.

Goddard, Y. L., Goddard, R. D., & Tschannen-Moran, M. (2007). A theoretical and empirical investigation of teacher collaboration for school improvement and student achievement in public elementary schools. *Teachers College Record, 109*, 877-896.

Herman, R., Dawson, P., Dee, T., Greene, J., Maynard, R., Redding, S., & Darwin, M. (2008). *Turning around chronically low-performing schools: A practice guide* (NCEE 2008-4020). Washington, DC: National Center for Education Evaluation and Regional Assistance, Institute of Education Sciences, U.S. Department of Education. Retrieved from http://ies.ed.gov/ncee/wwc/publications/practiceguides

Honigsfeld, A., & Dove, M. (2010, April 27). *Teacher collaboration to support English language learners.* Retrieved from http://www.kdp.org/teachingresources/podcastsechapter.php#learn

Leonard, L., & Leonard, P. (2003, September 17). The continuing trouble with collaboration: Teachers talk. *Current Issues in Education, 6*(15). Retrieved from http://cie.ed.asu.edu/volume6/number15/

CHAPTER 13

VOICES FROM THE FIELD

Teachers' Reflections on Coteaching Experiences

Judith B. O'Loughlin

The origins of coteaching in the United States began with the progressive education movement of the 1960s. Legislation prescribing ways to address diverse school populations followed in the 1970s, and then in the 1990s, studies emerged pointing toward the effectiveness of collaborative practices in K-12 education. The research focused mainly on special education students, and the overall results indicated that, through the application of collaborative and inclusive instructional practices, students demonstrated improvement in attitudes toward school, self-concept, and relationships with peers, as well as academic achievement (Villa, Thousand, & Nevin, 2008).

WHAT IS COTEACHING?

The No Child Left Behind Act of 2001 (Pub. L. No. 107-110) and the Individuals with Disabilities Education Improvement Act of 2004 (Pub. L. No. 108- 446) promoted the goals of academic achievement for all students in the United States. These measures required educators to be highly qualified in the subjects they teach and to use the most effective research-based strategies for comprehensive curriculum planning of all academic content. Additionally, this legislation promoted inclusion of students with both special education and second language development needs in mainstream classroom settings, which has prompted school districts across the country to develop *push-in* or coteaching models of instruction.

Researchers Villa et al. (2008) and Cook (2004) defined coteaching as follows:

- teaching responsibility, including planning, instruction, and evaluation shared by two or more certified educational staff;
- instructing a single but diverse (e.g., English to speakers of other languages [ESOL], general education, or special education) group of students in specific content area and for specific content objectives;
- sharing ownership and responsibilities for coteaching, including pooled resources and joint accountability; and
- demonstrating a shared belief system in the cooperative process of positive interdependence as coteaching partners and individual accountability to be responsible for lesson development, instructional planning, and implementation for all students.

Coteaching models were originally designed for special education and general education collaborations (Vaughn, Schumm, & Arguelles, 1997) and have been adapted and expanded for a setting that includes English language learners (ELLs) because of the continued growth of this student population in U.S. schools (McClure & Cahnmann-Taylor, 2010). Cook (2004) identified the following coteaching models:

- one teach, one observe;
- one teach, one drift;
- parallel teaching;
- station teaching;
- alternative teaching; and
- team teaching or "tag team" teaching

A thorough description of each configuration appears in Cook (2004), Dove and Honigsfeld (2010), Friend and Cook (2007), and Vaughn et al. (1997).

ESOL PRACTITIONER VOICES

Although there is a developing body of research defining and configuring models to implement coteaching (Cook, 2004; Cook & Friend, 1995; Dove & Honigsfeld, 2010; Honigsfeld & Dove, 2010), it is also important to hear the *voices* of actual ESOL practitioners. Based on results of a questionnaire administered to a sample of ESOL teachers, this chapter focuses on the reflections of ESOL teachers as collaborative practitioners in coteaching settings from three distinct regions of the United States: the East Coast, Southeast, and Midwest.

Data Collection

The questionnaire, developed by the chapter author, explored the following topics: (a) descriptions of coteaching partnerships, (b) student demographics (numbers of native English speakers and ELLs), (c) levels of English proficiency, (d) content areas of instruction, (e) the decision maker in determining the coteaching classes, (f) the choice of the coteaching team, (g) preparation time and/or how preparation time was organized, (h) the coteaching formats used, and (i) types of assessments determined and implemented. In addition, ESOL teachers were asked to summarize their experiences as coteachers by choosing one or more of five levels of ESOL and general education teacher collaboration from a table of descriptive key characteristics for each level (Davidson, 2006, as cited in McClure & Cahnmann-Taylor, 2010).

Coteaching Practices

According to the reported demographics in this sample, ESOL teachers cotaught in one or more of the core content grade-level classrooms. Some English as a second language teachers *pushed in* to more than one content area each day, while some cotaught in only one classroom setting, usually K-5 for reading and/or writing instruction. In one self-reported situation, a first-year English as a second language teacher was assigned to coteach (with a special education and a general education teacher) a test preparation course for students who had failed the state graduation assessment. In all of these classrooms, English was the language of instruction.

One bilingual special education teacher reported that she cotaught sixth-, seventh-, and eighth-grade mathematics with a bilingual mathematics teacher. In each of the grade levels, the prescribed language of instruction (English and Spanish) and percentage of language usage varied, depending on the class make-up, second language proficiency levels, and number of proficiency-level groupings in each class. For example, Spanish-only instruction was used with beginners; intermediate students received instruction 50% in Spanish and 50% in English; whereas more proficient students were taught 70% in English and 30% in Spanish for reinforcement of concepts.

Numbers of ELL students varied from setting to setting. In some classrooms, there were only a few nonnative English speakers (e.g., 2-3 in a class of 25-30). In other settings, up to one half of the students were ELLs. Besides the bilingual mathematics middle school classrooms described above, there were multiple first-language groups represented in each of the classrooms. English as a second language teachers reported that ELLs in their coteaching settings were of mixed abilities, ranging from beginners to students near transition out of ESOL designation and into general education courses without ESL support.

Coteaching Implementation

With the exception of two out of more than 30 settings, teachers reported that the decision to implement a coteaching model for one or more classrooms was determined by the administration. In some situations, an assistant superintendent and/or a school site principal made the decision; in others, the school principal worked with a director or coordinator assigned as the director of ESOL teachers. In one district, the assistant superintendent responsible for ESOL instruction and the ESOL teacher made the determination to pilot a coteaching model. Two teachers, a sixth-grade coteaching team, indicated that their principal made an effort to match teachers who would be compatible. Only one ESOL teacher reported that she and general education third- and fifth-grade teachers approached the building administrators and asked to pilot the model so general education teachers could learn instructional techniques to use with ESOL students.

Administrative Support

For almost all settings, coteachers received little or no professional development to prepare them to teach together and/or to support their first year as a team. In one school district, only the general education teachers were trained in the Sheltered Instruction Observation Protocol (SIOP) model (Echevarria, Vogt, & Short 2008). In a few other districts, general education and ESOL teachers were trained in the SIOP model, with the ESOL teacher providing turnkey training for other general education teachers. In one other setting, in which there were six ELLs in a Grade 12 language arts cotaught classroom, the team of teachers received only two professional development sessions.

Many teachers reported that the administration had not been able to provide them with common preparation time to coplan, create instructional materials, and select and grade student class work, written homework, projects, or instructional assessments. A few reported that during their first year of coteaching they had common preparation time with their general education coteacher, but as they entered subsequent years coteaching with the same or other teachers, the schedule did not allow for common planning time. Most teachers were creative in their efforts to meet and plan together; some teaching teams met before or after school, ate lunch together, or emailed one another with lesson plans and other instructional documents. A few ESOL teachers expressed frustration about not knowing ahead of time what lessons their general education partners were to teach. The ESOL teachers were not able to consider ELL lesson modifications because they did not receive their coteachers' plans before the beginning of each school day.

Coteaching Instruction Formats

When asked to describe the coteaching formats used for instruction, these ESOL teachers named a variety of roles that they fulfilled in the general education classroom. Few if any of these roles fit the models of instruction described by Friend and Cook (2007) or Dove and Honigsfeld (2010). Most ESOL teachers reported that they were underutilized by the general education teacher and that, most of the time, they were asked to circulate in the classroom to ensure that students were on task, check student work, or discipline students, similar to the "one teach, one drift" model (Cook, 2004). Many teachers reported that they were not respected and that their knowledge of ESOL students, language acquisition, and differentiated instructional strategies was never utilized. These teachers considered themselves to be no more than classroom aides. In spite of feeling underutilized, some ESOL teachers reported that they were able to do the following:

- develop visuals to introduce and preteach vocabulary;
- create vocabulary games to practice standardized test vocabulary;
- work with a small group to introduce or review concepts;

- chart information that the general education teacher taught;
- help students one-to-one with "on-the-spot" needs; and
- conduct parallel instruction outside but near the mainstream classroom.

A few teachers described coteaching configurations that demonstrated both planning and parity. One teacher described both teaching and charting (one teacher instructs and the other writes notes) and teaching and adding (one teacher instructs and the other provides paraphrases or adds information), similar to the team teaching or tag team teaching model (Cook, 2004), for a variety of eighth grade language arts lessons. In one setting in which three teachers (a general education, a special education teacher, and an ESOL teacher) cotaught, the lesson was divided into parts, with the special education teacher introducing the vocabulary words, the ESOL teacher creating practice activities for vocabulary, and the general education teacher teaching the main content focus of the lesson.

One teacher reported that, in her fifth grade social studies assignment, students viewed both teachers as coteachers who worked with all students during small group and whole class lessons. They described a *flow* between them, in which either could interject additional information or instructions during the lesson, regardless of who was leading. One team of teachers in a transitional bilingual self-contained sixth-grade class related that they worked well collaboratively, teaching lessons together and easily sharing instructional ideas. As a result, the students were very receptive to having coteachers.

Some teachers reported that it was difficult to work with beginners in an academic coteaching setting. ESOL teachers agreed that, ideally, beginners and low intermediate students benefited more from instruction in an ESOL pull-out setting or a combination of both push-in and pull-out models of instruction and assessment. A few teachers responded that their schedules accommodated this combined format. They described that, with the additional pull-out sessions, they were able to review academic vocabulary and content concepts, use supplementary materials, and create and implement alternate assessments. Teachers who were unable to schedule pull-out services for beginners reported frustration due to their inability to create the optimal instructional configurations for their ESOL students.

Many teachers reported that they were given few, if any, opportunities to scaffold or differentiate instruction or assessment. One teacher described her good intentions to tailor lessons for the needs of all of her students at the beginning of the school year. These objectives dissipated and had to be abandoned within a few weeks because of the demands of mandated district time frames within which district-required topics of instruction had to be completed. With regard to formative and summative classroom assessments, few ESOL teachers reported the accommodations such as extended time, oral directions, ESOL teacher-designed review materials (e.g., flash cards, manipulatives), test variations (e.g., with word banks, fewer short answer and/or multiple choice questions), or grading variations (e.g., rubrics, observation checklists, portfolio). However, most responding ESOL teachers agreed that state-mandated assessments drove both instruction and assessment such that modifications were not used.

Levels of Collaborative Practice

At the end of the questionnaire, ESOL teachers were asked to evaluate the levels of collaboration with a general education partner, using descriptions of five levels of collaboration (Davidson, 2006; McClure & Cahnmann-Taylor, 2010):

- *Pseudocompliance or Passive Resistance*: expectation that there will be no positive outcomes from coteaching, investing little or no time in the partnership.
- *Compliance*: expression of good intent, with efforts made to implement the model but with frustration and stress due to limited understanding of roles and responsibilities and/or conflicting school demands; expectation of external professional development and rewards.
- *Accommodation*: demonstration of positive attitude and willingness to experiment with the model, with achievement of model perceived as implementing strategies; expectation of external professional development.
- *Convergence*: demonstration of highly positive attitude, willingness to engage in experimentation and adoption of coteacher's ideas and strategies; developing belief in peer-led rather than external professional development.
- *Creative Coconstruction*: demonstration of belief that coteaching is the preferred teaching model for ELLs; perception that ESOL and mainstream teacher roles, although distinct, can be interchangeable; engagement in action research, peer-led professional development, and critical reflection on the developed model.

Although a majority of respondents assigned their current or past coteaching situations within a range from pseudocompliance to accommodation, several respondents reported that their experiences were at the level of convergence or creative coconstruction.

Several reflective comments pointed toward a positive attitude toward current and future coteaching assignments. One ESOL teacher stated that working with the same general education teacher over the past few years had provided benefits of learning together how to balance instruction, assessment, and classroom management. Another teacher reported that she had agreed with her coteacher that the ESOL teacher would not be considered a *visitor* in the content classroom and that working together produced a class that was *our class*. One team stated that the cotaught class worked because the team had taught summer school together earlier, had the opportunity to get to know each other, and began their planning in the summer. One ESOL teacher argued that teachers should not be forced to work together because it fits the schedule, but they must have the same common goals to create highly effective instructional settings for ELLs; the teacher described coteaching as "a marriage in which both partners have to clearly communicate, share common goals, and want to make it work."

SUMMARY AND FUTURE DIRECTIONS

The questionnaire provided only a small sampling of reflections on coteaching by 30 ESOL teachers in a small number of classrooms. Nonetheless, teachers' responses point to the need for future study of the challenges faced by ESOL and general education teachers to provide equitable learning environments for ELLs. This position supports conclusions reported by McClure and Cahnmann-Taylor (2010), Dove and Honigsfeld (2010), and Friend and Cook (2007), as well as Villa et al. (2008). The questionnaire revealed the following fundamental requirements of coteaching and collaborative practices for ELLs:

- sustained involvement of administrators;
- daily common preparation time for coteachers built into the scheduling;
- autonomy for teachers in the decision-making process;
- sustained professional development in coteaching methodologies;
- compatibility of coteaching partners;
- parity of partnerships–not *your* students or *my* students, but *our* students;
- clear lines of communication and a shared belief system about coteaching;

- an agreed collaborative decision-making process for differentiation of instruction, assessment, and grading.

In support of the need for sustained professional development, Cook (2004) noted, "A hallmark of inclusive schools is the sense that there is always new information that can help teachers better address student needs" (p. 11). Cook highlighted the importance of coteaching partner parity and of students viewing coteaching relationships as truly collaborative. Coteaching, according to Cook, should occur only if both teachers participate willingly. From the results of this questionnaire, it appears that only a few instances of coteaching were voluntary; most ESOL teachers and classroom teachers were not given a choice.

York-Barr et al. (2007) identified collaborative and common planning time as a key factor in the success of the program design, issues of parity, quality of instruction, and creating a true collaborative partnership, similar to the results from the responding ESOL teachers. McClure and Cahnmann-Taylor (2010) addressed the compatibility issue and suggested that "coteachers must engage in dialogue together for the explicit purpose of taking direct action to change their teaching partnership for the better" (p. 125). They suggested that it is important for teachers to be given multiple opportunities for dialogue and relationship building, with the goal of moving toward best practices. This research supports the teachers' responses concerning the need for common planning time and a shared belief system about coteaching.

Administrative support is crucial: administrative leadership is essential for the development of a schedule that provides a secure daily common preparation time for coteachers. With a dedicated common planning time, relationships start, academic conversations begin, and teachers build partnerships that eliminate possible perceived feelings of powerlessness. Designing and selecting instructional approaches and making assessment decisions can occur only when teachers have time to plan together regularly.

Beyond the need for administrative support and leadership at the beginning of the process, sustained involvement from supportive administrators is central to the success of coteaching collaborations. These teachers' reflections indicated that, after instructional decisions were made and schedules were created, administrators were no longer involved in the day-to-day implementation of the cotaught classes. The ESOL and general education teachers who cotaught classes expressed the need for administrative support throughout the school year. The supports could include securing additional resources, such as needed instructional materials, as well as providing opportunities for professional development (Dove & Honigsfeld, 2010). Administrators might also act as sounding boards at regularly scheduled meetings with coteaching partners to discuss their concerns.

The voices from the field suggest that coteaching requires all stakeholders in the school share common goals, communicate openly, and express a desire to make collaboration and coteaching work. As suggested by one ESOL teacher when referring to ELLs, they are not *my students* or *your students*; they are *our* students.

REFERENCES

Cook, L. (2004, April). *Co-teaching: Principles, practices, and pragmatics.* Paper presented at the New Mexico Public Education Department Quarterly Special Education Meeting, Albuquerque, NM. Retrieved from http://www.ped.state.nm.us/seo/library/qrtrly.0404.coteaching.lcook.pdf

Cook, L., & Friend, M. (1995). Co-teaching: Guidelines for creating effective practices. *Focus on Exceptional Children, 28*(3), 1-16.

Davidson, C. (2006). Collaboration between ESL and content teachers: How do we know when we are doing it right? *International Journal of Bilingual Education and Bilingualism, 9*, 454-475. doi:10.2167/beb339.0

Dove, M., & Honigsfeld, A. (2010). ESL coteaching and collaboration: Opportunities to develop teacher leadership and enhance student learning. *TESOL Journal, 1*(1), 3-22.

Echevarria, J., Vogt, M. E., & Short, D. (2008). *Making content comprehensible for English language learners: The SIOP model* (3rd ed.). Boston, MA: Allyn & Bacon.

Friend, M. P., & Cook, L. (2007). *Interactions: Collaboration skills for school professionals* (5th ed.). Boston, MA: Pearson.

Honigsfeld, A., & Dove, M. (2010). *Collaboration and co-teaching: Strategies for English learners.* Thousand Oaks, CA: Corwin Press.

Individuals with Disabilities Act. (2004). Retrieved from http://idea.ed.gov/

McClure, G., & Cahnmann-Taylor, M. (2010). Pushing back against push-in: ESOL teacher resistance and the complexities of coteaching. *TESOL Journal, 1*(1), 101-129.

No Child Left Behind Act. (2001). Retrieved from http://www2.ed.gov/policy/elsec/leg/esea02/index.html

Vaughn, S., Schumm, J. S., & Arguelles, M. E. (1997). The ABCDE's of co-teaching. *Teaching Exceptional Children, 30*(2), 4-10.

Villa, R. A., Thousand, J. S., & Nevin, A. I. (2008). *A guide to co-teaching: Practical tips for facilitating student learning* (2nd ed.). Thousand Oaks, CA: Corwin Press.

York-Barr, J., Ghere, G. S., & Sommerness, J. (2007). Collaborative teaching to increase ELL student learning. *Journal of Education for Students Placed at Risk, 12*, 301-335.

CHAPTER 14

ASSURING ELLS' PLACE IN THE LEARNING COMMUNITY

Leadership for Inclusive ESL

George Theoharis and Joanne E. O'Toole

School leaders have been called the "single most important factor in the effectiveness of a program for ELLs [English language learners]" (Hamayan & Freeman, 2006, p. x). To have the impact implied by this assertion, they must be well-informed about what constitutes quality education for ELLs, committed to ELLs' equitable education, and visionary about how such goals can effectively and realistically be implemented in their specific school context. The two school leaders whose actions are highlighted in this chapter were just such leaders: knowledgeable, committed, and visionary about possibilities for ELLs in their schools.

This chapter does not focus on the schools' restructuring decisions or designs. Rather we describe each school's inclusive service delivery to provide context. Prior to inclusive reform, both operated a pull-out English as a second language (ESL) program where ELLs were removed from general classrooms for 30-70 minutes each day. Restructuring was initiated to create inclusive ESL services within the general classroom.

Coteaching and Other Collaborative Practices in the EFL/ESL Classroom:
Rationale, Research, Reflections, and Recommendations, pp. 141–151
Copyright © 2012 by Information Age Publishing
All rights of reproduction in any form reserved.

TWO SCHOOLS COMMITTING TO INCLUSIVE ESL SERVICES

Bay Creek was a kindergarten through second grade school with approximately 380 students—16% ELL—run by Principal Lea. Green Tree was a kindergarten through fifth grade school with approximately 420 students—18% ELL—run by Principal Luke. The names of schools and principals are pseudonyms.

We present these two schools because they created inclusive services for ELLs, increased ELL family-school connections, and raised achievement for all students, in particular ELLs. For example, on state and local assessments, ELLs at Bay Creek surpassed ELLs across their district and state, with 90% of Latino students achieving at grade level. ELL student achievement at Green Tree rose from 17% reading at grade level to over 90% as a result of restructuring the service delivery.

Bay Creek's schoolwide restructuring pooled allocations that had previously been designated as ESL, Title I reading, and talented and gifted teachers as well as targeted aid to students of color. Pooling allocations from previously separate programs resulted in supporting four full-time teachers, which were then reconfigured as general classroom teachers. This reconfiguration created a net gain of four classrooms while eliminating pull-out Title I, ESL, targeted assistance for students of color, and talented and gifted—all of which had previously been pullout programs. As a result, classroom teachers became responsible for delivering all instruction for all learners—including ELLs—within their classrooms. Class size decreased from 21-24 students to approximately 16. This fund reallocation required district, state, and federal permission and sufficient numbers of dual-certified teachers in general elementary and ESL/bilingual education.

Green Tree adopted a coteaching approach to serve ELLs inclusively, creating teams at each grade level of one or two general education teachers and an ESL teacher. The two ESL teachers each serviced two to three grade levels. Teams collaborated to coplan and coteach all students within their classrooms with the assistance of bilingual paraprofessionals.

While the leaders of these two schools were key to creating inclusive ESL programs, a single leader's vision is insufficient for reform (Hamayan & Freeman, 2006; Shaw, 2003). It is through collaboration and shared commitment that schools become most effective for ELLs, a "unitary vision for academic change" (Walquí, 2000, p. 203). In these schools, the unitary vision was evident as leaders and staffs engaged in (a) professional development for the instruction of ELLs, (b) created inclusive classroom compositions under new service models, (c) built community, and (d) actively involved ELL families in their children's schools. The rest of this chapter draws on scholarly literature and practical examples from each school to highlight these four key components of leadership for inclusive ESL reform.

PROFESSIONAL DEVELOPMENT

A well-intended vision for schoolwide ESL reform becomes effective when everyone charged with implementing it has the capacity to do so. Professional development for the instruction of ELLs, well-designed and delivered, enables educators to build confidence in meeting ELLs' needs (Thomasson, 2006), cultivates asset-based perspectives of ELLs (Xu & Connelly, 2010), and aims to improve ELLs' learning and achievement (Stritikus, 2006). It is an ongoing, recursive process (Coady et al., 2008; Thomasson, 2006) that prepares principals and staffs to develop a coherent program for ELLs (Echevarria, 2006) and build capacity for creative problem solving (Musanti & Pence, 2010).

Bay Creek

Bay Creek conducted extensive ELL professional development to raise staff capacity to meet ELLs' needs. Principal Lea arranged for an ESL professor to offer courses at Bay Creek toward an ESL teaching certification.[1] Nearly 90% of staff voluntarily participated in substantial professional learning about ELLs, including the office secretary, custodian, art, music, and physical education teachers, principal, paraprofessionals, and classroom teachers. Principal Lea funded this professional development with money from a federal comprehensive school reform grant. Several visible and fruitful outcomes resulted from this initiative: About 10 teachers became dually certified in early childhood or elementary education and ESL; staff engaged in regular discussion and learning around issues of language, culture, and race; and shared understandings and vocabulary promoted the staff's ability to communicate effectively on behalf of ELLs.

Green Tree

Principal Luke—with district office support—garnered a state grant to fund a part-time collaboration facilitator. This facilitator, a district teacher knowledgeable about collaboration, coteaching, and adult learning, facilitated Green Tree teachers' transition to coteaching by working with ESL and classroom teachers over a 3-year period.

Principal Luke also assured that professional development opportunities, previously offered exclusively to classroom teachers, were now extended to ESL teachers. Together Green Tree staff engaged in ongoing, professional study and dialogue around ELLs and their families—some that was voluntary for staff and some was required. Professional learning and support were provided in literacy, collaboration, differentiation, and mathematics.

Existing resources (the literacy coach, collaboration facilitator, math instructional resource teacher, and former talented and gifted teacher) delivered on-site classes and workshops, and in-classroom coaching and planning sessions. Principal Luke provided interested teams time and substitute funds for half-day planning meetings with funds from three meager budgets: a district professional development fund, a principal's discretionary fund provided by the parent organization, and federal money for school improvement.

Principal Luke saw two primary outcomes of this work. The first was attitudinal, as staff began to think about students and instruction differently. Secondly, the new models involved and valued all teachers as they sought to educate all learners together.

INCLUSIVE CLASS COMPOSITION

School leaders who promote ELL reform understand the importance of inclusive placements. When ELLs are fully included in the general classroom, they have equitable access to resources and curricula (Coady et al., 2008). Access to resources and curricula, however, is not sufficient for learners whose linguistic needs must also be met (Gibbons, 1991). Pull-out ESL—by removing ELLs from the general classroom—disrupts the intended nature of inclusion by segregating ELLs from their peers on a regular basis. To the contrary, inclusive ESL services that provide linguistic support in the classroom, affirm ELLs as full-time members of their classroom learning communities.

ESL services, by design, focus on ELLs' acquisition of English. Yet, among the resources ELLs bring to the classroom is their knowledge of a language other than English. Assuring equity for ELLs in the classroom requires providing both English and home language support (Gibbons, 1991). When the classroom teacher, ESL teacher, and/or bilingual paraprofessional facilitate instruction with ELLs' home languages, ELLs maximize their capacities and linguistic resources, "one of the greatest resources they bring to school" (Gibbons, 1991, p. 62). In addition, the classroom offers opportunities for ELLs' linguistic resources to enrich the entire learning community.

Both contextual and learner variables come into play when schools plan for the delivery of home language support (de Jong, 2006). Clustering ELLs by age and language allows them to access their full conceptual and linguistic repertoire while optimizing language instruction and peer support (de Jong, 2006; Gibbons, 1991). When educators deliver instruction through the ELLs' home language and English, they deliver highly tailored instruction with the potential to close the achievement gap (Zehr, 2006).

Bay Creek

Bay Creek staff believed that ELLs would be best served if placed in heterogeneous classrooms with peers who spoke their home language. Therefore, "when possible and appropriate," (Principal Lea) students were "slightly clustered" in some rooms at each level by language. With a 16% school ELL population, clusters ranged from 10% to 30% of the class. Spanish-speaking students, whenever possible, were clustered with teachers proficient in Spanish. Over the course of our involvement with Bay Creek, the number of teachers who spoke Spanish grew from one to five. In addition, bilingual paraprofessionals who shared ELLs' language—Spanish or Hmong—were scheduled into these classrooms. Slight clustering allowed them to remain in those classrooms for longer blocks of time.

Green Tree

The collaborative teaching model at Green Tree also resulted in ELLs being slightly clustered into one or two general classrooms per grade level. Prior to this reform, each ESL teacher worked with students from approximately half of the 27 classrooms. After restructuring, the full-time ESL teacher cotaught with four to five classroom teachers, and the half-time ESL teacher cotaught with two to three. In restructuring, particular attention was paid, according to the collaboration specialist, to "not overloading any one classroom and to maintain close to the natural proportion of the school." Given that ELLs made up about 18% of the school, this meant that 10% to 30% of a given class was ELLs.

Green Tree teachers and administration felt that ELLs should be placed with peers who spoke their home language. While there were 12 languages spoken at Green Tree, the most common were Spanish and Hmong. As a result, at least two Spanish- or Hmong-speaking students were clustered in the designated classrooms. Bilingual paraprofessionals were assigned specific times to work in classrooms with these students. Under the general classroom teacher's direction, bilingual paraprofessionals tutored students, ran centers, pretaught concepts, translated stories, and interpreted whole-group instruction.

Green Tree staff dedicated several meetings each spring to creating balanced classrooms, an essential part of their inclusive reform mission. Before inclusive reform, class placement took about 30 minutes per grade level and only general education teachers participated. After inclusive reform, placement meetings typically involved all grade-level teachers who worked with the students and often lasted 2 to 4 hours. Not always easy, these meetings took place over multiple days and were filled with debate.

COMMUNITY BUILDING

Being a member of a community creates a sense of belonging (Kriete, 2003), a basic human need that lays the foundation for successfully negotiating social and academic environments (Schaps, 2003). A sense of belonging develops over time as people come to share knowledge and experiences (Kriete, 2003). ELLs, however, may come to school with little shared knowledge or common experiences with their native-English speaking peers. For them, a teacher's attention to community building is essential for helping them develop that sense of belonging.

Bay Creek

The teachers at Bay Creek embraced and integrated community building within each classroom and throughout the school day. Bilingual paraprofessionals worked with all learners while providing home language support in the classroom for the Spanish and Hmong speakers. After assisting with a bilingual classroom read-aloud, one paraprofessional commented,

> It was very important for all the students to hear and value the Hmong language, both the Hmong students and their classmates.... Being in the classrooms also meant that I knew what was going on there, and I got to know the teachers. With this knowledge, I could better support the teachers when I worked with families in the community.

Although Spanish-English instruction was more prevalent, Hmong-speaking paraprofessionals assured that the Hmong language permeated classrooms and encouraged English-speaking students to learn some

Hmong. Students of all backgrounds at Bay Creek could regularly be heard counting in Hmong, Spanish, or English together. They sang the school song with verses in English, Hmong, and Spanish.

Green Tree

The foundational principle of the coteaching approach is inclusion: inclusion of ELLs with their English-speaking peers and inclusion of ESL teachers and their expertise in the planning and delivery of instruction for ELLs. Teachers at Green Tree used ongoing community building activities to help learners come to value and understand one another. All teachers participated in professional development around the community building approach they adopted called Tribes (Gibbs, 2000) and were expected to use it to build strong classroom communities. This approach also informed school rules, discipline procedures, and professional activities.

Inclusion and community building for staff involved several strategies, including staff community building (Tribes) activities, social events, and decision-making and leadership teams. These teams made substantial decisions about the operations of the school, most significantly the creation of teaching teams to coplan and codeliver instruction. The team teaching approaches used mirrored those found in inclusive practices for learners with special educational needs, such as station teaching, tag team teaching, and parallel teaching (Friend & Cook, 2006), where both teachers share responsibility for determining goals, instruction, and assessment to address children's needs.

INVOLVING FAMILIES

School leaders in effective schools for ELLs place a high value on assuring that the school and ELL families are connected (Coady et al., 2008; Lucas, Henze, & Donato, 2004; McLaughlin & McLeod, 1996; Stritikus, 2006; Walquí, 2000). They welcome ELL families and encourage their involvement in the school (Lucas et al., 2004). These leaders facilitate involvement in innovative ways (McLaughlin & McLeod, 1996) and in the families' home languages (Wenger et al., 2004). Additionally, bilingual educators who communicate authentically with ELL families help them mediate home-school differences, build school-family relationships, and empower the families to participate more fully in their children's education (Wenger et al., 2004).

Bay Creek

In response to wishes and concerns expressed by Latino and Hmong parents, Bay Creek teachers organized *parent empowerment groups*. These groups—facilitated by a bilingual paraprofessional and attended by ELL families, the principal, and teachers—held regular meetings to enhance home-school communication. Despite some objections to the noninclusive nature of these meetings from some White, native-English speaking families in the community, Principal Lea supported them as "a way to better connect with families that, in this city and around the country, are denied access to their children's schooling." These meetings have been maintained and regularly attended by 20 to 50 Latino parents and 15 to 25 Hmong parents.

Prior to the parent empowerment groups, no Latino or Hmong families attended Parent Teacher Organization (PTO) meetings. Subsequently, Latino parents are active in the PTO with some serving as officers. Although no Hmong parents became officers in the PTO, one Hmong father ran and was elected to the citywide school board. While we are uncertain whether the parent empowerment group meetings sparked the emergence of these families' school, PTO, or school board involvement, it is important to note that the changes in the kind and quantity of involvement of families of color and specifically ELL families seen at Bay Creek were not evident in other district schools or parent organizations.

Green Tree

A significant role developed for bilingual paraprofessionals at Green Tree was to facilitate home-school communication with ELL families. Together Principal Luke and the bilingual paraprofessionals designed a system to relay information from teachers, staff, and administration to Hmong- and Spanish-speaking families. This communication system involved: (a) translating or relaying schoolwide notes to ELL families, (b) arranging quarterly conferences with ELL families to discuss student progress, and (c) sending translated recorded messages to ELL families via the automated phone system.

CONCLUSION: WHAT CAN LEADERS LEARN FROM THESE SCHOOLS?

A key element to both Principal Lea's and Principal Luke's work was the sense of responsibility to drive ESL program restructuring. This sense of personal responsibility or agency (Theoharis & Causton-Theoharis, 2008) was instrumental in leaders' courage and momentum to make changes and in stark contrast to school leaders who abdicate responsibility for ELL programs to ESL or bilingual educators. However, according to both principals, that sense of agency was not enough.

In observing these schools and their leaders, it is clear that each leader committed to sustained professional learning tied directly to their inclusive ESL model. Classroom creation was a careful process that responded to student needs, natural proportions of ELLs, and available staffing. Too often leaders create overloaded classrooms with overly dense clusters of students with particular needs, in this case ELLs, in attempts to offer more inclusive services. The leaders featured in this chapter created a new reality in which a balance was struck between efficient services and truly heterogeneous classrooms.

Creating an inclusive classroom composition was not enough either. The leaders understood that students and staff needed to feel connected in order to develop a sense of community to truly become inclusive. They worked with their staffs to create that feeling of community for students within classrooms and for staff across the school. Finally, committing to inclusive ESL services required reaching out and connecting with ELL families in new and meaningful ways.

The two principals and their schools provide practical examples of leadership committed to inclusive schools and classrooms for ELLs. This work positions issues of inclusion beyond classroom membership to valuing and involving all members of a school community.

ACKNOWLEDGMENT

This chapter is based on a study that was originally presented at the University Council of Educational Administration annual convention in 2007 in Washington DC.

NOTE

1. This professor was new to this city the year Bay Creek was planning their inclusive reform. She shared that she was supportive of the idea of the Bay Creek plan, but was not a part of planning process and not a part of this research. After the reform was implemented, she did conduct her own collaborative research with teachers at Bay Creek about their pedagogy and ESL practices.

REFERENCES

Coady, M., Hamann, E. T., Harrington, M., Pacheco, M., Pho, S., & Yedlin, J. (2008). Successful schooling for ELLs: Principles for building responsive learning environments. In L. S. Verplaetse & N. Migliacci (Eds.), *Inclusive ped-*

agogy for English language learners: A handbook of research-informed practices (pp. 245-255). New York, NY: Erlbaum.

de Jong, E. (2006). How should English language learners be grouped for instruction? In E. Hamayan & R. Freeman (Eds.), *English language learners at school: A guide for administrators* (pp. 118-119). Philadelphia, PA: Caslon.

Echevarria, J. (2006). How do you ensure that the mainstream teachers and English as a second language teachers collaborate with each other to effectively address the content and language needs of the English language learners? In E. Hamayan & R. Freeman (Eds.), *English language learners at school: A guide for administrators* (pp. 114-116). Philadelphia, PA: Caslon.

Friend, M., & Cook, L. (2006). *Interactions: Collaboration skills for school professionals* (5th ed.). Boston, MA: Allyn & Bacon.

Gibbons, P. (1991). *Learning to learn in a second language.* Portsmouth, NH: Heinemann.

Gibbs, J. (2000). *Tribes: A new way of learning and being together.* Sausalito, CA: Center Source Systems.

Hamayan, E., & Freeman, R. (2006). *English language learners at school: A guide for administrators.* Philadelphia, PA: Caslon.

Kriete, R. (2003). Start the day with community. *Educational Leadership, 61*(1), 68-70.

Lucas, T., Henze, R., & Donato, R. (2004). The best multilingual schools. In O. Santa Ana (Ed.), *Tongue-tied: The lives of multilingual children in public education* (pp. 201-213). Lanham, MD: Rowman & Littlefield.

McLaughlin, B., & McLeod, B. (1996). *Educating all our students: Improving education for children from culturally and linguistically diverse backgrounds.* Santa Cruz, CA: National Center for Research on Cultural Diversity and Second Language Learning.

Musanti, S. L., & Pence, L. (2010). Collaboration and teacher development: Unpacking resistance, constructing knowledge, and navigating identities. *Teacher Education Quarterly, 37*(1), 73-89.

Schaps, E. (2003). Creating a school community. *Educational Leadership, 60*(6), 31-33.

Shaw, P. (2003). Leadership in the diverse school. In S. R. Schecter & J. Cummins (Eds.), *Multilingual education in practice* (pp. 97-112). Portsmouth, NH: Heinemann.

Stritikus, T. T. (2006). Making meaning matter: A look at instructional practice in additive and subtractive contexts. *Bilingual Research Journal, 30,* 219-227.

Theoharis, G., & Causton-Theoharis, J. (2008). Oppressors or emancipators: Critical dispositions for preparing inclusive school leaders. *Equity and Excellence in Education, 41,* 230-246.

Thomasson, K. (2006). How do you ensure that teachers and staff have the professional development they need to implement an effective program for English language learners? In E. Hamayan & R. Freeman (Eds.), *English language learners at school: A guide for administrators* (pp. 182-184). Philadelphia, PA: Caslon.

Walquí, A. (2000). *Access and engagement: Program design and instructional approaches for immigrant students in secondary school*. McHenry, IL: Delta Systems for the Center of Applied Linguistics.

Wenger, K. J., Lubbes, T., Lazo, M., Azcarraga, I., Sharp, S., & Ernst-Slavit, G. (2004). Hidden teachers, invisible students: Lessons learned from exemplary bilingual paraprofessionals in secondary schools. *Teacher Education Quarterly, 31*(2), 89-111.

Xu, S., & Connelly, F. M. (2010). On the need for curious and creative minds in multicultural and cross-cultural educational settings: Narrative possibilities. In C. J. Craig & L. F. Deretchin (Eds.), *Cultivating curious and creative minds* (pp. 252-266). Lanham, MD: Rowman & Littlefield.

Zehr, M. A. (2006, December 6). Team-teaching helps close language gap. *Education Week*, pp. 26-29.

PART III

EMPIRICAL STUDIES ON COLLABORATION

CHAPTER 15

UNDERSTANDING BY DESIGN AS A TOOL FOR COLLABORATIVE PLANNING

Laura H. Baecher

Given both the prevalence and importance of coteaching when working with English language learners (ELLs), how can institutions of higher education prepare English as a second language (ESL) teachers to master their roles as language development specialists in the context of collaborative content-area planning? If teacher educators are like classroom teachers, tending to work in isolation (Hargreaves & Shirley, 2009; Lortie, 1975), are teacher candidates in teaching English to speakers of other languages (TESOL) programs adequately exposed to models of collaboration, tools for coplanning, or opportunities to work with content-area teacher candidates—all of which could foster their capacity to coplan and coteach when eventually in the field? This chapter describes one approach to curriculum design, *Understanding by Design* (UbD) (Wiggins & McTighe, 2005), and how it was used as a tool to better prepare ESL teacher candidates for collaborative planning with content teachers.

METHODOLOGY

As a consequence of findings from a previous study, which indicated that collaborative planning in the school setting between ESL and content area teachers was the exception rather than the rule (Baecher, 2009), the intervention designed for this project was training ESL teacher candidates in an approach to curriculum design that would enable them to speak the language of content-area specialists. For example, approaches such as the Sheltered Instruction Observation Protocol (SIOP) (Echevarria, Vogt, & Short, 2007) and the Cognitive Academic Language Learning Approach (CALLA) (Chamot & O'Malley, 1994) offer clear direction for content and language planning in ESL. Yet, these are models generally presented in training programs only to ESL teacher candidates. In order for collaborative planning to occur, ESL and content/classroom teachers need a common language to guide their discussions about curriculum and a common frame of reference to plan instruction.

The current and well-regarded approach to curriculum design developed by Wiggins and McTighe (2005), *Understanding by Design* (UbD), was selected for this intervention because of its adaptability to any content area and because of its widespread use in K-12 schools. Yet, ESL teachers tend to be unfamiliar with this approach to curriculum planning. Over the course of three semesters, a series of workshops to train ESL teacher candidates in UbD was developed by the author, in collaboration with content area faculty at Hunter College, New York. The participating ESL teacher candidates were followed into their second and third year of teaching, and through qualitative methods, the following research questions were examined:

1. In what ways had the UbD training prepared ESL teacher candidates for content-based planning?
2. How had the UbD training provided a structure for collaborative planning?
3. To what extent had the UbD training served as a tool for collaborative planning in the school setting?

Setting

The schools in which participating teachers worked were all public, urban, elementary, middle, and high schools in New York City. The ESL teachers served in push-in, pull-out, self-contained, and sheltered models of ESL programs.

Participants

The participants included two cohorts of ESL teacher candidates (25 in each group). All had received their Bachelor's degrees and were obtaining a master's and state certification in ESOL through the New York City Teaching Fellows program, which places teacher candidates in high-needs schools as full-time teachers while they simultaneously pursue their degrees. Other participants included the professors who had collaborated in the planning for this course, who are teacher educators at the college in the discipline areas of mathematics, social studies, and science education, as well as the author, who is a professor of TESOL at the same college.

Procedure for Data Collection and Analysis

Data sources included (a) the teaching journal kept throughout two summers by the researcher; (b) lesson plans, reflection papers, and unit plans created by teacher candidates; (c) open-ended questionnaires completed by the participating teachers once they were in their second and third year of teaching; (d) interviews with the visiting content-area professors, and (e) interviews with two third-year teachers who kept records of their planning process as they worked with UbD after graduation. Data collected were analyzed qualitatively by coding and reviewing for core concepts.

IMPLEMENTATION OF UBD TRAINING FOR ESL TEACHER CANDIDATES

Phase 1: Introduction to UbD

To begin, ESL teacher candidates were assigned to curriculum planning teams in one of the following content areas: mathematics, science, social studies, or literature. One ESL class at one team member's school was selected as the anchor site for all the planning. Team members spent time in person and online collaboratively planning a 4-6 week unit of content-based ESL, and each member was responsible for developing lesson plans that fit into the curriculum map for the unit.

Planning instruction through UbD requires curriculum designers to begin with the end in mind—to identify the key understandings they wish to develop in their learners over the course of the unit. These key understandings, referred to as *Big Ideas* and *Essential Questions* in UbD, often are generated by considering state standards and breaking them into their subcomponents. Once teacher candidates determined the desired understandings their students need to develop by completing the unit, they then turned to the assessments—what would their ELLs have to do to show mastery of these understandings?

The last step was to determine the types of activities that would occur in the unit and the sequence in which to present them. Due to the order in which UbD curriculum is planned, the process is known as *backward design*. This type of curriculum organization works against the tendency for teachers to plan activities they find enjoyable and then tack on the purpose later, thereby generating a series of engaging activities which may not add up to the development of deep understanding. Or, teachers may become so consumed with preparing students for high-stakes standardized tests, there is a rush to *cover* the curriculum, which leaves many students disengaged.

Phase 2: Bring on the Content

Since K-12 ESL teachers must have familiarity with all the content areas in order to be successful and equal partners in coplanning, current practice in each field was demonstrated. In mathematics, when we read the story *The Doorbell Rang* (Hutchins, 1986), teacher candidates replicated the story's act of sharing real cookies and verbally described what they did. By doing so, they performed the operation of division and identified the quotient, divisor, and dividend—but without using any of these mathematical terms. These hands-on math lessons embodied current best practices from the field (Brahier, 2009), which emphasized:

- the use of narrative, to lower the affective filter;
- experiential learning, in the form of manipulatives; and
- avoidance of technical terms, to allow students to process the concepts using familiar words.

For social studies, teacher candidates began by examining a photo in a small group, describing it in detail. A representative from each group was then asked to line up according to the order they thought the photos were taken and explain how the group arrived at the decision, citing fashion styles or makes of automobiles that provided the clues. Teacher candidates were surprised to learn that the photos were all taken from the same intersection in Brooklyn over the course of 100 years. When they were asked to describe their experience, they realized that they acted as historians, using evidence to understand change over time (Beal, Bollick, & Martorella, 2009; Levstik & Barton, 2005; Sunal & Haas, 2008). The social studies approach emphasized:

- the use of primary source documents, in the form of pictures, quotes, maps;
- the use of talk as a means to process preconceptions and opinions; and
- an inductive, rather than a deductive, orientation to learning history.

To demonstrate techniques in the teaching of literature, teacher candidates read a poem aloud, and then crafted their own poems, fashioned after the writer's. Candidates added lines and changed words to make the poem their own, using the original as mentor texts. The study of literature provided an opportunity for candidates not only to become writers, but to analyze *voice* with specific evidence (Russell, 2009). The literature approach emphasized:

- enjoyment of literature precedes analysis of literature;
- the use of writers' styles as models for students' own writing; and
- opportunities for creative writing.

In science, teacher candidates were asked to guess how many bones are in a human hand. Their best guesses were recorded. They explained how they arrived at these guesses—some heard a number before, others tried feeling their hands to make their guess. When they examined an X-ray image and counted up the bones, they realized that their guesses were inaccurate. They were then asked to make a similar prediction about the bones in their feet, but they now requested the X-ray—thus evolving as scientists in the inquiry cycle (Bass, Contant, & Carin, 2009; Driver, Newton, & Osbourne, 2000). The science approach emphasized:

- anticipating and planning ways to confront students' misconceptions;
- a cycle of inquiry involving prediction, exploration, and observation; and
- the use of talk to negotiate meaning.

Science, in particular, powerfully communicates the message of UbD. Students make predictions based on their prior knowledge and background, participate in an experience, talk and communicate their findings, write up their findings, and set forth on the next exploration. Experience must be the basis of real concept development; for the concept to be fully developed in the students' mind, it must be communicated and talked about using language that is understandable to the student. It can then be named, read about, and written about in abstract,

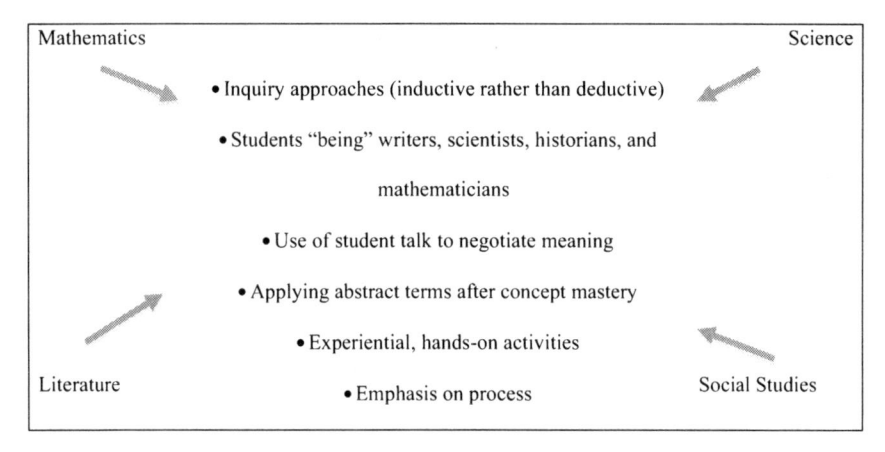

```
Mathematics                                                          Science
           • Inquiry approaches (inductive rather than deductive)
           • Students "being" writers, scientists, historians, and
                                mathematicians
              • Use of student talk to negotiate meaning
              • Applying abstract terms after concept mastery
                 • Experiential, hands-on activities
Literature      • Emphasis on process                          Social Studies
```

Figure 15.1. Current curricular approaches across the content areas.

technical, or academic terms; however, if these terms are introduced too early in the process, comprehension will be in jeopardy.

Although the ESL teacher candidates struggled with a sense of touching only superficially on all the content areas, the training provided a wide-lens view of what is being practiced across the disciplines (see Figure 15.1).

Phase 3. Bring Back the Language

Teacher candidates became so engrossed in planning for key understandings and generating interactive and engaging activities to develop concepts in the content areas, they had to be reminded that their primary role is to develop their students' English language proficiencies. Teacher candidates demonstrated their understanding of the relationship of content and language instruction through their lesson plans, specifically their content and language objectives. By using a lesson plan format that demanded both types of objectives be identified, teachers focused on aligning content and language instruction.

EFFECTIVENESS OF UBD AS A COMMON PLANNING TOOL

All 50 participants in the training later reported that their familiarity with UbD was supportive of their work in their school settings, even where the opportunities to plan collaboratively were limited. The themes which arose in their responses were that preparation in UbD:

1. created opportunities for planning units of learning for ELLs that were content-rich;
2. guided them in planning a structured unit even when planning alone; and
3. increased their capacity to coplan with content teachers.

Preparing ESL Teachers to Plan Content-Rich Units

In order to partner with a content area or classroom teacher for collaborative planning and teaching, ESL teachers need to be able to anchor their language instruction in meaningful content (Cummins, 1994; Thomas & Collier, 1997). Teachers reported that the UbD training enabled them to revisit the excitement generated by the study of content. In many cases, the ESL teachers were reading or re-reading texts they had not worked with in years or engaging in research in order to be well-versed in the subject matter of the unit.

Providing a Structure that Guides Independent Planning

Teachers' comments indicated that their training in UbD served them once in the field when they approached planning independently. The concept of backward design was one that they called upon to direct and redirect their planning process.

> Even at a micro level, I use UbD when I plan my thematic units by gearing my mini lessons by contemplating the take-home point to lead up to the final ideas I'd like them to learn. Although I think it was hard to understand when we were in class, I think I am starting to understand that it's really about teaching with a purpose—a very defined purpose. I wholeheartedly agree with this ideology because, as with anything, you won't get to where you want to go if you don't know where you're going in the first place.

Building Capacity for Planning With Content Teachers

Teachers reported that their training in UbD provided a platform from which they could better advocate for their ELLs. Familiarity with UbD earned them respect from colleagues and administrators, a necessary condition for successful collaboration (Creese, 2002; Friend & Cook, 2003).

> When my administrator discovered that I was familiar with UbD, he was really happy that we could 'speak the same language' and actually put me in

charge of designing a content-based ESL curriculum for new immigrant students to our school. I think he didn't expect an ESL teacher to really be prepared to plan a content unit.

IMPLICATIONS FOR FUTURE EXPLORATIONS

The potential of UbD to facilitate collaboration for the instruction of ELLs has just started to be explored. It may lead to a number of directions to investigate; for example, researchers may:

- examine the possible effects on student learning if teachers plan through UbD;
- seek to better understand how UbD may provide a frame for ESL and content/classroom teachers to coplan;
- investigate how schools using a common planning approach can facilitate collaborative work; and
- explore the impact of training in collaborative planning on subsequent teacher collaboration.

RECOMMENDATIONS

As expectations to coteach continue to increase, schools will need to devote time and resources to considering where and when ESL and classroom teachers can collaboratively plan (Honigsfeld, 2009). Consequently, schools of education will need to consider alternative approaches to preparing teachers and administrators in their orientation to coplanning and coinstruction. In schools of education, program departmentalization reinforces the boundaries between content area experts and TESOL specialists. In order to support collaborative planning and coteaching to be employed in the school setting, curricular and departmental boundaries in schools of education also must be crossed. How can this be achieved? By reaching across into content-area courses to bring awareness and education about ELLs and the role of the ESL teacher through:

- TESOL faculty visiting content-area methods classes (and vice versa);
- creating assignments in fieldwork that would require coplanning and coteaching;
- developing a common format for lesson planning that would be used across programs that calls for addressing the needs of ELLs; and

- agreeing to use a common language for curriculum design across program areas.

At schools of education, where elementary and secondary teachers are prepared alongside ESL teachers, and future school administrators are trained, there exists an often unexplored opportunity to model coteaching and coplanning practices through collaboration between faculty of such programs and field experiences that would require the practice of these skills (DelliCarpini, 2008). This is an exciting direction to continue to explore.

ACKNOWLEDGMENTS

The author would like to acknowledge the following Hunter College, School of Education faculty: Dr. Anne Ediger, TESOL, for her support of interdepartmental course visitation; Dr. Frank Gardella, mathematics, Dr. Lynda Kennedy, social studies, and Dr. Laura Eiditis, science, for sharing best practices in their fields; and to the TESOL Teaching Fellows for their commitment to the ELLs of New York City.

REFERENCES

Baecher, L. (2009, November). *Considerations in the implementation of push-in ESL.* Paper presented at the 39th Annual Conference of New York State TESOL, White Plains, New York.

Bass, J., Contant, T., & Carin, A. (2009). *Methods for teaching science as inquiry* (10th ed.) Boston, MA: Pearson.

Beal, C., Bolick, C. M., & Martorella, P. (2009). *Teaching social studies in middle and secondary schools* (5th ed.). Boston, MA: Pearson.

Brahier, D. (2009). *Secondary and middle school mathematics* (3rd ed.). Boston, MA: Allyn & Bacon.

Chamot, A. U., & O'Malley, M. (1994). *CALLA handbook: Implementing the cognitive academic language learning approach.* Reading, MA: Addison-Wesley.

Creese, A. (2002). The discursive construction of power in teacher partnerships: Language and subject specialists in mainstream schools. *TESOL Quarterly, 36,* 597-616.

Cummins, J. (1994). Knowledge, power, and identity in teaching English as a second language. In F. Genesee (Ed.), *Educating second language children: The whole child, the whole curriculum, the whole community* (pp. 33-58). New York, NY: Cambridge University Press.

DelliCarpini, M. (2008, August). Teacher collaboration for ESL/EFL academic success. *The Internet TESOL Journal, 14.* Retrieved from http://iteslj.org/Techniques/DelliCarpini-TeacherCollaboration.html

Driver, R., Newton, P., & Osbourne, J. (2000). Establishing the norms of scientific argumentation in classrooms. *Science Education, 84*, 287-312.

Echevarria, J., Vogt, M., & Short, D. (2007). *Making content comprehensible for English learners: The SIOP Model* (3rd ed.). New York, NY: Pearson.

Friend, M., & Cook, L. (2003). *Interactions: Collaboration skills for school professionals* (4th ed.). New York, NY: Longman.

Hargreaves, A., & Shirley, D. (2009). The persistence of presentism. *Teachers College Record, 111*, 2505-2534.

Honigsfeld, A. (2009). ELL programs: Not 'one size fits all.' *Kappa Delta Pi Record, 45*(4), 166-171.

Hutchins, P. (1986). *The doorbell rang*. New York, NY: Greenwillow.

Levstik, L., & Barton, K. (2005). *Doing history: Investigating with children in middle and elementary schools* (3rd ed.). Mahwah, NJ: Erlbaum.

Lortie, D. (1975). *Schoolteacher: A sociological study*. Chicago, IL: University of Chicago Press.

Russell, D. (2009). *Literature for children* (6th ed.). Boston, MA: Allyn & Bacon.

Sunal, C. S., & Haas, M. (2008). *Social studies for the elementary and middle grades* (3rd ed.). New York, NY: Pearson.

Thomas, W. P., & Collier, V. P. (1997) *School effectiveness for language minority students*. Washington, DC: National Clearinghouse for Bilingual Education.

Wiggins, G., & McTighe, J. (2005). *Understanding by design* (2nd ed.) Alexandria, VA: Association for Supervision and Curriculum Development.

CHAPTER 16

DOES THE DEVIL LAUGH WHEN TEAM TEACHERS MAKE PLANS?

Christopher Stillwell

The administrators of a new language program at a private university in western Japan were tasked with bringing great change to the way language is taught, and this change was to take place very quickly. Gone would be the lecture-style, grammar-translation classes with 60+ students. In their place a group of experienced native-English teachers was to establish a culture of interactive, communicative language learning, with a curriculum tailor-made to the students. These students were not language majors or even studying in the humanities, and were perhaps unsurprisingly not known for being motivated toward or skilled at using English. Success would require every tool the teachers and administrators had at their disposal. To make sure they were truly doing everything they could, they added one more: team teaching.

Written by one of the administrators responsible for implementing the team teaching, this chapter will recount key aspects of the initiative in its first semester. It will document how the foundations were laid for collaborative teaching, and it will share lessons that can be drawn from the successes of the program as well as the unforeseen challenges it faced. The chapter will draw from data collected through three anonymous teacher surveys administered before, during, and after the semester; anonymous student surveys administered in the last week of class; an informal focus group with senior lecturers; and interviews and informal conversations with various participants.

CONTEXT

Most team teaching circumstances involve teachers with different backgrounds (for example, native speaker and nonnative speaker; content specialist and language teacher), but in our case the teams would consist almost entirely of paired native-English speaker language teachers (with the exception of one team that included a Japanese learning advisor). Still, a literature review on team teaching conducted during the semester planning phase suggested many ways that this collaborative practice should be ideally matched to the needs of the new program, as it could allow pairs to benefit from individuals' strengths, facilitate differentiated instruction, build a shared institutional culture, and foster program continuity, among many other things (Armstrong, 1977).

Coinciding with the implementation of the new language program was the opening of a new self-access learning center (SALC). Team teaching could boost the effectiveness of the center and its staff by creating opportunities for the SALC learning advisor and administrator to join the classroom as coteachers, thus enhancing their ability to identify student needs and to tailor and promote SALC offerings accordingly. Extending the inclusiveness of the initiative to incorporate program administrators as well could additionally reduce barriers and facilitate a greater exchange of ideas and cohesion across the faculty, simultaneously creating opportunities for collaborative professional development.

In addition, as all teachers had to adapt a single original curriculum to their varied classes, team teaching might naturally create opportunities for teachers to exchange ideas and share what they had learned from using the material in other nonteam taught classes, naturally leading to a better curriculum overall. In short, though team teaching is widely known for demanding considerably more planning time than traditional teaching, there seemed to be reason to hope that in this particular instance it might result in greater efficiency in many other areas.

Perhaps the greatest anticipated benefit of the team teaching was that it would provide valuable and necessary support as the students underwent the transition to a completely new culture of communicative language learning through increased teacher-student interaction. Resources would only allow for 6 out of the 27 classes to be team taught, but the benefits of the practice could extend to the nonteam taught classes as well, in most cases by allocating slightly more students to the team taught classes and by placing those students thought to be most at risk of having difficulty with the program (as identified by low scores on a placement test) in the team taught classes. While team taught students could get the increased teacher attention that struggling students need the most, the other classes would also be smaller, containing students who had done better on the placement test.

TEAM TEACHING WORKSHOP

A review of the literature on team teaching proved valuable for informing the establishment of the program. One common theme was the need for adequate training of teachers (Goetz, 2000, Richards & Farrell, 2005, Stewart, Sagliano, & Sagliano, 2002). Prior to the first week of classes, the seven teachers, three administrators, and one learning advisor were therefore convened for an orientation workshop on team teaching. The projected coteaching partners were first divided into two separate groups to collaboratively brainstorm a list of pros and cons of team teaching. In this fashion, the participants could naturally share concerns and learn from one another's insights. At the same time, they would generate points of entry for discussion of key coteaching principles.

Whole-group discussion of the lists combined insights from the participants with those found in the literature. It was found that team teaching could promote collaborative learning among teachers (Richards & Farrell, 2005) and it could permit teams to (a) take advantage of the individuals' strengths, (b) spur creativity as teachers teach for their colleagues as well as their students, and (c) facilitate individualized instruction by allowing each learner to get more attention from teachers (Armstrong, 1977). The groups also noted that it could create opportunities to model realistic and authentic conversations and could also facilitate creative use of the classroom space for increased interaction.

Among the problems discussed were that team teaching "makes more demands on time and energy, thus members must arrange mutually agreeable times for planning and evaluation sessions," and "group decisions are slower to make" (Buckley, 2000, p. 13). In addition, it can lead to power struggles and conflict between partners (Bailey, Curtis, & Nunan, 2001). Workshop participants also expressed concern that team teaching could lead to overly teacher-dominated lessons and could confuse the students in terms of who is the *teacher* and who is the *aid*.

The following segment of the workshop focused on secrets of success for team teaching, including the need for:

- a balance between self-confidence and appreciation for the partner's strengths (Shannon & Meath-Lang, 1992);
- an atmosphere of trust and mutual respect between partners as well as agreement on shared goals (Bailey, Dale, &Squire, 1992);
- acceptance of colleagues as equals and readiness to improvise (Richards & Farrell, 2005); and
- administrators who actively team teach as well to understand the commitments involved (Stewart et al., 2002).

Participants then worked with their future team teaching partner to rate six models outlined in Goetz (2000) in terms of (a) benefit to students, (b) use of both teachers' expertise, (c) ease of planning, (d) clarity of roles, and (e) practicality. These models varied in terms of configuration of classes and division of work, but all fell within our program's requirements that team teachers share:

1. planning;
2. teaching, with both teachers actively involved in the class at all times;
3. postlesson reflection/evaluation; and
4. responsibility for assessment

The closing portion of the workshop focused on helping pairs develop consensus on how to address problems. In this segment, partners read a personal account of a team teaching experience that had gone poorly (adapted from Bailey et al., 2001). Partners identified what had gone wrong, why, and what alternative actions might have been more fruitful.

ADMINISTRATIVE SUPPORT

Anonymous teacher surveys administered 1 month into the team teaching initiative indicated that everything was on track. The majority of participants expressed that they were following the requirements and that their team teaching brought them enjoyment of working with their partner and a useful perspective for their other classes. In addition, half the respondents agreed or strongly agreed that it brought easier development and adaptation of classroom material for their lessons in general, fostered greater openness to trying alternative teaching approaches in the classroom, and increased creativity.

Another discussion about team teaching was held as part of a general meeting at the end of the second month. At the end of the third month, an informal focus group discussion was held with senior lecturers (the four teachers with several years' experience at the program's parent school). Aside from the final anonymous teacher surveys at the end of the semester, administration did not become directly involved in team teaching apart from one instance in which a teacher requested assistance addressing interpersonal challenges unique to the particular partnership.

STUDENT SURVEYS

All students were given anonymous surveys at the end of the semester in which to share their impressions on the course and the progress they had made. The responses were quite positive, particularly in light of the fact that studies conducted prior to the start of the program indicated that students were unlikely to appreciate student-centered English classes. Of 687 respondents, 78.3% rated the course *good* or *excellent*, 77% said their interest in English had increased, and although only 8.8% stated that English instruction was one of their reasons for enrolling in the school, 63.3% expressed plans to take the optional English class in the following semester (and in actuality enrollment numbers were much higher).

Students in the team taught classes were given additional survey questions, the results of which were even more enthusiastic (see Table 16.1). Of 141 respondents, more than 83% agreed that team teaching helped them

Table 16.1. Survey Responses From Team Taught Students (141 Respondents)

	Agree/ Strongly Agree
Benefits of having two teachers	
• Having two teachers helps me learn more.	83%
• Having two teachers makes a better English class.	84.4%
• Having two teachers gives me more chances to talk to a teacher.	89.4%
• I get more attention from my teacher in this class than I would in a class with one teacher.	85.1%
• Having two teachers helps me get used to speaking English with partners.	75.9%
• I enjoy English class more with two teachers.	82.9%
• In the SILC, I would prefer to have two teachers in English class.	80.8%
Drawbacks of having two teachers	
• I am confused by having two teachers.	7.1%
• With two teachers, sometimes I do not know which one is in charge of the class.	12%

learn more, made a better English class, and provided more attention from the teacher. Additionally, 80.8% said they prefer to have two teachers in English class.

TEACHER DATA COLLECTED LATER IN THE SEMESTER

Toward the end of the semester a third anonymous teacher survey, informal conversations with staff, and the focus group with senior lecturers revealed a number of positive outcomes. SALC staff noted that the team teaching kept them connected to the classroom, a connection that could help them in their work of advising learners and tailoring SALC materials to students' needs. Three of the ten participants noted additional crossover insofar as the practice had led to other opportunities for professional development with their partner, and six stated that joint planning had given them ideas for teaching the curriculum in general. Survey questions intended to find out the extent to which common team teaching problems were surfacing in our context revealed little difficulty apart from 50% of the respondents reporting "lack of sufficient planning," "difficulty sharing the planning,", and "difficulty taking equal responsibility for grades."

Still, teachers' responses to presemester and postsemester questions borrowed from a survey by Bailey et al. (1992) showed that their beliefs about team teaching took a negative turn over the course of the semester (see Table 16.2). It appears that teachers came to find the additional

Table 16.2. Beliefs About Team Teaching, Before and After the First Semester (10 Respondents)

	Percent Agree/Strongly Agree	
	Pre-semester	Post-semester
Team teaching is more trouble than it's worth	10	60
The amount of time necessary to collaborate on goal setting, syllabus design, and lesson planning is more trouble than it's worth	10	70
Planning together is the most valuable part of team teaching	40	10
Working in class together is the most valuable part of team teaching	50	40
Only teachers themselves should decide whether or not to enter into a team teaching arrangement.	20	70
Only teachers themselves should decide who their teaching partners will be	10	50

demands of team teaching much more challenging as the semester went on, with the number of teachers expressing that team teaching was not worth the effort rising from 1 to 7, and joint planning proving particularly unpopular. In spite of this, 8 of the 11 participants opted to maintain the status quo and continue teaming with their partner in the second semester when given the choice.

LESSONS LEARNED

A distinct characteristic of the team teaching in our context is that ten out of the eleven participants were native speaker language teachers. Although this appears to have been beneficial in many ways, one interpretation of the data is that this characteristic may have intensified some common difficulties of team teaching, particularly in two areas. While many other team teaching partnerships involve pairs of teachers with different skills and strengths (e.g. a language specialist and a content specialist, or a native speaker and a local nonnative speaker), the teams in our context had a great deal of overlap in terms of experience and abilities.

As a result, difficulties may have arisen in making distinctions between the partners' roles. And if it were not plain to see that each teacher brought something essential to the partnership, the time demands of coplanning may have seemed onerous and unnecessary. The following sections will explore these two difficulties in greater detail.

Who's the Boss?

One pair of team teachers interviewed individually noted difficulty finding the balance in the classroom, as "someone always has to be the lead" but "you're never quite sure who is in charge." Another confirmed that in a team comprised of two native speaker language teachers, having less clearly defined roles "initially makes it a bit more difficult." This teaching pair found it useful to address the issue by delineating individual responsibilities in terms of taking roll, marking papers, monitoring students, and teaching the core content.

In the conversation with senior lecturers, a great deal of discussion focused on the fact that the three teachers and one learning advisor who were new to the program were each paired with someone who had worked previously in the program's parent school and thus had more seniority. This resulted in a situation where all teaching pairs consisted of partners who were roughly equal in terms of professional training, but none were equal in terms of the institution's hierarchy.

As one put it, "It's okay to say 'I'm not a manager, we are working together,' etc. Can that happen? Difficult." The director of the program had set up the pairs in this fashion to facilitate new teachers adapting to the institutional culture by working with those experienced with the program, but this may have been a source of teacher dissatisfaction as "perhaps all people feel there is not an equal relationship happening in the classroom.... If this is what's happening it's not really team teaching.... Maybe these people feel they are being spied on."

This power imbalance seems likely to have been most acutely felt in the two partnerships between a new teacher and an administrator, and it may be no coincidence that they are the only two teams to break up in the second semester, though other reasons have been given. Although Stewart et al. (2002) stated that "administrators need to be fully aware of the time and energy required to teach in linked courses" (p. 41), and Richards and Farrell (2005) recommended accomplishing this by having administrators "actively team-teach to better understand the commitments involved" (p. 169), this advice should perhaps only be followed if team teaching can be arranged between administrators or friends. In our case, the third administrator-teacher partnership consisted of teachers who have been friends for years, and who expressed total willingness to continue in the second semester.

Who Has the Time?

Shannon and Meath-Lang (1992) stated that "team teaching should not be viewed as a solution to time constraints or to staff efficiency issues" (p. 139). In our context, the survey responses and discussions concurred, showing time and planning issues to be the most consistent concern from the start to the finish of the semester. It seems possible that pairing native-speaker language teachers may actually have intensified the perception of time used inefficiently. As opposed to a class taught by a content specialist and a language specialist—in which drawing on each teacher's expertise is essential to a successful lesson—our teachers would have firsthand experience of teaching the exact same material solo in other classes, without having lost the extra time that group decision making requires. This may be a reason team teaching was consistently viewed by some as only useful for crowd control. Still, in the words of one participant there are additional advantages to the pairing of language teachers: "In this context you are learning more. If you are with someone teaching sociology, maybe you are not learning much" in terms of activities and methods practically applicable to language teaching.

DO WE HAVE A CHOICE?

Going forward, it is to be hoped that awareness of the complications inherent in our particular team teaching situation can lead to better administration of the program. Bailey et al. (2001) argued that choice with regard to whether to participate and with whom has a major impact on teachers' feelings about the practice, which seems to be the case here: on end-of-semester surveys, 70% agreed that "only teachers themselves should decide whether or not to enter into a team teaching arrangement" (see Table 15.2). When given the choice, all but two partnerships opted to continue.

In future semesters, particular care will have to be taken when partnering administrators. In addition, it will probably also be useful to explicitly designate a couple of hours in the schedule to collaborative planning work for all. Ideally, teachers will have a choice of using such shared time to meet a range of institutional needs. Team teachers can use the time for joint planning, reflection, and evaluation while nonteam teachers attend to other responsibilities such as collaborative materials development and peer review (for more on this, see Honigsfeld & Dove, 2010).

CONCLUSIONS

As of this writing, the program is entering its second semester, and it has a lot to be proud of. In general, student performance in terms of attendance and ability to meet exit competencies has been better than anyone had dared to hope. Those students who were team taught expressed strong support for the practice. Those who were not team taught may have unknowingly received indirect benefits as their less motivated or less skilled peers were placed into the team taught classes for the additional teacher attention it would permit. Though teachers expressed some dissatisfaction with team teaching, it is difficult to know whether the program would have met the same level of success without it. In addition, other relatively intangible benefits may have disappeared, as team teaching naturally fostered connections across teachers' offices, exchanges of ideas about the curriculum, and avenues for discussing the everyday challenges of language teaching.

REFERENCES

Armstrong, D. G. (1977). Team teaching and academic achievement. *Review of Educational Research, 47*(1), 65-86.

Bailey, K. M., Curtis, A., & Nunan, D. (2001). *Pursuing professional development: The self as source*. Boston, MA: Heinle & Heinle.

Bailey, K. M., Dale, T., & Squire, B. (1992). Some reflections on collaborative language teaching. In D. Nunan (Ed.), *Collaborative language learning and teaching* (pp. 162-178). Cambridge, England: Cambridge University Press.

Buckley, F. (2000). *Team teaching: What, why, and how?* Thousand Oaks, CA: SAGE.

Goetz, K. (2000). Perspectives on team teaching. *EGallery. 1*(4). Retrieved from http://people.ucalgary.ca/~egallery/goetz.html

Honigsfeld, A., & Dove, M. (2010). *Collaboration and co-teaching: Strategies for English learners*. Thousand Oaks, CA: Corwin Press.

Richards, J., & Farrell, T. (2005). *Professional development for language teachers*. Cambridge, England: Cambridge University Press.

Shannon, N. B., & Meath-Lang, B. (1992). Collaborative language teaching: A co-investigation. In D. Nunan (Ed.), *Collaborative language learning and teaching* (pp. 120-140). Cambridge, England: Cambridge University Press.

Stewart, T., Sagliano, M., & Sagliano, J. (2002). Merging expertise: Promoting partnerships between language and content specialists. In J. Crandall & D. Kaufman (Eds.), *Content-based instruction in higher education settings* (pp. 29-44). Alexandria, VA: TESOL.

CHAPTER 17

SUMMER BOOK CLUBS FOR ENGLISH LANGUAGE LEARNERS

Teacher Collaboration for Promoting Academic Achievement

Susan Spezzini and Abby P. Becker

> *I was thinking about how our ELLs were having difficulty with the summer novels. Then, it came to me: "We can have book clubs and provide sheltered instruction." I called my coteacher, and we worked out a plan.*

The epiphany described here by Angela Wilson[1]—an English as a second language (ESL) teacher—provided a new direction for academic achievement among English language learners (ELLs) at Southeast High School (SHS). Of the five 12th-grade ELLs at SHS in 2005-06, only one graduated. A major obstacle to graduation was credit accrual, a situation that concerned Angela and her fellow ESL teacher Jane Harris.

Angela and Jane discovered that many ELLs started their fall semester English class with an almost insurmountable point deficit from not having done the summer assignments. To help ELLs meet expectations, Angela and Jane collaborated with English teachers in creating summer book clubs that fostered language development and offered accessible academic content.

Spurred by anecdotal evidence, a mixed-method study examined the book clubs' effect on the ELL pass rate. Quantitative data came from ELLs in summer book clubs and fall English classes. Qualitative data came from interviews with teachers who organized the book clubs and with interns who delivered instruction. Results showed summer book clubs contributing to statistically significant increases in ELLs' fall pass rate. Findings suggested two unanticipated outcomes: high school orientation for ninth-grade ELLs and professional development for mainstream teachers. These outcomes respond to calls for additional research on secondary ELLs (Genesee, Lindholm-Leary, Saunders, & Christian, 2005) and on professional development for effective ELL instruction (Ballantyne, Sanderman, & Levy, 2008). Findings are critical in areas like "North and South Carolina, Georgia, and Alabama—states with limited prior experience in serving their educational needs" (Rubinstein-Avila, 2007, p. 572), where ELLs have a 56% graduation rate compared to 74% overall (Zehr, 2009).

SUMMER PROGRAMS FOR ELLS

ELLs tend to lose ground during summer (Shin & Krashen, 2007). To offset potential losses, summer programs target language, academic, and social goals. They can provide learning opportunities in critical subject areas, offer structured transition to high school, expedite progress toward graduation through credit-recovery courses and proactive credit accrual, or prepare ELLs for exams and higher education (Jordan, 2008; Zehr, 2008). By hosting university internships, some programs have further enhanced their support for ELLs (Cohen, 2007; Kirkland, Camp, & Manning, 2009).

Focused on literacy, one voluntary program reduced summer losses through ample access to compelling books (Kim, 2003). Another showed higher gains in an experimental self-selected group than in a control group (Shin & Krashen, 2007). Yet, most studies of ELL summer programs lack empirical data regarding their effectiveness (Zehr, 2008). Also lacking are data on how teacher collaboration can enhance ELLs' academic development.

METHODOLOGY

This mixed-method study was designed to respond to two research questions:

1. To what extent did SHS summer book clubs contribute to an increased ELL pass rate in fall English classes?
2. What other outcomes resulted from these book clubs?

Setting

Located 5 miles from a prominent research university, SHS is in a school district further comprised of a middle school and three elementary schools. This district serves a small city situated in a southeastern state's largest metropolitan area. Though mainly middle-class, its population ranges from low to high socioeconomic status.

SHS experienced a steady increase of ELLs from 1995 to 2005 and a 45% surge over the following 2 years. By fall 2008, 67 of its 1,000 students (nearly 7%) were ELLs: 49 (73%) Spanish speakers (Mexico, Dominican Republic, Honduras, Argentina, Peru), 12 (18%) Arabic speakers (Yemen, Jordan), 2 (3%) Swahili speakers (Kenya, Tanzania), and 4 (6%) speakers of other languages—French (Guinea), Gujarati (India), Japanese (Japan), and Thai (Thailand).

Participants

Study participants included students, teachers, and interns. The students were ELLs who took English in the fall (49 in 2006, 62 in 2007, and 67 in 2008). Of these, some also participated in summer book clubs (25 in 2007 and 19 in 2008). The teachers, Angela and Jane, organized and monitored the book clubs. Angela held a master's degree in ESL, was certified in three fields (ESL, English, and Spanish), and had taught 6 years at SHS. Jane held a master's degree in collaborative education, was certified in four fields (ESL, special education, English, and French), and had taught 17 years at SHS. The interns, Emmy Barnes and Gail Bennett, delivered instruction in summer 2007, and Mark Stewart and Ramona Simmons did so in 2008.

Instructional Intervention

In January 2007, Angela and Jane shared their book club idea with SHS administrators. The administrators approved the book clubs, earmarked Title III funds for the summer salary of one ESL teacher, and requested interns from the local university. Each of the four book clubs was allotted 15 hours—3 hours daily for 5 days. To leverage administrative, clerical, and custodial support, the SHS administrators scheduled

Table 17.1. Summer School and ELL Book Clubs

June	4-Week Summer School	1-Week ELL Book Clubs	
	7:30 - 3:30	8:00 - 11:00	12:00 - 3:00
Week 1	9th-12th		
Week 2	9th-12th	9th (Section 1)	10th
Week 3	9th-12th	9th (Section 2)	11th and 12th
Week 4	9th-12th		

the weeklong ELL book clubs concurrently with the credit recovery summer school as is shown in Table 17.1.

In February, Angela and Jane collaborated with English teachers in selecting graphic novels for each grade: ninth grade, *Black Beauty* (Sewel, 2000); 10th grade, *Huckleberry Finn* (Twain, 2006); 11th grade, *Red Badge of Courage* (Crane, 2006); and 12th grade, *Dr. Jekyll and Mr. Hyde* (Stevenson, 1998). Guided by best practices in ESL (Echevarria, Vogt, & Short, 2009), these ESL and English teachers collaboratively designed alternative projects, identified instructional strategies, and determined accommodated assessments.

In March, Angela and Jane sought support from counselors and the middle school ESL teachers for encouraging ELLs to register for the book clubs. They also contacted ELL parents. In April, Angela and Jane met with the interns and internship supervisor. In May, they helped interns plan lessons based on the Sheltered Instructional Observation Protocol (Echeverria et al., 2009).

In June, the interns taught the book clubs by implementing sheltered instruction lessons. They made novels comprehensible to ELLs by utilizing background knowledge, emphasizing key vocabulary, highlighting language features, using graphic organizers, restating concepts, providing scaffolding, promoting learning strategies, and incorporating oral interactive techniques. The interns also helped ELLs complete their assigned summer projects by doing illustrations, time lines, character wheels, and biopoems. On the first day of the fall semester, ELLs took their projects from the ESL classroom to their English classrooms, where they were assessed by their fall English teachers.

Research Procedure

Quantitative data consisted of the pass rates of ELLs in fall English, from 2006 to 2008, and the number of ELLs who participated in the summer book clubs. Qualitative data were provided by Angela, Jane, and Mark, who were interviewed by the second author and also by Emmy, Gail, and Ramona who provided electronic responses to the protocol questions. Content analysis (Patton, 2002) included triangulation of data from two sources (teachers and interns) and insights from a third source (school/university partnership director).

RESULTS

Effects from Book Clubs on ELLs' Pass Rate in English

The number of ELLs in fall English classes is provided in Table 17.2, along with the pass/fail data from fall 2006 (before book club implementation) and from fall 2007 and 2008 (after book club implementation).

The pass rate increased from 76% (preprogram) to 95% (2007) and 93% (2008). Such year-to-year postprogram consistency provided internal validity. Although the fourth column illustrates the combined data from 2007 and 2008, it does not represent a totality of different students. Many ELLs were enrolled in SHS English classes in both fall 2007 and fall 2008. Yet, because continuing students were in different classes each year, and because the pass rate was related solely to one class for a given semester, calculating a combined total was useful for analysis purposes.

The increased pass rate from 76% preprogram to 94% combined postprogram suggests a positive effect gained from summer book clubs. Of 129 ELLs, 44 had participated in a book club, with 41 passing English. The 3 failures were due to attendance issues.

To better understand the effect of these book clubs, a significance test was used to compare preprogram data (Column 1) with postprogram data (Column 4). Because the resulting chi square of 11.8874 was higher than

Table 17.2. Number of ELLs who Passed or Failed English in Fall

ELLs in Fall English Classes	Before Book Clubs	After Book Clubs Were Implemented		
	2006	*2007*	*2008*	*2007 & 2008*
Passed (*N*)	37	59	62	121
Failed (*N*)	12	3	5	8
Enrolled (*N*)	49	62[a]	67[b]	129
Fall pass rate (percent)	76%	95%	93%	94%

Note: $\chi^2 = 11.8874$, $df = 1$, $\alpha = .05$. [a]Of 62 ELLs, 25 participated in the 2007 book club. [b]Of 67 ELLs, 19 participated in the 2008 book club.

the critical value of 3.841, a statistically significant relationship existed between the book clubs and the pass rate (Aron, Aron, & Coups, 2005). In short, after book clubs were introduced, the pass rate increased significantly.

In the interviews, the ESL teachers confirmed that the book clubs had contributed toward a greater number of ELLs passing the fall English classes. According to Angela, the problem of ELLs failing because of the summer reading project "has pretty much disappeared now that we've got this program."

Other Outcomes From the Summer Book Clubs

The ESL teachers felt that the book clubs also served as high school orientation for rising ninth graders. Angela explained that, after book clubs were introduced, the first day of the school year progressed more smoothly. Jane agreed that familiarity with campus allowed ELLs to transition more easily to high school. Previously, ESL teachers had spent time directing ELLs to class. After the book clubs were in place, they saw ninth-grade ELLs helping non-ELL classmates navigate the halls. Moreover, because book clubs took place in the ESL classrooms, ELLs knew where to find their ESL teachers and could obtain assistance when needed. Gail noted that the book clubs welcomed ninth graders and introduced them to high school expectations: "Students came a bit nervous and unsure. By the end of the week, they had new friends, familiarity with campus, and work to be proud of."

Though summer book clubs were created to help ELLs meet expectations for their fall English classes, they also helped English teachers learn about effective ELL instruction. In the spring preparation stage, English teachers collaborated with ESL teachers in planning the book clubs. In the summer implementation stage, English teachers received inclusion support during their credit-recovery classes. In the fall assessment stage, English teachers assessed ELLs' accommodated projects. Through firsthand experiences and improved learner outcomes, these teachers learned about comprehensible input, first language support, accommodations, scaffolding, sheltered instruction, and alternative assessments.

FINDINGS

The SHS summer book clubs significantly contributed to increased fall pass rates for ELLs. This outcome corroborates with results from a summer reading program that contributed to increased fall reading scores for multiethnic preadolescents (Kim, 2003). According to Stephen Krashen (personal communication), the SHS success may have stemmed from (a) voluntary participation having attracted motivated students, (b) novels having supported language acquisition and literacy, or (c) ELLs having received orientation to school. Because comparison studies were not conducted with volunteer groups in other types of programs, reasons for this success remain a conjecture. Nonetheless, the first research question can be answered positively—summer book clubs contributed to raising the ELLs' fall pass rate. Regarding the second question, summer book clubs provided two unanticipated outcomes—high school orientation for rising ninth graders and professional development for mainstream teachers.

DISCUSSION

The book clubs clearly addressed a call for closing the achievement gap for ELLs (Forrest, 2006). They were curriculum-centered (graphic novels for the fall English classes), learner-centered (sheltered instruction based on language levels), and educator-centered (collaboration between ESL and English teachers). Their impact exceeded the goal of improving ELL pass rates in fall English. Jane explained how ELLs—upon successfully completing English—were experiencing greater success in subsequent semesters and with other subjects. Her observations resemble how "intensive strategy instruction in a summer course brought lasting results" and "improvement in reading began with the jumpstart received in the summer literacy program" (Cohen, 2007, pp. 164, 173). With reachable goals and doable strategies, ELLs started to see themselves as academically capable.

Jane illustrated this transition by describing two typical ELLs—Aisha and Francisco. For Francisco, the book club seemed to trigger a major turn-around effect. Upon arriving in the United States, Francisco had been placed in the sixth grade. When he participated in the 2007 book club, Francisco had just finished his second year at SHS but had accrued less than 1 year of credit. Because Francisco often talked about dropping out, Jane was surprised that he had preregistered for the book club, and even more surprised that he actually came all 5 days. It might have been his girlfriend's presence that initially drew Francisco to the book club. Yet, once there, something clicked. Perhaps it was technology and multimodal texts. Perhaps it was hands-on help to become a better student (Heron, 2003). Two years have passed since Francisco attended his first book club. Not only is he still at the SHS, but he is on track for graduation.

When Aisha attended her first book club, she had recently arrived in the United States. Although SHS had several Arabic speakers, none were from Aisha's country, and she kept to herself for 5 months. The book club changed the high school experience for Aisha. The personal environment provided more than linguistic and academic support. Not only was Aisha finally able to make friends, but she realized that her emerging biliteracy was appreciated—she began to thrive. When Aisha returned to school that fall, she seemed like a new person. And, when she attended her second book club the following summer, she eagerly helped classmates who were still in the silent period (Krashen, 2003).

These characterizations represent ELLs who, according to Jane, were empowered by the book clubs to draw strength from their nonmainstream backgrounds and to emerge from silence, which "is not to be interpreted or construed as resistance to learning English, a lack of English competency, or as underachievement" (Rubinstein-Avila, 2007, p. 587). By believing they had control over their own academic achievement, they knew they could do it and so they did. Jane's explanation of these ELLs' enhanced sense of agency is similar to how "agency functioned in an inquiry-based summer school program for incoming ninth graders who struggled to succeed in math and language arts during middle school" (Heron, 2003, p. 569).

IMPLICATIONS FOR RESEARCH

Because this study is limited to one school, care must be taken when attempting to apply its findings to other settings. More specifically, because SHS participants were self-selected, intervention effects may not hold for ELL populations in other programs. Future studies could focus on the book club elements that are instrumental for promoting ELLs' academic achievement such as curricular components (Forrest, 2006) and collaborative mentoring (Spezzini, Austin, Abbott, & Littleton, 2009). Studies could also examine long range effects of the summer book clubs on ELLs' sense of agency (Heron, 2003) and credit accrual.

RECOMMENDATIONS

Given the positive outcomes in this study, we encourage collaboration between ESL and English teachers for implementing summer book clubs. Based on our experiences, we offer these recommendations:

1. ESL teachers should be experienced and highly trained, preferably at a master's level. They should have already established a positive working relationship with mainstream teachers.

2. ESL teachers and English teachers must be willing to collaborate in ELL book clubs during three stages: spring preparation, summer implementation, and fall assessment.
3. University interns should be secured from a nearby ESL teacher education program.
4. Administrators should understand effective ELL instruction and be willing to support the summer book clubs. Such book clubs should be scheduled concurrently with the regular summer school to leverage administrative, clerical, and custodial support.
5. Federal programs officers should earmark Title III funds for the ESL teacher's salary during the length of the summer program.

CONCLUSIONS

Angela's plan and successful implementation of the summer book clubs forged a new path at SHS for increasing the ELLs' pass rate. Implemented through teacher collaboration, this program both promoted academic achievement and enhanced credit accrual. To that end, summer book clubs may indeed be a key for enabling ELLs to unlock the credit accrual labyrinth toward graduation.

ACKNOWLEDGMENTS

We thank SHS administrators for their support, ESL teachers and interns for their participation, Julia Austin for her guidance, Maryann Manning and Stephen Krashen for their insights, and Patrick Chappell and Heidi Goertzen for their reviews.

NOTE

1. In this chapter, all names are pseudonyms.

REFERENCES

Aron, A., Aron, E. N., & Coups, E. J. (2005). *Statistics for the behavioral and social sciences: A brief course* (3rd ed.). Upper Saddle River, NJ: Pearson Prentice-Hall.

Ballantyne, K. G., Sanderman, A. R., & Levy J. (2008). *Educating English language learners: Building teacher capacity*. Washington, DC: National Clearinghouse for English Language Acquisition.

Cohen, J. (2007). A case study of a high school English-language learner and his reading. *Journal of Adolescent and Adult Literacy, 51*, 164-175.

Crane, S. (2006). *The red badge of courage*. Irvine, CA: Saddleback.

Echevarria, J., Vogt, M. J., & Short, D. J. (2009). *Making content comprehensible for secondary English learners: The SIOP model* (3rd ed.). Boston, MA: Pearson—Allyn & Bacon.

Forrest, S. N. (2006). Three foci of an effective high school Generation 1.5 literacy program. *Journal of Adolescent and Adult Literacy, 50*(2), 106-112.

Genesee, F., Lindholm-Leary, K., Saunders, W., & Christian, D. (2005). English language learners in U.S. schools: An overview of research findings. *Journal of Education for Students Placed at Risk, 10*, 363-385.

Heron, A. (2003). A study of agency: Multiple constructions of choice and decision making in an inquiry-based summer school program for struggling readers. *Journal of Adolescent & Adult Literacy, 46*, 568-579.

Jordan, J. (2008, July 18). Program at Gainesville State offers English language learners high school credit. *The Gainesville Times*. Retrieved from http://www.gainesvilletimes.com/news/archive/7090/

Kim, J. (2003). Summer reading and the ethnic achievement gap. *Journal of Education for Students Placed at Risk, 9*, 169-188.

Kirkland, L. D., Camp, D., & Manning, M. (2009). Changing the face of summer programs. *Childhood Education: Infancy through Early Adolescence, 85*(2), 96-101.

Krashen, S. (2003). *Explorations in language acquisition and use*. Portsmouth, NH: Heinemann.

Patton, M. Q. (2002). *Qualitative research and evaluation methods* (3rd ed.). Thousand Oaks, CA: Sage.

Rubinstein-Avila, E. (2007). From the Dominican Republic to Drew High: What counts as literacy for Yanira Lana? *Reading Research Quarterly, 42*, 568-589.

Sewell, A. (2000). *Black beauty*. Carson, CA: Learning Advantage.

Shin, F., & Krashen, S. (2007). *Summer reading: Program and evidence*. Boston, MA: Pearson—Allyn & Bacon.

Spezzini, S., Austin, J., Abbott, G., & Littleton, R. (2009). Role reversal within the mentoring dyad: Collaborative mentoring on the effective instruction of English language learners. *Mentoring & Tutoring: Partnership in Learning, 17*, 297-314.

Stevenson, R. L. (1998). *Dr. Jekyll and Mr. Hyde*. Ranch Dominguez, CA: Educational Insights.

Twain, M. (2006). *The adventures of Huckleberry Finn*. Irvine, CA: Saddleback.

Zehr, M. A. (2008). Summertime studies give English learners path to sharper skills. *Education Week, 27*(44), 10-11.

Zehr, M. A. (2009). Graduation rates on ELLs a mystery. *Education Week, 29*(3), 1 & 20-1.

CHAPTER 18

POWER DIFFERENTIALS

Pseudo-Collaboration Between ESL and Mainstream Teachers

Nelson Flores

One of the challenges of teacher collaboration is that it is sometimes interpreted differently by those viewed to be in a position of power as compared with others perceived to have less power. Corrie (1995) documented such a dynamic and argued in her research that, in many instances, what was called collaboration by those in a position of power was actually *pseudo-collaboration* that served to mask power differentials between the parties involved.

A few scholars have explored the presence of pseudo-collaboration, a hindrance to true collaboration, in team-teaching situations between English as a second language (ESL) and mainstream teachers (Arkoudis, 2003). This chapter seeks to expand on such prior work by documenting the challenges of one high school's attempt at implementing collaborative team teaching between an ESL teacher and mainstream teachers. In particular, it explores power relations that emerged between mainstream teachers and the ESL teacher, and shows that what mainstream teachers interpreted as collaboration was a pseudo-collaborative relationship from the perspective of the ESL teacher, which prevented her from effectively advocating for her students.

PSEUDO-COLLABORATION BETWEEN MAINSTREAM AND ESL TEACHERS

Educators interested in creating more collaborative, team-teaching relationships between ESL and mainstream teachers must challenge instances of pseudo-collaboration that may undermine the educational services provided to English language learners (ELLs). These power relations are particularly important to recognize because it is often common for ESL teachers to have a much lower authority status in schools than mainstream teachers (Arkoudis, 2003). In a survey of secondary school teachers, Reeves (2006) noted that most mainstream teachers did not value professional development in ESL, implying a lack of respect for the methodologies in which ESL teachers are trained. In addition, in a qualitative study of an innovative approach to improving collaboration between ESL teachers and mainstream teachers, Duke and Mabbott (2000) found many condescending attitudes on the part of mainstream teachers toward ESL teachers. The perceived inferiority of ESL teachers and the knowledge they have to offer to mainstream teachers can present a great challenge to the collaboration between the two. In many cases, ESL teachers' expertise may not be valued, and these second-language acquisition specialists may not be able to effectively meet the needs of ELLs.

To illustrate this power dynamic, Arkoudis (2000) described how the collaboration between an ESL teacher and a science teacher transpired. She found that the difference in subject status between science and ESL in the larger school culture created an imbalance of power; the ESL teacher was constantly placed in the position of deferring to the expertise of the science teacher. Unfortunately, the expertise of the ESL teacher was undervalued, despite that fact that she had more years of teaching experience. Arkoudis attributed this phenomenon to the larger social and political context of education and argued that:

> While science is an academic subject, the status of ESL as a subject is questionable. ESL is clearly not a traditional academic subject in the same sense as science. Indeed, in many secondary schools.... ESL does not exist as a separate discipline area, but as part of the English curriculum. (p. 62)

In other words, secondary schools categorize teachers by academic subject, and ESL is not treated as a separate subject. This in turns subordinates the ESL teacher to teachers with a *real* academic discipline. Subordination is a considerable challenge to collaborative team teaching and must be addressed directly in order to create truly collaborative relationships between ESL teachers and mainstream teachers.

In order to further explore the phenomenon of pseudo-collaboration between ESL and mainstream teachers, what follows provides empirical evidence of the power relations that emerged between an ESL teacher and three mainstream teachers at one New York City high school. It chronicles the cooperative activities between an ESL teacher and a science teacher, where the power relations were very apparent, and the same ESL teacher's relationship with both a math and a social studies teacher, which appeared to be more collaborative though pseudo-collaborative in the end. The reporting of this evidence is not meant to argue against implementing collaborative team teaching in ESL but rather hopes to unpack the characteristics of pseudo-collaboration in order to challenge these power relations.

PSEUDO-COLLABORATION IN A SCIENCE CLASSROOM

Based on interviews and analysis of face-to-face and online planning meetings, there was much evidence to support the idea that the science collaborative team-teaching situation was pseudo-collaborative. A description of a regular team-teaching day according to the ESL teacher was as follows:

> The most common pattern that comes to mind is maybe an [introductory activity] usually decided by [the science teacher], and we'd discuss it, and then we'd get into the lecture. Now the lecture usually [the science teacher] would deliver, and I would chip in every now and then. There'd be questions that students would ask, and depending on which teacher they're asking, the teacher would answer back or say it's not part of the lesson; we'll get to that later.

In this interview, the ESL teacher describes a dynamic where the science teacher is calling the shots, and she is taking a backseat and following his lead. An administrator who observed the class confirmed this dynamic:

> In the classroom, it was the content teacher dominating while the ESL teacher was taking not a back seat but her presence wasn't as strong as the content teacher, which if it's going to be collaborative team teaching, it should be both teachers.

In this situation, the ESL teacher was delegated into a secondary role in which she would help students with group work but contributed little during whole class discussion. The same inequitable power dynamic was also evident in the curriculum planning time of the two teachers. While the science teacher claimed that planning disagreements were openly discussed and compromises reached, the ESL teacher provided another story, which depicted the science teacher as always having the upper hand and not being receptive to the input she gave. This description of events was verified by transcriptions of online chats the two teachers had as they were planning the week's lessons:

> ESL teacher: I have been doing a little looking around on the WWW for ideas on how to get Ss to understand the diffusion, osmosis and active/passive transport, and there was one quick experiment involving an egg in water. (Maybe salt water.) I'm thinking for the 10th graders for that one, but maybe for the 9th graders when they get to that topic too.
> Science teacher: It's good you looked. We did osmosis in the lab, so we won't do it again in class. Did you find any images of budding, etc?
> ESL teacher: No images of budding. What was the osmosis lab?
> Science teacher: Onion skin in a wet mount slide. They observed and drew the image. Then we added a salt solution, which caused the water to diffuse out of the cell. And finally we washed off the salt with more water solution and the cell returned to the prior shape. This was a 3-week lab. I'd like to stick to the topics I sent you earlier for this week. OK?

It was clear from this interaction that the mainstream teacher had all of the power in determining the subject topics and would not consider the suggestions made by the ESL teacher. In addition, his tone at the end suggested that the topic was no longer open for discussion, and they indeed move on to the next topic, with the ESL teacher deferring to the Science teacher's decision.

The previous interaction was not an isolated phenomenon. Another example can be found from the transcription of Internet chats from another day:

> ESL teacher: I disagree with one of your suggestions. I think it's important to mention the nucleolus ... the nucleolus is important for students to go back to later on when we introduce the concepts of reproduction. Can't leave that one out.
> Science teacher: Just let it go and things will be fine. If the kids can figure out there is a nucleus, cell membrane, and

                cytoplasm, I will be very happy. Don't bring in the
                nucleolus ... that's the level that the students need
                to be at. Anything further is unnecessary ... do you
                trust me on the nucleolus?
ESL teacher: Sure.

Once again, the ESL teacher was put into the position of deferring to the science teacher without any evidence that the science teacher even considered what she was saying.

While the science teacher never discussed any of these interactions in his interview, he did mention that he believed the ESL teacher lacked content knowledge and advocated more content training for ESL teachers. The issue for the science teacher was that the ESL teacher was not qualified to express opinions about the content because she was not trained in the content area; his statement suggested he saw a role for the ESL teacher in providing information on how to effectively deliver the lesson and how to meet the language needs of ELLs. However, the ESL teacher stated that even her ideas of how to deliver lessons were oftentimes not seriously considered:

> If I were to ask [the science teacher] what is it about this teaching strategy that has proven effective in the past, and his stock answer is, "This is how it's done. This is how it's always been done so we're going to do it." And to me, that reasoning is lost on me ... I don't base teaching decisions on what's been done in the past ... I wasn't successful at finding a language to talk back and understand his reasoning in terms of pedagogy.

Even in terms of pedagogy, the science teacher still did not seriously consider her input, and she still felt powerless to effect change.

PSEUDO-COLLABORATION IN MATH AND SOCIAL STUDIES

As opposed to the science classroom where pseudo-collaboration was apparent, in the math and social studies classrooms power relations were much more subtle. The dynamic that emerged in the math and social studies classrooms appeared to be in stark contrast to the one that had emerged in the science classroom. Describing an average day in math class, the mainstream teacher noted:

> We split up our lesson plan which is simple to do because it's usually examples, and then the group work, and the do now, so [the ESL teacher] can do maybe the debrief and the [introductory activity] and group work, and I'll go over maybe two or three of the examples. We always make sure that there

is not just one person standing around and the other person doing all of the work. The students know that they have two real teachers.

The ESL teacher confirmed this teaching dynamic by adding the following:

> The minilesson either [the math teacher] or I take it over. We sort of switch. I'm not really sure what the pattern is. And then we have some example problems that we then show or model, and we switch on that.

The same dynamic was evident from discussions with both the social studies teacher and the ESL teacher. They both noted that they divided the work up in terms of delivering the lesson and stressed to the students that they were both the teachers in the classroom. In addition, the ESL teacher noted that she had a better rapport with these two teachers than the science teacher, particularly when they disagreed, something that the social studies teacher seconded:

> We work real well together. Sometimes we don't get to sit down the way we need to. Sometimes things happen; we get here, and we'll [be] right on the same page with each other ... I think that for the most part, I think both of us are very respectful toward the other and what the other has to offer when the other one makes recommendations.

The relationship that emerged from the two collaborative team teaching experiences here appeared to be much more egalitarian than in the science classroom. Both teams of teachers were treated as equal in their respective classrooms, and all teacher contributions were respected.

While these collaborative relationships were more equitable, there was still evidence of privileging of the mainstream teacher over the ESL teacher. One theme that emerged was that the mainstream teachers believed team teaching worked with the ESL teacher because all teachers agreed philosophically. They related this would not be the case if there were significant philosophical differences. As the social studies teacher noted:

> It wouldn't work. I mean we'd still come to work to do our job but it really wouldn't work. I wouldn't like it actually. I wouldn't want to team teach anymore.

The math teacher expressed a similar sentiment concerning teaching skills when she stated:

> You know I wouldn't choose to work with another person unless it was necessary. Given the fact [the ESL teacher] is very easy to work with and is very competent and works very hard has minimized the amount of communication that we need. I really appreciate it. So I don't know if I would be able to team-teach if it was with somebody who didn't have that overall skill set.

Both of these highly supportive teachers expressed that the only reason they felt positive concerning team teaching was because the ESL teacher did not challenge their teaching style significantly. The implication of this is that should she or another ESL teacher significantly challenged their style, the power dynamic might change considerably in favor of the mainstream teacher. Although these team teaching situations were more collaborative than with the science teacher, power still remained in the hands of the mainstream teachers who felt entitled to dismiss the ESL teacher should she begin to seriously challenge their perspective as mainstream teachers.

The decision-making superiority of the mainstream teachers was confirmed in interviews with the ESL teacher. Although she gave high praise to these teachers, she expressed sentiments similar to her science team-teaching situation. With the math and social studies teachers, when there were disagreements over content, the ESL teacher oftentimes felt unable to disagree because she was not a content area specialist. In addition, she noted that she sometimes still felt unable to teach the class in the way she thought was best, a sentiment that neither the math or social studies teacher expressed. One example she gave was:

> With [the math teacher] I think she would say things like, "Oh well, that's not on the Regent's exam" or in the classroom when students ask, "What's the difference between a hexagon and a hectagon?" like today, and her answer was, "Did I ever talk about hectagon? No? Ok ... then go home after school and look it up on the computer." Now I know that's her way of managing time constraints, but ... that's not exactly me.

The ESL teacher, although having serious reservations about this time-management approach, did not mention her misgivings to the mainstream teacher because she felt the mainstream teacher knew how to pace the curriculum better than she did, even though she felt the pacing was inappropriate for her ELLs. In short, the ESL teacher, while feeling more empowered in these two team-teaching situations and treated as an equal in terms of presenting the lesson and planning the lesson, still showed evidence of deferring to the mainstream teachers and not expressing her opinion in certain situations, a sign of pseudo-collaboration and not true collaboration.

IMPLICATIONS

In theory, collaborative team teaching provides ELLs access to high quality content instruction that has been made comprehensible by the ESL teacher and the mainstream teacher working together as a team (Clegg,

1996). Yet, as demonstrated by the collaborative practices of these teachers, true collaboration can oftentimes remain an elusive goal. The challenges of developing true collaboration indicate the need for more professional development for ESL and mainstream teachers on how to effectively work together and the need to make them more aware of the risk of falling into a pattern of pseudo-collaboration. Mainstream teachers and ESL teachers cannot simply be paired up and left to their own devices. Instead, strategic and rigorous training in collaborative practices as well as support in implementation of team-teaching approaches must be provided.

Yet, the fact remains that in many school contexts, including the one described above, ESL teachers are not seen as having equal status to mainstream teachers, and it indicates that professional development is not enough. This is especially true at the secondary level, where content expertise is seen as the most valuable characteristic of teachers. All educational institutions serving ELLs require a school-wide effort that challenges the commonly held idea that content expertise is more valuable than expertise in ESL methodology. Until the expertise of ESL teachers and mainstream teachers are seen as equally important, barriers to true collaboration between ESL and mainstream teachers will persist. In short, collaborative team teaching in ESL will not be effective without a challenge to larger discursive constructions of what makes a *real* teacher.

One way to challenge this privileging of content over second language development is to make this dichotomy less apparent in the organization of teacher education and teacher professional development. During teacher preparation and professional development, ESL teachers should receive more content knowledge while mainstream teachers should receive more training in ESL methodology. Perhaps then, ESL teachers may feel more confident in their status in the classroom while mainstream teachers will have more appreciation for the expertise that ESL teachers bring to the table. This greater appreciation of what the other brings to the table may avoid some of the power dynamics observed in this study and make disagreement less of a one-sided relationship in favor of mainstream teachers. This change in teacher development can open up the road to true collaboration, which would then shape classrooms where the needs of ELLs are at the center of instruction.

REFERENCES

Arkoudis, S. (2000). 'I have linguistic aims and linguistic content': ESL and science teachers planning together. *Prospect, 15*, 61-71.

Arkoudis, S. (2003). Teaching English as a second language in science classes: Incommensurate epistemologies? *Language and Education, 17*, 161-173.

Clegg, J. (1996). *Mainstreaming ESL: Case studies in integrating ESL students into the mainstream curriculum.* Bristol, PA: Multilingual Matters.

Corrie, L. (1995). The structure and culture of staff collaboration: Managing meaning and opening doors. *Educational Review, 47*, 89-99.

Duke, K., & Mabbott, A. (2000). An alternative model for novice-level elementary ESL education. *MinneTESOL/WITESOL Journal, 17*, 11-30.

Reeves, J. (2006). Secondary teachers' attitudes toward including English language learners in mainstream classrooms. *The Journal of Educational Research, 99*, 131-142.

CHAPTER 19

BARRIERS TO COLLABORATION BETWEEN ENGLISH AS A SECOND LANGUAGE AND CONTENT AREA TEACHERS

Beth Lewis Samuelson, Faridah Pawan, and Yu-Ju Hung

> The responsibility is up to all parts of the community to make the transition from home to school successful for all students not just English language learners. (Marina, 4th grade resource teacher)

The rough ground of collaboration between English as a second language (ESL) or English as a foreign language (EFL) teachers and their mainstream content area colleagues has only recently begun to achieve attention in academic research (Arkoudis, 2006). ESL teachers are often viewed as members of a helping profession without ownership of a content area or specific learning goals (Creese, 2002; Pawan & Craig, 2011; Pawan & Ortloff, 2011). The current study identified three areas presenting challenges for collaboration: (a) lack of administrative support; (b) lack of time for professional collaboration; and (c) misinformed attitudes toward (English language learner) ELLs and the second language acquisition process. Each of these areas is directly linked to the status of ESL as a profession in K-12 schools.

This chapter draws on teacher voices from a professional learning community that provided a secure space in which teachers could express their views and discuss their experiences. Teacher knowledge communities of this type can be "safe storytelling places where educators narrate the rawness of their experiences, negotiate meaning and authorize their own and other's interpretations of situations" (Craig, 2009, p. 600). The teacher professional learning community examined here has been characterized by collaboration, sharing of values, concern for student achievement and well-being, and dialogue on shared knowledge and practices (Gilles, Wilson, & Elias, 2010). These qualities have been supported and developed primarily through online forums and a cohort-based model for in-service professional development.

Online professional development was critical to the success of this model program. Other studies related to this work have documented that collaborative interactions between students in online learning environments can support deepening critical thinking and collaboration (Pawan, Paulus, Yalcin, & Chang, 2003). The terrain described may appear rough, but mapping the territory is an essential step in enabling teachers and teacher trainers to better identify the ways that they can collaborate and communicate to ensure that all learners are successful.

THE STUDY

The teachers whose insights and stories are presented here frequently commented on the obstacles that they encountered in their attempts to improve collaboration between ESL and content area teachers. In this study, we asked what these complexities might be: What obstacles might ESL and content area teachers in urban high-needs schools face in establishing meaningful collaboration with each other?

The study was a substudy of ongoing research on a 5-year professional development program, the Collaborative Teaching Institute (CTI), which enrolled K-12 teachers, whether they were content area or specialized bilingual/ESL teachers, in an 18-month sequence of online courses in ESL instruction and assessment. The federally-funded program, which ended in 2010, was designed to assist teachers in Indiana in teaching and working with ELLs and led to an add-on teaching license or endorsement in teaching ESL (Pawan & Ward, 2007). The current study draws on the forum discussions in course on basic linguistics for teachers, which was required for all CTI participants. The forum discussions were characterized by student-student interactions in which the teachers were able to collaborate and share their perspectives freely (Kamhi-Stein, 2000).

Table 19.1. Teacher-Participants and Their Characteristics

Name	Gender	ESL/bilingual or Content Area	Grade level
Amy	F	ESL	Elementary
Athena	F	Elementary, all subjects (CA)	5th
Cecelia	F	Bilingual	2nd
Daisy	F	ESL	Elementary
Denise	F	ESL	Elementary
Flor	F	ESL	Secondary
Hannah	F	English (CA)	8th
Holly	F	Elementary, all subjects (CA)	3rd
Honoria	F	ESL	H.S.
Lacey	F	ESL	K-5
Magdalena	F	Bilingual	6th
Maria	F	Bilingual	K
Marina	F	Resource teacher, special educ. (CA)	4th
Mary	F	ESL	Elementary
Susan	F	ESL	Elementary
Totals	15 females 0 males	8 ESL teachers 3 bilingual teachers 4 CA teachers	12 Gr. K-6 3 Gr. 7-12

The Participants

Table 19.1 provides a summary of the 15 teachers, their gender, teaching area, and grade level. All names are pseudonyms. All the students in this all-female class were working toward a license addition or endorsement in ESL. (One additional participant, a full-time graduate student, was excluded from this study because she was not teaching). Four were currently working as content area teachers—middle school English, elementary traditional classes, and special education—while earning their ESL endorsements. All of the remaining participants (11) were ESL and bilingual teachers.

Most were experienced nontraditional, part-time graduate students. They had completed two courses each semester while continuing to teach full-time.

Data Collection and Analysis

The texts for this study were collected during one semester in a distance education course. The main sources included:

1. one thousand five hundred forty-nine asynchronous online forum postings over 15 weeks;
2. eight transcripts from synchronous chat sessions in small groups of 4-5; and
3. five hundred twenty-six messages sent in the online course environment.

The dataset was analyzed recursively (Bogdan & Biklen, 1998; Lincoln & Guba, 1985), first using an open coding scheme that identified all of the challenges encountered by the teachers that might become obstacles to their effective practice as ESL teachers, including obstacles to effective collaboration between ESL teachers and content area teachers. The dataset was coded twice by two independent raters. Three categories dealing with professional issues emerged as especially pertinent: collaboration with administrators, school staff, and colleagues (see Table 19.2). Each of these areas yielded insights into the kind of support that ESL and content area teachers need for effective collaboration.

RESULTS AND DISCUSSION

The results of the data analysis revealed three primary areas in which the participants experienced barriers to collaboration: lack of support from administrators and staff, lack of time for planning between ESL and content area teachers, and encounters with negative or misinformed attitudes toward ESL. The discussion that follows explains the results and addresses the positive contributions that dialogue and sharing of expertise can make toward providing support for ESL and content area teachers.

Lack of Administration and Staff Support as a Barrier to Collaboration

One barrier to effective working relationships between ESL and content teachers is the lack of support from the nonteaching staff and administration at their schools. Lacey emphasized that administrators are the "'law' of the school" (Table 19.2, line 1a). Administrative decisions related to scheduling and resource allocation have direct and significant impact on the quality of teacher collaboration. The ESL teachers provided accounts of how they needed more administrative support in order to be able to work effectively with ELLs and address their academic needs.

The roles that school secretaries and other front-line staff members have with English language learners and their families are critical for

Table 19.2. Coding Scheme for Professional Issues Dealing With Administrators, Staff, and Colleagues

Code	Subcode	Examples
Professional issues: administrators	1a. support from administrators	"Administrators need to be involved because they are the "law" of the school. If the administrators are on board with the collaboration and are aware of ESL issues then they will be able to help the teachers learn how to collaborate with one another." (Lacey)
	1b. administrator attitudes towards ESL teachers and students	"This is a brand new ESL site. Our director stressed to us that ESL was not wanted. So yes, we feel like the 'black sheep.' ... There are 5 of us working in one room. We have nowhere to take our groups." (Amy)
Professional issues: staff	2a. support from staff	"I actually tried to call you a couple weeks ago because I have one of your old students. Of course we requested his info and did not receive it. Then I called and asked to speak to you and they became extremely annoyed and a little defensive. Short story, short ... never received anything. We just retested." (Flor)
Professional issues: colleagues	3a. time for collaboration	"My experience with collaboration with general education teachers has been very frustrating. There is just not enough time to collaborate. They collaborate during their prep time which is during the day while I'm teaching. My prep time is when they are all teaching math. If I collaborated with just the teachers of my level 1-2 students, I would need to meet with more than 11 teachers. At this point we are spread so thin that it is impossible. The collaboration that does happen is always initiated by me. I go to the teachers and talk to them when I can." (Susan)
	3b. teacher attitudes toward ESL teachers and students	"I struggle with helping teachers change their beliefs. The best way I feel to help them is to work side by side in class with them to show them that ESL children can do things just like the other children. Also, to expose teachers to articles that help to widen their knowledge base of ESL learners." (Athena)

helping new students adjust, but often the work of settling new ELLs is left to the ESL teachers. "As an English-as-a-New-Language (ENL) teacher," explained Mary, "I have had many families come to school to enroll and the secretaries send them straight to my office." When they arrive in her office, they do not know anything about the school calendar, how to order school lunches, how to arrange for bus transportation and other basics. "It takes so much time to talk to them about this," Mary continued, "that I get backlogged on those days. In our district, the case load for ENL teachers is much higher than that of the Special Needs teachers. A lot of Special Needs teachers in the building have 12 students on their case load compared with 75+ ENL. This is wrong." Flor revealed a similar situation in which staff at a student's old school did not respond to requests to send over ESL diagnostic test records (see Table 19.2, line 2a).

Lack of Time for Collaboration Between ESL and Content Area Teachers

The lack of time for teacher collaboration was a complicated issue for both ESL and content area teachers. In Table 19.2, line 3a, Susan explains how even teachers who wish to collaborate can be hindered by scheduling patterns that provide them with no common time for working together. She has found collaboration with content area teachers to be very frustrating because of scheduling conflicts and the numbers of teachers who are working with her ESL students. She stated, "If I collaborated with just the teachers of my level 1-2 students, I would need to meet with more than 11 teachers. At this point we are spread so thin that it is impossible." She initiates collaboration work when possible, but mostly the burden to do so falls on her shoulders.

This difficulty was experienced by the content area teachers as well. Holly, an all-subjects elementary teacher, also emphasized pressures that made it difficult for them to work with ESL teachers:

> As a content teacher, I also feel like sometimes I really need that time to do other things instead of collaborate with the ENL teacher even though I know it is crucial to the success of the upcoming lessons being taught. Sometimes she comes in to meet with me, and I just haven't had time to think about the next week yet; I am still focusing on the current week. It is frustrating for both of us.

These accounts illustrate how teachers on both sides, ESL and content area, can experience tensions due to the competing demands of their time commitments.

Athena added the perspective of the mainstream teacher in need of more assistance but unable to receive it from her ESL colleague. As a content area teacher, she felt that she got no support from the ESL teacher at her school. She wrote:

Our ESL teacher pops in once every two weeks in the middle of my prep to see what she can do to help me. I give her suggestions, ask for help, then just wait until she pops in two weeks later. It is frustrating. She says she doesn't help me as much because "I know what I am doing." But, 1/3 of my class is ESL students, all of which come with different needs. I would love for her to help me preteach vocabulary. But, it never happens.

The discussions and examples thus far demonstrate that collaboration between content area teachers and their ESL colleagues is often challenged by factors not always within their control.

Negative and Misinformed Attitudes Toward ESL as Barriers to Collaboration

In addition to lack of administrative and staff support and lack of time for working together, the participants frequently encountered negative attitudes toward ESL students and teachers on the part of teaching and non-teaching staff at their schools. Negative attitudes resulting from misinformation about ESL as a discipline were manifested in administrative decisions and presented serious difficulties for good working relationships between ESL and content area teachers. As Amy noted, ESL teachers can feel that they and their students are the "black sheep" of their schools (Table 18.2, line 1b).

Content area teachers often entertain misinformed and flawed ideas about the language abilities of the ELLs in their classrooms. Flor's account sums up this attitude: "Some teachers do not believe that ESL is a *real* class anyway. If a student can carry on a conversation, then they believe that they do not need to be there [in the ESL class]." Teachers who do not think that teaching ESL students requires professionalism and craft do not see the need to work with the ESL teachers to improve their practice. Athena explained that the teacher across the hall loved having ESL children in her classroom because they were "easy." Athena often tried to engage her colleague with strategies for giving the students the attention that they deserve. "I LOVE ESL children, but 'easy' wouldn't be how I would describe them," she stated.

Such misconceptions could result in low English proficiency being viewed equivalent to a learning deficit or disability. As a result of minimal understanding of the nature of language proficiency and the needs of English language learners, many mainstream teachers allow their ELLs' language proficiency to influence their assessment of how much those students could learn or accomplish. Amy, a former content area teacher now working as an ESL teacher in elementary school, described how her colleagues' misperceptions about the English abilities of their ELLs had an impact on their teaching:

> In my former role as a classroom teacher, I felt that all ENL students could participate at some level in my classroom. Unfortunately, many of my mainstream teaching colleagues disagreed. In my opinion, the teachers who do not believe ENL students can participate in the mainstream classroom are not seeking to provide or do not believe in providing comprehensible input.

Even mainstream teachers who were well-meaning sometimes did not understand how to best help their ELLs. Lacey gave an account of how teachers who did not understand the difference between Basic Interactional Conversation Skills (BICS) and Cognitive Academic Language Proficiency (CALP) could misconstrue language abilities of their students (Cummins, 1991; Cummins & Man, 2007). She wrote:

> I have heard teachers say, "This student speaks English well. He should be able to write and understand English, too." I think that sometimes the teachers assume that the students should already have knowledge of concepts when they do not. I have seen teachers that do not understand that some things may need to be taught, like vocabulary or certain phrases which we say in America.

At the secondary level, Flor gave an account of how language attitudes on the part of teachers, monolingual students, and administrators could overwhelm students.

> I have a mixed hour of junior high and high school students, and they are terrified about making mistakes. The general population, not to mention a few teachers, has been extremely ugly to them. They are just getting to the point where they really trust me and are willing to take some chances in class.

Mary complained that many administrators and classroom teachers do not understand the need for providing accommodations for limited English proficient students or how to deliver them. She explained:

> In my experience, [LEP children] are lumped with the lowest performing groups.... LEP students need exposure with native speakers who are at grade-level.... Despite the professional development given to classroom teachers, many still just don't "get it." Many don't provide the correct accommodations out of ignorance of the needs of LEPs. The actual colleagues who are more educated about teaching LEPs are very limited. Just because a teacher has LEPs in their rooms for some number of years does not make them an expert.... Administrators are in similar situations. Many

in my area have had minimal education in working with LEPs. Again, they make generalizations that are not based in research.

This study maps out some significant obstacles that ESL and content area teachers might face in their attempts at serious collaboration. Some of the areas that presented the greatest challenges were lack of administrative support, lack of time for substantive collaboration, and misinformed attitudes toward ELLs and the second language acquisition process. Teachers lack administrative support for the work they do when they are expected to manage large case loads and take on roles that staff members normally fill, such as introducing new students and their families to school culture. The lack of time is an area closely related to administrative support, as the decisions for scheduling ultimately reflect the priorities of the administration. Also, administrators can make the collaboration between ESL teachers and content area teachers possible by practicing their role as the law of their schools to schedule meeting time or arrange meeting opportunities between two groups and making them accountable for the collaboration.

Meeting together to discuss teaching concerns and barriers to their effective collaboration is the first step for these teachers. Creating accessible and safe spaces for ESL and content area teachers is critical in order for them to sustain conversations over a long period of time and thus to develop trusting relationships. The online community created by this distance education course and by the Collaborative Teaching Institute provides one such example of ways that teachers can work together to address the barriers that they are experiencing. Further research, however, is needed to understand how teachers who might otherwise be isolated by structural and administrative barriers can collaborate via Internet forums and social media.

The research also suggests that much more work can be done to combat misunderstandings about the nature of second language acquisition and the needs of ESL students in preservice and in-service teaching training programs in all grade levels and subject areas, as well as in training programs for administrators. Inviting all teachers and administrators to participate in the education of ESL students—an initiative that is analogous to the promotion of the concept that all teachers are literacy teachers—would help to promote better awareness of the optimal conditions for learning and teaching language. In that regard, in its new reiteration, CTI will expand its recruitment to include not only teachers but also administrators in its joint teacher training programs.

This survey highlights the voices of the teachers, thereby emphasizing that the teachers are the experts who are most familiar with the challenges and barriers they face in their particular schools and districts. Any initiative to address barriers to collaboration and improve the preparation of non-ESL teachers and administrators must be founded on ESL teachers' voices and ESL teachers' expertise. The rough terrain described here need not be a barrier, but merely a map of the territory that enables teachers and teacher trainers to better identify the ways that they can work together to ensure that all learners are successful.

REFERENCES

Arkoudis, S. (2006). Negotiating the rough ground between ESL and mainstream teachers. *International Journal of Bilingual Education and Bilingualism, 9*, 415-433.

Bogdan, R. C., & Biklen, S. K. (1998). *Qualitative research for education: An introduction to theory and methods* (3rd ed.). Boston, MA: Allyn & Bacon.

Craig, C. (2009). Research in the midst of organized school reform: Versions of teacher community in tension. *American Educational Research Journal, 46*, 598-619.

Creese, A. (2002). The discursive construction of power in teacher partnerships: Language and subject specialists in mainstream schools. *TESOL Quarterly, 36*, 597-616.

Cummins, J. (1991). Language development and academic learning. In L. Malave & G. Dugnette (Eds.), *Language, culture and cognition* (pp. 161-175). Clevedon, England: Multilingual Matters.

Cummins, J., & Man, E. (2007). Academic language: What is it and how do we acquire it? In J. Cummins & C. Davison (Eds.), *International handbook of English language teaching* (pp. 797-810). New York, NY: Springer Science+Business Media LLC.

Gilles, C., Wilson, J., & Elias, M. (2010). Sustaining teachers' growth and renewal through action research, induction programs, and collaboration. *Teacher Education Quarterly, 37*(1), 91-108.

Kamhi-Stein, L. D. (2000). Looking to the future of TESOL teacher education: Web-based bulletin board discussions in a methods course. *TESOL Quarterly, 34*, 423-455.

Lincoln, Y., & Guba, E. (1985). *Naturalistic inquiry*. Beverly Hills, CA: SAGE.

Pawan, F., & Craig, D. (2011). ESL and content area teacher responses to discussions on English language learner instruction. *TESOL Journal, 2*, 293-311.

Pawan, F., & Ortloff, J. H. (2011). Sustaining collaboration: English-as-a-second-language, and content-area teachers. *Teaching and Teacher Education: An International Journal of Research and Studies, 27*, 463-471.

Pawan, F., Paulus, T. M., Yalcin, S., & Chang, C. -F. (2003). Online learning: Patterns of engagement and interaction among in-service teachers. *Language Learning and Technology, 7*(3), 119-140.

Pawan, F., & Ward, B. (2007). Integrated curriculum (Indiana). In F. Pawan & G. Sietman (Eds.), *Helping English language learners succeed in middle and high schools: Collaborative partnerships between ESL and classroom teachers.* Alexandria, VA: TESOL.

CHAPTER 20

PULLING AWAY FROM PULL-OUT

Coteaching ELLs in the New Latino South

Greg McClure

It is the last day of the quarter and the two teachers in the classroom appear to be in the middle of a synchronized instructional dance. Eva, the fourth-grade teacher, is seated in a chair at the back of the room with the students gathered on the carpet in front of her. As Eva reads aloud to the students from Patricia Polacco's Babushka's Doll, Leila, the English for speakers of other languages (ESOL) teacher who coteaches with Eva during this daily literacy block, hops up from her spot on the carpet and comes to life as Babushka's doll. Perched at the edge of a desk, Leila transforms herself into the doll on Babushka's shelf, mimicking her every move as Eva reads the story. Eva tells how the doll begins to swing her legs, and Leila points to her own swinging them back and forth. For the remainder of the story, Leila performs as a live version of the magical doll from the story, using pantomime and facial cues to accentuate key events and clarify vocabulary terms. In a matter of moments, she has brought the story to life and provided real-time visual scaffolding to the oral reading of the text.

DEMOGRAPHIC AND INSTRUCTIONAL TRENDS

The scene above comes from a year-long case study of two coteachers in a fourth grade classroom in the southeastern United States, a region that has experienced tremendous growth in its English language learner (ELL) population since the mid-1990s (Hamann & Harklau, 2010). Recent data confirm that southeastern states in the United States continue to experience some of the fastest growth rates of ELLs. For example, South Carolina, the state with the largest percent increase between 1998 and 2008, experienced an increase of more than 800% in its enrollment of ELLs (Batalova & McHugh, 2010). Unfortunately, academic achievement has not paralleled this demographic growth. The National Center for Educational Statistics (NCES) reported that Latino students, who represent the majority of ELLs, have a dropout rate of 27 % compared with 7.3% of their White counterparts (as cited in Kaufman, Alt, & Chapman, 2004).

Facing these realities, grade-level teachers with little or no professional development in second language instruction (Antunez, 2002) struggle to create teaching practices that support the language and content development needs of the ELLs in their classrooms. As a result, many districts have turned away from pull-out models that remove ELLs from the mainstream classroom and are implementing more inclusive and collaborative approaches like coteaching between ESOL teachers and grade-level teachers. In this study coteaching is conceptualized as an instructional practice where two or more educators share instructional responsibility for students assigned to the same classroom (Villa, Thousand, & Nevin, 2008).

While the notion of collaborating to meet the needs of ELLs is not a new one (Nunan, 1992), coteaching for ELLs in U.S. public schools is relatively unexplored in empirical studies. With the exception of recent work by Honigsfeld and Dove (2010) and McClure and Cahnmann-Taylor (2010), most of the empirical work examining coteaching has occurred in international contexts (Arkoudis, 2006; Creese, 2005; Davison, 2006; Gardner, 2006; Glazier, 2004). While these studies have established a significant baseline on coteaching ELLs, findings from international settings cannot necessarily be mapped onto the U.S. context without further inquiry. Given the unique reality of the U.S. context resulting from the shifting demographic landscape and the prevailing climate of accountability, the lack of empirical work on coteaching in U.S. schools constitutes a significant gap in our knowledge regarding how to best educate ELLs. Consequently, this case study aims to address this gap by documenting how coteachers collaborate to support language and content learning for ELLs in a fourth grade classroom in northeastern Georgia.

Table 20.1. Site and Participant Profile

	Westside Elementary Percentage	Eva & Leila's Class Percentage
Asian	2	7
Black	37	7
Hispanic	40	68
Multiracial	4	7
White	17	11
English language learners	29	77
Free/reduced lunch	78	89
	Eva	*Leila*
Years teaching	3	3
Education	BS Elem. Ed.	MS Ed. TESOL
Languages	English	English, Arabic

CONTEXT AND METHODS

Westside Elementary School (WES) is a medium-sized neighborhood school in an urban district in northeast Georgia. Table 20.1 provides key demographic data for the school and the fourth grade classroom where this study took place. Eva, the fourth grade teacher, and Leila, the ESOL teacher, cotaught a 2-hour literacy block every day.

Data Sources

Data for this study were collected mainly from ethnographic field notes, transcripts from interviews and Coteaching Inquiry Group (CIG) meetings, and documents and artifacts. Beginning in October 2008 and ending in May 2009, the author conducted weekly classroom observations in Eva and Leila's classroom that generally lasted 2 hours. To provide a framework for reflection and analysis, the author and the coteachers created the CIG and met several times during the year to discuss issues the teachers were facing as well as patterns noticed from observations. This idea was in direct response to Davison's (2006) assertion of the need for coteachers to spend time together reflecting on and breaking down their coteaching experiences. All CIG meetings took place in Eva and Leila's classroom at WES and generally lasted 2 to 3 hours.

COTEACHING ELLS AT WESTSIDE ELEMENTARY SCHOOL

At WES Eva and Leila drew on a number of instructional resources and coteaching arrangements, one of which was team teaching. According to Friend and Cook (2003), team teaching is defined as both coteachers being responsible for the planning and instruction for all students. They add that team teaching may involve a number of different arrangements, from alternating the teaching of minilessons to taking turns in leading discussions. Leila and Eva reported that although team teaching required significant coplanning to coordinate their lessons, it was their preferred approach to coteaching.

Team Teaching

Scholars have suggested that ELLs, especially in the upper elementary grades and beyond, are faced with the increasingly challenging task of simultaneously developing English proficiency, mastering content knowledge, and developing academic literacy (Echeverria, Vogt, & Short, 2008; Gibbons, 2002). When Leila and Eva engaged in team teaching, they were often able to address these challenges, effectively scaffolding each other's verbal instruction and content concepts. They were also able to attend to procedural aspects of instructional tasks. Examples of this are seen in the opening vignette in this chapter and are further evidenced below.

Team teaching for Leila and Eva always occurred during writing instruction in the last hour of the day. Typically, one of the teachers would lead a minilesson while the other actively supported the lesson using the interactive whiteboard to pull up images or color-code pieces of text on the screen. The teachers were quite effective at playing off of each other's instruction in what Eva referred to as *tag teaming back and forth* to add concrete examples or to help clarify what had been said. One lesson on descriptive writing illustrates this tag teaming. Eva, the grade-level teacher, started the lesson by asking the class "Who can tell me what a sensory detail is?" As hands went into the air, Leila jumped in (TAG!) from her position back at the whiteboard and offered to Eva and the class, "Maybe we should review the five senses first. Who can name one of the five senses?" As students generated a list of the five senses, Leila was calling on students, and Eva was now at the whiteboard (TAG!) writing down student responses and quickly drawing appropriate body parts next to each one (an eye for sight, a nose for smell, and so on).

When I asked Leila to comment on this example of team teaching, she indicated that she simply realized "in the moment" that revisiting the five senses would help ELLs with the ultimate task of incorporating sensory details into their own writing. Additionally, while Leila confirmed the author's perception that tag teaming was largely unplanned and improvisational, she also offered a different perspective. She attributed her willingness to jump in more frequently as being directly related to having planned together with Eva. In her words, "having a better sense of where the lesson was going and what the final task would be" was critical and helped Leila decide what types of instructional support and scaffolding ELLs would need.

Validating Language and Culture Through Coteaching

While team teaching encouraged collaborative sequences like tag teaming that effectively scaffolded students' participation in academic tasks, it also allowed the teachers to develop lessons that capitalized on the collaborative possibilities afforded by coteaching. During the last quarter of the year, Leila and Eva developed an extended poetry unit that exemplified effective coteaching for ELLs. The unit addressed key content concepts in language arts and also provided meaningful opportunities for students to develop their language skills in ways that validated their linguistic and cultural resources in the process. Further, in planning the unit, both teachers expressed interest in making the project more creative than typical poetry units that explore a variety of poetic forms and culminate in an individual poetry portfolio. Leila, who has experience as a photojournalist, suggested incorporating photos into the project. Further discussion quickly led to the idea of connecting the project to students' families and thus, the Multicultural Family PhotoPoetry Project was born.

To begin the unit, the teachers took turns leading minilessons to cover basic characteristics of a variety of poetic forms (haiku, free verse, sonnets, and others). They also shared examples of their own poetry, collaboratively wrote a poem with the whole class, and led an outdoor nature walk to collect artifacts to use in writing haikus. One of the assessment products of the unit involved individual student contributions to the class's multicultural, multilingual alphabet book. Students were each assigned a letter from the alphabet and were asked to talk with their families to come up with a couple of words for their letter that were important to them and their families in some way (e.g., *Amigos* for "A"). Students were then given time in class to choose one word and develop a poem for that word. Students were told they could write in English, their native language, or to write bilingually; however, emphasis was placed on paying attention to the conversations they had had with family members. Students worked individually on their poems and conferenced with both teachers while crafting their work.

Xi Zon Bing
By Eli

Xi Zon Bing
Card games
Play seriously
Entire family
Fears losing
They laugh
When they win.

Source: Photo by Monira Silk.

Figure 20.1. *Xi Zon Bing* by Eli.

As the poems began to take shape, Leila worked with students to stage photos that captured the tone and meaning of their poems. One highlight of the project occurred towards the end as the class was filling in some of the letters that still needed a poem. The perennial issue of alphabet books, the letter X, was immediately solved when Eli volunteered to compose the poem for X. Eli wrote about *Xi Zon Bing*, a Taiwanese card game that his family plays around Chinese New Year (see Figure 20.1). This was a significant event, as Eli was the only Asian student in the classroom and seldom had the opportunity to see his language and culture represented in significant ways. The authenticity of the project was further manifested at the annual Community Poetry Picnic when the students shared a digital version of their alphabet book with families and community members.

CELEBRATION AND HESITATION

This project was successful on many accounts. From a coteaching perspective, team teaching allowed the teachers to effectively trade off between leading minilessons and supporting each other's instruction. Additionally, by incorporating their specific talents the teachers were able to extend the unit in creative ways. Connecting the alphabet book to students' home language and culture emerged largely because Eva wanted to do more than the typical poetry portfolio. Similarly, Leila's photography expertise moved the students' poems from two-dimensional texts to multimodal works of art that were brought to life with color and images of the students themselves. It is critical to note that both teachers mentioned that knowing they had the support of the other was a key factor in taking some risks with this project and extending their work.

By all accounts, Leila and Eva enjoyed coteaching together. Although coteaching required significant planning on their parts, in interviews and in final written reflections both teachers indicated they would like to continue coteaching with one another in the future. In addition to agreeing that it was the most effective approach for working with ELLs, both Leila and Eva also recognized coteaching as a form of ongoing professional learning. For Leila, team teaching was like "performing in the presence of a colleague," and for her this was a major motivator to be prepared and to develop "well thought-out and prepared lessons." Eva added, "I think we both prefer teaching the whole group—when we had the time to plan, our teaching was more fluid. And too, you learn a lot about your teaching when you're coteaching at the same time with someone."

Despite their preference for coteaching, both teachers expressed some frustration and disappointment that they attributed to elements in the broader sociopolitical context in which they were teaching. Equally important, both also independently cited lack of common planning time as their greatest barrier to developing their practice. In closing, it is critical to discuss how these factors impacted Eva and Leila's work together, as examining these factors may provide insight into how to best support and sustain coteaching models for ELLs.

Regarding the school, district, and state positions on coteaching, Leila and Eva agreed that there was an obvious contradiction between the glossy institutional rhetoric surrounding coteaching and the reality that they lived out as coteachers. School and state documents officially promoted coteaching as the preferred approach for working with ELLs (Georgia Department of Education, 2008); however, few tangible resources were provided to help coteachers fully realize the model. For example, formal improvement plans at both the district and the school level emphasized "increasing instructional time by limiting interruptions, expanding the ESOL push-in model, and supporting collaboration between classroom teachers and ESOL teachers" (WES, 2006, p. 14). However, when asked about training and professional development, neither Eva nor Leila indicated that they had received any professional development on coteaching, nor were they granted any common planning time to facilitate their collaborative work.

CONCLUSION

Much of what Leila and Eva experienced throughout the year is congruent with current literature on coteaching. As in many studies of coteaching in special education contexts (Murawski, & Dieker, 2004; Scruggs, Mastropieri, & McDuffie, 2007), lack of institutional support in terms of resources and professional development were key factors impacting Leila and Eva' ability to implement coteaching to the degree they would have liked. Beyond these logistical elements though, the teachers described needing time to develop their coteaching beyond just planning lessons, more from a relational perspective. In final interviews and written reflections, the teachers discussed the role of the CIG sessions in meeting this need. Their responses confirm the value of such an approach:

> I've never been able to really talk with Leila [outside of the CIG meetings] where we are not using all our time to just plan this or that for tomorrow. Our group meetings really allowed us to deal with some of the interpersonal issues that come up when you're sharing a classroom. (Eva)

> I would say the biggest benefit [of the CIG meetings] is that we were able to kind of step away from the actual teaching and offer each other feedback. I really don't know what my other coteachers thought about having me in their classroom all year but I know what Eva thought because we shared it in this group! So I felt like we were able to take more risks that way with each other because we were more comfortable. (Leila)

Regardless of the format employed (such as parallel, team, or other arrangement), coteaching is a collaborative instructional practice that, at the core, is about human relations. It involves two teachers navigating the process of sharing instructional space, resources, decision making, and practices and how that process translates into teaching and learning experiences with diverse students. As indicated in the teachers' comments about the role of the CIG, coteachers need an explicit framework or process to facilitate critical reflection and dialogue on their practice. The CIG meetings provided that framework for Eva and Leila. School districts considering coteaching and other collaborative practices for working with ELLs need to recognize coteaching from a relational perspective as well as an instructional one.

The practice of coteaching holds great promise as an instructional model for facilitating language and content development for ELLs, as well as for promoting creative and nurturing professional partnerships for coteachers. Indeed, ESOL and grade-level teachers have much to learn from one another. Finally, as ESOL teachers work more in *mainstream* classrooms, there exists the opportunity to change the perception that ESOL work is merely support work on the periphery of teaching and learning in schools. In addition to the direct benefits to students and teachers, coteaching partnerships that are supported by a framework for dialogue and reflection have a significant opportunity to positively impact whole-school culture regarding ESOL teachers, students, and knowledge.

REFERENCES

Antunez, B. (2002). *The preparation and professional development of teachers of English language learners.* Washington, DC: ERIC Clearinghouse on Teaching and Teacher Education.

Arkoudis, S. (2006). Negotiating the rough ground between ESOL and mainstream teachers. *International Journal of Bilingual Education & Bilingualism, 9,* 415-433.

Batalova, J., & McHugh, M. (2010). *Number and growth of students in US schools in need of English instruction.* Washington, DC: Migration Policy Institute.

Creese, A. (2005). *Teacher collaboration and talk in multilingual classrooms.* Clevedon, England: Multilingual Matters.

Davison, C. (2006). Collaboration between ESOL and content teachers: How do we know when we are doing it right? *International Journal of Bilingual Education & Bilingualism, 9,* 454-475.

Echevarria, J., Vogt, M., & Short, D. (2008). *Making content comprehensible for English language learners: The SIOP model* (3rd ed.). Boston, MA: Allyn & Bacon.

Friend, M., & Cook, L. (2003). *Interactions: Collaboration skills for school professionals* (5th ed.). Boston, MA: Pearson.

Gardner, S. (2006). Centre-stage in the instructional register: Partnership talk in primary EAL. *International Journal of Bilingual Education & Bilingualism, 9,* 476-494.

Georgia Department of Education. (2008). *Georgia high school graduation requirements: Preparing students for success.* Atlanta, GA: Georgia Department of Education.

Glazier, J. (2004). Collaborating with the "other": Arab and Jewish teachers teaching in each other's company. *Teachers College Record, 106,* 611-633.

Hamann, E. T., & Harklau, L. (2010). Education in the new Latino diaspora. In E. G. Murillo (Ed.), *Handbook of Latinos and education* (pp. 157-169). New York, NY: Routledge.

Honigsfeld, A., & Dove, M. (2010). *Collaboration and co-teaching: Strategies for English learners.* Thousand Oaks, CA: Corwin Press.

Kaufman, P., Alt, M., & Chapman, C. (2004). *Dropout rates in the United States: 2001* (NCES 2005-046). Washington, DC: US Department of Education.

McClure, G., & Cahnmann-Taylor, M. (2010). Pushing back against push-in: ESOL teacher resistance and the complexities of coteaching. *TESOL Journal, 1*(1), 101-129.

Murawski, W. W., & Dieker, L. A. (2004). Tips and strategies for co-teaching at the secondary level. *Teaching Exceptional Children, 36*(5), 52-59.

Nunan, D. (1992). *Collaborative language learning and teaching.* New York, NY: Cambridge Press.

Scruggs, T. E., Mastropieri, M. A., & McDuffie, K. A. (2007). Co-teaching in inclusive classrooms: A metasynthesis of qualitative research. *Exceptional Children, 73,* 392-416.

Villa, R., Thousand, J., & Nevin, A. (2008). *A guide to co-teaching* (2nd ed.). Thousand Oaks, CA: Corwin Press.

Westside Elementary School. (2006). *School improvement plan 2006-2009.* Atlanta, GA: Author.

PART IV

COLLABORATIVE PRACTICES TO SUPPORT MENTORING AND PROFESSIONAL DEVELOPMENT

CHAPTER 21

COTEACHING AS PROFESSIONAL DEVELOPMENT

Francesca Mulazzi and Jon Nordmeyer

This chapter describes a changing role for English for speakers of other languages (ESOL) teachers and considers how schools can implement a more collaborative approach as ESOL teachers move from isolated language teachers to integrated language specialists. It outlines how one department redefined itself and then established structures to integrate a new role for ESOL teachers within the larger school community.

This professional evolution raised questions among ESOL teachers who held differing perspectives on their role, and motivated teachers to develop new skills, attitudes, and knowledge in order to implement a collaborative approach to serving English language learners successfully. For some veteran teachers, in particular, it challenged a prevailing notion that teaching ESOL means working with students rather than colleagues.

OUR CHANGING CONTEXT

The Shanghai American School (SAS), in Shanghai, China, is the second largest international school in the world, and one of several serving the diverse expatriate community in Shanghai. More than 350 faculty mem-

---

Coteaching and Other Collaborative Practices in the EFL/ESL Classroom:
Rationale, Research, Reflections, and Recommendations, pp. 219–229
Copyright © 2012 by Information Age Publishing
All rights of reproduction in any form reserved.

bers, including 18 full-time ESOL staff members, teach 3,000 students in prekindergarten through high school across two campuses. A private, nonprofit school, governed by a board of directors and accredited by the Western Association of Schools and Colleges, SAS has a rigorous college-preparatory curriculum, which offers high school students a choice of International Baccalaureate and Advanced Placement courses. More than half of SAS students hold passports from the United States and Canada. While over 30 home languages are represented, the nonnative English speaking student population at SAS is primarily composed of Chinese and Korean speakers. At SAS, the authors each served in dual roles of ESOL teacher and K-12 Coordinator on their respective campuses.

The ESOL program at SAS is based on a sheltered immersion model, in which all students take the same core curriculum and are taught using sheltered instructional approaches in all classes (Echevarria, Vogt, & Short, 2000). Twenty percent of students enrolled at SAS also receive ESOL support: in the form of content-based language development classes, in-class support or both. The rapid growth of our school's enrollment (doubling from 1,500 to 3,000 students in 10 years) mirrored the cultural and linguistic diversity of the Shanghai expatriate community. An effort by the ESOL department to redefine *mainstream* by honestly describing our student population resulted in roughly sixty percent of our students being identified as *English language learners*, with a wide range of English proficiency levels. Since every SAS classroom had bilingual learners, this necessitated a new understanding of how ESOL teachers could serve as resources for all teachers within our school community.

In the field of K-12 TESOL, collaboration has become a more common practice in the past decade, and there is a growing recognition of the role that language plays in all classes. "Viewing language teaching as an integrated process rather than a discrete discipline introduces new ways of engaging with colleagues. Collaboration across subject areas not only supports student learning but also facilitates professional growth" (Nordmeyer & Barduhn, 2010, p. 7). Our student demographics, along with the trends of integration and collaboration in K-12 education, provided the need for our faculty to rethink our approach to serving English language learners (ELLs) and the opportunity to redefine the role of the ESOL teachers.

TWENTIETH VERSUS TWENTY-FIRST CENTURY MODELS

We recognized that teachers were operating with two different views of ESOL. The twentieth century model of ESOL (Figure 21.1) reflected a traditional medical perspective, which placed responsibility on the ESOL

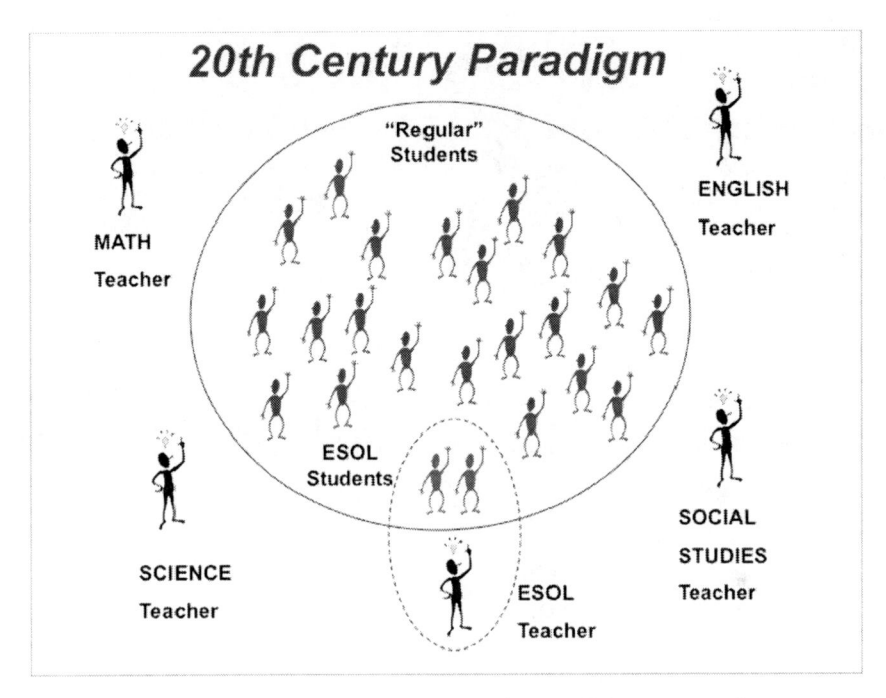

Figure 21.1. Twentieth century model of serving English Language learners.

teacher to *cure* the student of her language problems in a pull-out class. In this view of ELLs, students have only two options: they are either in the ESOL program and receiving treatment, or out of the ESOL program and ready to return to the mainstream classroom, where they can begin to do their *real* learning. From this binary perspective, the purpose of the core classroom teacher is to teach the majority of the *regular* students and to welcome the ELLs once they are *cured* of their English-language deficiency.

In contrast, the twenty-first century model (Figure 21.2) is built on a different view of students, which necessitates a different view of teachers' roles. From this perspective, ELLs are viewed along a continuum, on which *all* students are developing academic English proficiency. Students are seen as different *in degree* with a wide range of English proficiency, and continue to move along this developmental continuum (Freeman, 2005). As, Mohan, Leung, and Davison (2001) observed, "There is more recognition of areas of common ground: that, differences notwithstanding, both ESL learners and native speakers are learning language for academic purposes, and both groups are using language to learn" (p. 218).

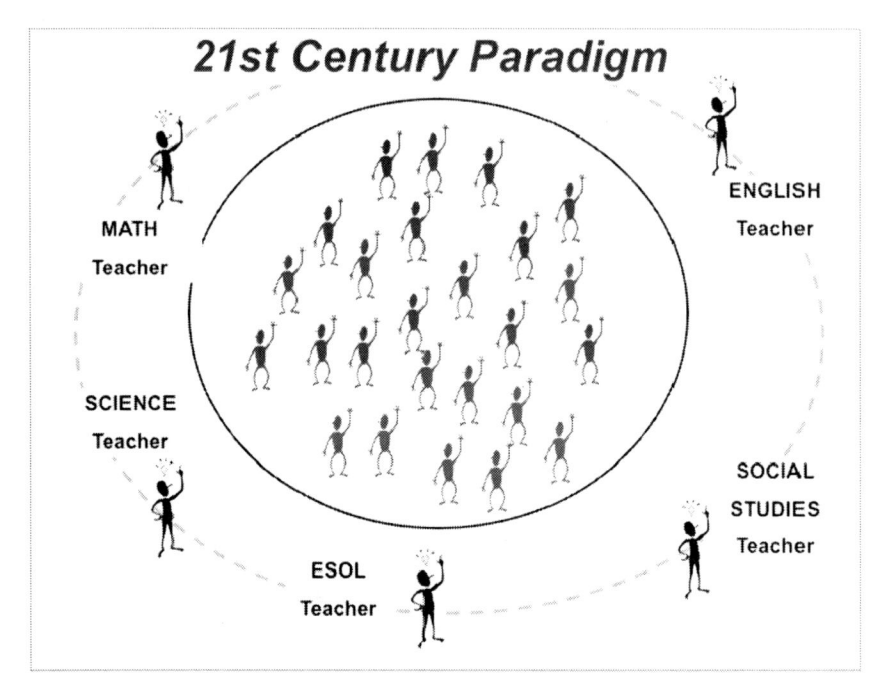

Figure 21.2. Twenty-first century model of serving English language learners.

In the twenty-first century model, on the other hand, teachers take a collaborative and integrative approach to working with ELLs because ALL teachers share responsibility for ALL students. The ESOL teacher is an integrated part of a team working to develop both content and language, but with specific roles defined.

> This type of integration of language and content does *not* mean that ESOL teachers are becoming obsolete, or that all teachers need to be English teachers. On the contrary, elementary classroom teachers and secondary content teachers are *still* primarily responsible for teaching the grade-level curriculum, but they need to do it in ways that make that content accessible for ELLs.
>
> ...
>
> Likewise, ESOL teachers are *still* the ones responsible for teaching English. Especially in the case of students with beginning English proficiency, intensive English language development is critical and ESOL teachers need to meet this need. However, ESOL teachers need to consider how they can also connect language development with content learning. (Nordmeyer, 2008, p. 38)

COTEACHING AS PROFESSIONAL DEVELOPMENT

We recognized this shift in the role of ESOL teachers at our school and explored how to add a dimension of reciprocal professional growth to the process of coplanning and coteaching. Such an integrated role can be difficult to define and is often complicated by labels such as *coach, mentor, teacher-trainer,* or *professional developer.* However, as a professional learning community, our ESOL teachers needed to move beyond the false dichotomy of serving as either *peer* or *mentor.* In this new role, we considered coteaching as professional development, both for ESOL teachers and non-ESOL teachers. Collaboration that only benefits students but does not foster professional growth is a lost opportunity.

We saw professional learning as a welcome byproduct of collaboration to support students; this helped to create additional incentives for colleagues to coteach with ESOL teachers. For example, coteaching provided evidence for teachers' performance evaluation portfolio. At SAS, all teachers must demonstrate professional growth based on a set of standards for teacher evaluation. One standard addresses differentiating instruction to meet the needs of all students, and in particular, differentiating by English proficiency level. This provided a particularly salient connection between professional development and coteaching: a chance to immediately apply principles of teaching ELLs in an authentic context. By embedding professional learning in our day-to-day work, growth was contextualized, relevant, and hopefully sustained. By directly serving student needs through coteaching and building professional development into ongoing collaboration, ESOL and core teachers worked together to accomplish both goals.

As ESOL teacher-leaders, we tried to promote the importance of coteaching as a form of professional learning by developing a schoolwide plan for professional development to serve ELLs. This plan presented the rationale that English is the language of instruction at our school and all students must have access to the same curriculum. It also proposed that ELLs need support in learning grade-level content while developing academic English proficiency, and that ESOL teachers cannot do this job alone. Two key ideas to this view of serving ELLs are:

1. The entire school community must take responsibility for all its students, and
2. Professional development is essential in creating educational opportunities for all students admitted to our school.

With enthusiasm, we worked as K-12 ESOL coordinators to promote this new role for our ESOL department and our school's administrative team. Collaboration seemed to be a win-win situation, benefitting ELLs with increased support and helping teachers through on-site, relevant professional development. Coteaching as embedded professional learning is also supported by the National Staff Development Council (2001) *Standards for Professional Development*: "The most powerful forms of staff development occur in ongoing teams that meet on a regular basis, preferably several times a week, for the purposes of learning, joint lesson planning, and problem solving" (Learning Communities section, para 2).

As the ESOL department teacher leaders, we recognized challenges. First, coteaching to support ELLs was still largely viewed as a special interest project of the ESOL department. Second, teachers and administrators in the different divisions varied in both their understanding and enthusiasm for increased collaboration and their viewing coteaching as professional development. Third, we needed to generate buy-in from the school community, starting with the ESOL teachers in each division. We initially focused on working within the ESOL department to develop skills and knowledge of coteaching while asking principals to work with their ESOL team to put the plan into action in each division.

MAKING MEANING AS A DEPARTMENT

As a department we reached a crossroads. Some teachers were excited to collaborate more, some felt uncomfortable that their job description seemed to be changing, and others were confused about expectations. To facilitate a discussion of how to move forward as new department, we used an intentional, structured process called the Future Protocol (Murphy, 2008) from *School Reform Initiative*. The protocol was designed to help us to envision and articulate a shared future.

- First we described the present as the past ("We used to …").
- Next, we articulated and imagined the ideal future ("Now we …").
- Finally we described the next steps as completed actions ("We implemented …").

We read and discussed articles about change, collaboration, and the impact of coteaching on student achievement. In the ensuing discussion, it emerged that the ideal future of the ESOL department varied widely. The first round of the protocol's conversation articulated that some teachers did not want to expand their roles to provide professional development for their colleagues. Differing views of the department's future included, "more emphasis on direct student support and less on teacher training," "know what is expected of me everyday," and "no distinction between me and classroom teachers." Some teachers wanted to be left alone with their ESOL students while others wanted to dive into the twenty-first century paradigm.

As K-12 coordinators, we tried to clarify the new role of an ESOL teacher at our school by creating new Standards and Benchmarks specifically for ESOL teacher portfolio-based performance evaluation. We built on the most relevant descriptors from the current standards for teachers and specialists used at SAS, all rooted in the work of Charlotte Danielson. These draft standards and benchmarks were then refined with input from the entire K-12 ESOL team on a wiki as another step in the evolution of the ESOL teachers' understanding. The new standards defined the dual roles of English teachers and language integration specialists through coteaching and helped to provide clarity to the ESOL teachers, and just as important, to administrators (see Table 21.1).

Taking Ownership

As a K-12 ESOL department we needed (a) to deepen our understanding of the new ESOL Teacher Standards and Benchmarks and (b) to identify areas of strength we shared. We completed an individual teacher self-assessment at a K-12 department meeting. Each teacher considered the

Table 21.1. New ESOL Teacher Standards and Benchmarks

Performance Area A: Planning and Preparation
- Demonstrate knowledge of current trends in ESOL and professional development
- Demonstrate knowledge of the school's ESOL program and the core grade-level program
- Demonstrate knowledge of students
- Plan the ESOL support program (Pull out and Push in) integrated with the overall school program

Performance Area B: Instruction and Assessment
- Motivate and engage all students in meaningful learning and growth
- Differentiate instruction to meet the needs of students
- Define learning expectations and provide timely evaluative feedback on individual student performance
- Integrate the use of technology in instruction and learning goals

Performance Area C: Delivery of Service
- Use appropriate assessment techniques to measure and report student learning
- Collaborate with teachers in the design of instructional units, lessons and assessments
- Engage colleagues in reciprocal professional learning

Performance Area D: Professional Responsibilities
- Coordinate work with counselor and other instructional specialists
- Participate in a professional learning community
- Engage in personal professional development

standards, one by one, and reflected on his or her own practice. We used a green light (*I am proud of this*), yellow light (*I am working on this*), red light (*I am concerned about this*) reporting format.

Using an online survey allowed us to immediately view our responses together as a group. It was clear that some areas were more comfortable for us, whereas others were more challenging. Taking a snapshot of our department was an immediate and tangible illustration of how we were in the process of changing our practice. It was reassuring to see that we had many areas that we considered strengths, and we identified areas to work towards for other goals.

While most teachers welcomed clarification of a new role, challenges remained in the form of perceived or real roadblocks to true collaboration. From both newer and more experienced teachers we heard many of the same complaints: it was impossible to truly collaborate because they lacked time or planning structures, collaboration couldn't happen if there were challenging relationships to navigate, and coteaching couldn't happen if there wasn't support from the administration. Some teachers expressed frustration that accountability varied from division to division, and a small but vocal minority in this group simply said, "Just let me shut my door and teach kids English."

Over the remainder of the year, most teachers embraced their new role and acknowledged they had the initial support they needed, although questions remained about implementation. This group of ESOL teachers continued to develop skills, create resources, share coteaching activities that worked, and plan with administrators how to expand coteaching within each division.

One way we attempted to implement coteaching—and simultaneously commit to continuous improvement—was to develop a *menu* of options to offer the mainstream teachers with whom we collaborate (see Figure 21.3). This menu defined the possibilities for collaboration in practical terms and grouped them into coplanning, coteaching, and coassessing strands. We presented this as a variety of choices and invited teachers to *order* from the menu as a way of taking tasks off their plate, instead of simply adding more to their list of things to do. By documenting and sharing what worked in the past, through the menu we also showcased successful teaching partnerships. Teachers could recognize specific examples of ways they collaborate with an ESOL teacher on the menu. As a next step, we customized this menu to reflect different student and teacher needs in each division.

Lessons Learned

Many of our colleagues welcomed the evolution of the ESOL department; others declined greater involvement of an ESOL teacher in their

COLLABORATION
A menu for supporting ELLs

ESOL DEPARTMENT

Starters: Co-Planning

- **Finding materials** - For history or science, the ESOL teacher can locate a short story, non-fiction text or image related to a particular topic, then write up a guide sheet with vocabulary list and comprehension/inference questions
- **Creating materials-** For social studies or language arts, the ESOL teacher can create graphic organizers and other scaffolding materials
- **Language objectives** - When doing long-term planning for a unit, the ESOL teacher may be able to suggest a specific language focus area
- **Pre-reading** - The ESOL teacher can preview a chapter or text to compile a vocabulary list, to highlight any potential language challenges, and plan teaser/sponge questions to access prior knowledge relevant to the text
- **Assessments-** plan for a variety of assessments or suggest alternative performance assessments accessible to ELLs
- **Task analysis-** Mainstream teacher gives a lesson plan (or the instructions for an assignment) to ESOL teacher, who does a task analysis. It's one way to flag "hard to see" difficulties and determine which supports might need to be created.

Main dishes: Co-Teaching

- **Small group work** - While class is working on projects or research in pair or small groups, teachers divide the groups so each teacher consults with half the students (perfect for debate)
- **Consultant** - While groups are working on a project, they can visit a "mini writing center" in one area of your class to get feedback on their text. Or one teacher sits in the hall, and students come out one by one to re-tell a plot or historical event, or to practice a speech.
- **Vocabulary expert-** while students are working/reading, both teachers circulate and respond to raised hands by giving "instant / impromptu" vocabulary lessons

Just Desserts: Co-Assessing

- **Co-assessing presentations** - Two teachers use the same rubric to evaluate oral presentations. Can focus on separate criteria or double up and moderate scores
- **Co-assessing writing-** Two teachers use the same rubric to evaluate a writing sample OR ESOL teacher can assess language (spelling, grammar, mechanics) and the other can evaluate content (organization, ideas, evidence).
- **Writing Process Check-in** - require students to come to the Writing Center to have their thesis statement checked before they can continue with their essay or research project
- **Co-creating assessments-** creating a mix of assessments over the course of a unit/semester that are beyond paper & pencil (ie- one oral presentation, a written work, in-class writing, at-home writing, speeches, etc.)
- **Co-writing rubrics-** make a rubric, create "models" that meet different levels of the rubric

What's cooking?

Side Dishes: On the spot collaboration

While one teacher is lecturing/explaining...
...the other teacher can be taking notes on the board/LCD

While one teacher is giving instructions orally...
...the other teacher can be modeling instructions or writing them on the board

While one teacher is handing out papers...
...the other teacher can be clarifying feedback or giving a new task

While one teacher is facilitating a silent activity...
...the other teacher can be reading aloud with a small group in another space

Adapted from Murawski & Dieker (2004)

Figure 21.3.   Collaboration menu.

classes. Obstacles included curricular ownership, lack of trust, unwillingness to change, or perhaps most frequently, lack of time to implement collaboration. We learned that is important for ESOL teachers to keep the following challenges in mind:

- Expectations for collaboration must be balanced with the reality of mainstream teachers' jobs. For example, a creative suggestion for differentiation from an ESOL teacher may not always be practical for a science teacher who has 80 students.
- Non-ESOL teachers' main responsibility is teaching their curriculum to students. While mainstream teachers are often willing to collaborate and may agree that developing language skills will help students to accomplish classroom tasks, at the end of the day they ultimately need to focus on their subject.

Accepting this prioritization of needs helps ESOL teachers to approach coteaching realistically.

Progress continues steadily. The entire ESOL department does not unanimously share the viewpoint of the twenty-first century model; however, many SAS ESOL teachers have moved their practice further along the continuum of collaboration. As ESOL coordinators, we have offered workshops during professional development in-service days, attended by mainstream and ESOL teachers eager for new strategies to improve student learning and to facilitate collaborative conversations in a professional learning community. Additionally, the elementary division established a schedule that allows ESOL teachers and mainstream teachers weekly time to collaborate, coplan, and coteach. Finally, middle school teams have engaged in curriculum mapping, articulating the writing and language focus for each unit, and inviting ESOL teachers to coteach more consistently and intentionally. Building on momentum, teachers are energized and empowered to continue the evolution of a more collaborative and integrated role for ESOL.

CONCLUSION

As our ESOL department evolved, we recognized that making the transition from isolated language teachers to integrated language specialists required attention to intentional steps of the process. After identifying and defining our new role and seeking input from the stakeholders, we worked actively with administrators to develop solid infrastructure and systems on which to build a more inclusive professional learning community.

Our program continues to develop, but as a result of this intentional change process described above, ESOL teachers no longer focus exclusively on a small percentage of students who are *in the ESOL program.* Instead, they collaborate with mainstream colleagues to intentionally scaffold, coteach, and assess the academic language skills and essential content knowledge that all students deserve. In the process, we are engaging in reciprocal professional growth, which engages both ESOL teachers and their colleagues in meaningful collaboration.

REFERENCES

Echevarria, J., Vogt, M., & Short, D. (2000). *Making content comprehensible for English language learners: The SIOP model.* Boston, MA: Allyn & Bacon.

Freeman, D. (2005). Teaching in the context of English language learners. In M. Sadowski (Ed.), *Teaching immigrant and second language students: Strategies for success* (pp. 7-20). Cambridge, MA: Harvard Education Press.

Mohan, B., Leung, C., & Davison, C. (Eds.). (2001). *English as a second language in the mainstream: Teaching, learning and identity.* Harlow, England: Pearson.

Murphy, S. (2008). *The future protocol.* Retrieved from http://schoolreforminitiative.org/protocol/doc/future.pdf

National Staff Development Council. (2001). *Standards for professional development.* Retrieved from http://www.learningforward.org/standards/index.cfm

Nordmeyer, J. (2008). Delicate balance. *Journal of Staff Development, 29*(1), 34-40.

Nordmeyer, J., & Barduhn, S. (Eds.). (2010). *Integrating language and content.* Alexandria, VA: Teachers of English to Speakers of Other Languages.

CHAPTER 22

PEER GROUP MENTORING

Preservice EFL Teachers' Collaborations for Enhancing Practices

Hoa Thi Mai Nguyen and Peter Hudson

LOCAL CONTEXT

There is an increasing demand worldwide for more competent English teachers and effective approaches to teacher preparation. In the Asian context, reforms in English as a foreign language (EFL) teacher education, including field experiences (practicum), aim to raise the standard for and quality of EFL teachers. English language education in Vietnam requires considerable reform to both preservice teacher education and existing teacher practice (Le, 2007). Tertiary education in Vietnam has been criticized for giving inadequate attention to preservice EFL teaching practice while focusing too much on the transmission of knowledge and teaching theory. These critiques suggest that preservice EFL teachers are inadequately prepared or trained for classroom practice (Pham, 2001).

For many years, practicum has been a compulsory component within preservice EFL teacher education programs, providing opportunities to practise teaching skills in authentic situations. Preservice teachers are expected to apply their university understandings to these real-life school contexts and work collaboratively with their teaching supervisors (mentors). While practicum plays a critical role in developing preservice teachers' professional practice, there are challenges in the mentoring arrangements.

CHALLENGES IN MENTORING

The quality of mentoring is limited by many factors including the need for substantial investments of time, money, effort, and resources. An important constraint on the traditional mentoring process is the availability of teachers as role models and mentors for preservice teachers. Some preservice teachers have claimed that their school-based practicum experiences were inadequate because of poor or limited mentoring (Morton, 2004). Consequently, there is a need for alternative approaches to develop preservice teachers' learning during the practicum. In addition, EFL teachers may not display personal attributes conducive to effective mentoring; characteristics such as sharing, reflection, and collaboration among colleagues are generally absent among Vietnamese EFL teachers (Le, 2007).

Considering the existing problems and issues with mentoring and university supervision, this study investigated alternative measures that may advance a preservice teacher's professional growth toward becoming an effective classroom practitioner. It focused on the application of a group of preservice teachers engaged in mentoring each other during a practicum in Vietnam, due to the limited opportunities for preservice teachers to develop teaching practice through mentoring by classroom practitioners.

THEORETICAL GROUND

The quality of school-based mentoring for preservice EFL teachers relies on collaboration and reflection on teaching practices. Preservice teachers involved in one study (Nguyen & Luong, 2007) considered their peers as a most useful source of support that provided a way to acquire new pedagogical skills and knowledge. Other studies (e.g., Le Cornu, 2005; Nguyen & Baldauf, 2010) investigated paired placement, peer supervision, peer observation, peer coaching, peer mentoring, and learning circles as formal peer collaboration during preservice EFL teachers' practicum experiences. These studies have documented the favorable outcomes and benefits of preservice teachers working together and supporting one another throughout a practicum.

We use the term *peer group mentoring* (PGM), in which *peer* includes educators and professionals working on a similar level, *group* is a collective of more than two, and *mentoring* is the vehicle for engaging in professional learning. PGM refers to the supportive process in which a group of peers are involved in mentoring one another.

Franzak (2002) advocated that a group of critical friends can work together collaboratively to improve the day-to-day teaching-learning process. Participants in these groups use structured protocols to explore teaching strategies, conduct peer observations, and analyze evidence of their students' achievements. When preservice teachers meet, they examine each other's practices and give feedback on improving their work, which implies a reciprocal learning. This interaction is underpinned by Vygotsky's (1978) social constructivism, contending that meaning is constructed through first-hand experiences and as a social exchange between individuals. In this process, each participant interprets, transforms, and internalizes new knowledge as a result of collective dialogues.

The PGM model in this research focused on peer observation and the provision of constructive feedback. It employed specific turn-taking rules and promoted constructive criticism from peer observations to ensure equitable arrangements for all concerned.

Context for Peer Group Mentoring (PGM)

Based on the key principles and practices of mentoring, the following model of PGM was integrated and implemented for preservice EFL teachers during a TESOL practicum in Vietnam. At the beginning of the 6-week practicum, the preservice teachers ($n=28$) attended one 3-hour orientation meeting during which they self-allocated into groups of three or four. The orientation included an explanation of the program's goals, philosophy, requirements, and expectations. The participants were required to observe their peers' teaching with the agreed observation criteria to be used during feedback meetings at least once a week. During each feedback session, the participants discussed what they had learnt from each other's teaching performances, and what they thought should be improved.

The process was intended to encourage: (a) observation of practice, (b) feedback on areas that appeared successful and those requiring improvement, (c) amendments to future planning, implementation of changes, and (d) peers observing this implementation for further feedback. Important to the PGM process was the alignment with reflective practices. The program aimed to provide the preservice EFL teachers with additional supportive strategies for developing their professional practice during their practicum.

A qualitative approach was used to explore the research inquiry. It permitted the researcher to study a selected issue in depth and in detail (Patton, 2002) and could "be used to obtain the intricate detail about the phenomena such as feelings, thoughts, processes, and emotions that are difficult to enact or learn from more conventional methods" (Strauss & Corbin, 1998, p. 11). Six 1-hour focus group interviews with four-to-six participants in each group were conducted to explore the participants' experiences in their peer group mentoring. Data analysis followed an iterative process employed in qualitative research where data analyses were revised and refocused based on emergent themes (Hittleman & Simon, 2006).

FINDINGS AND DISCUSSION

The findings in this study will be discussed along the following themes: (a) changes in teaching methods, (b) changes in work practices, and (c) sources of emotional support.

Changes in Teaching Methods

Participant comments that related to changes in teaching methods were categorized. The comments revealed that the preservice teachers considered the peer observations and subsequent meetings valuable and helpful for developing their teaching methods. Additionally, the majority of the preservice teachers across the six groups seemed to value their peer observation practices and feedback sessions. One of them claimed, "I learned from my peer observation more than from that of my school mentor." Most of them said that they valued the role of peer observation as an impetus for their self-reflection. Some reflected on their own lessons when observing their peers teaching a similar lesson:

> I always taught a lesson 2 days before my peer's same lesson. When observing her, I realized that her lesson was more successful than mine. The reason was that she used more interesting games.... Observing peers helped me reflect on my own teaching.

Working with peers and using peer feedback was said to have enabled these preservice teachers to report, to reflect, and to identify issues and concerns. Most of the preservice teachers claimed they reflected on their strengths and weaknesses when receiving their peer's feedback. The following quote illustrates what many preservice teachers expressed on the same topic: "I used to speak too fast, so the students didn't understand what to do. Also, I tended to move around too much in the class. My friend observed my lessons, and her comments helped me realize those weaknesses".

Study participants believed that their peers' feedback aided them to reflect on their lessons more accurately because they could not identify areas for improvement as readily themselves. Most of them agreed that peer observations were effective in helping them develop their teaching practice and cited reasons they believed this was the case, including mutual learning from peers, drawing benefit for improving their own lessons, and identifying teaching mistakes. They also mentioned some specific aspects of teaching that were improved such as motivational techniques, flexibility in teaching, use of the blackboard, time management, teaching behaviors, student management techniques, and effective communication strategies.

Changes in Work Practices

Another category of comments regarding preservice teachers' experience in the PGM concerned the development of positive work practices. One of the changes in their work practices was establishing skills to share practices. Some of the participants claimed that through being involved in the PGM process, they started sharing both personal and professional issues with their peers, and sharing became part of their professional practice. One of them remarked: "I think this intervention was very effective because it engaged us in working in groups. Otherwise, we worked on our own and did not care what others did. Now, we could build up our sharing habits in our groups".

Some of the preservice teachers claimed that they shared their feelings with their peers after the lessons, although this was an infrequent occurrence and only evident when peers were friends previously. One preservice teacher said,

> I shared my feelings about the lessons with Trang (my close friend at university), but not every lesson. It is a kind of stress relief for me. I never talked like that with other friends in the groups. We just met and talked about trivial things.

Some other preservice teachers from two different groups commented that they and their peers in the same class sometimes shared their personal concerns such as money problems. Sharing was reported to emerge as an important element for their learning culture.

Three preservice teachers reported that they liked observing their peers more than once per week even though it was not compulsory to do so. They said that observing their peers' lessons could be an effective work practice for their future professional development. Other preservice teachers reported that they were more disciplined as a result of working with their peers, especially in areas involving time scheduling for assigned work and responsibilities for completing work together. A preservice teacher commented, "I felt I needed to complete the work we discussed even though I felt too tired sometimes". The act of collaborating on work that had shared goals and similar concerns within the EFL context enabled them to develop positive work practices. Collaboration appeared to lead to changes in perceptions of working as beginning professionals in an academic environment.

Preservice teachers commented on their opportunities to participate in a community of practice. Most participants agreed that the PGM process enabled them to engage in a wider circle of learning among peers in the same school. With a total of 18 specific mentions of this involvement, the preservice teachers reported that they not only worked with their assigned peers, but also extended their interactions to other peers at the school. One teacher commented, "If I could not observe my peer on that day, I went to see others' lessons. I felt I could work with everyone in the group, and we did not only work in pairs." Two participants in the same focus group agreed with the previous comment. Some participants also reported that the effect of working in groups extended to a wider community of practice in which all preservice teachers worked together and challenged each other to create more effective teaching practices.

Additionally, it was observed that the PGM process may develop skills that prepare preservice teachers to participate in similar communities of practice in their future careers. This skill development was noted by a preservice teacher, "I liked the way our group worked together. It helped me to realize how important it was to share our issues together and work through them. I felt everyone in the group were my friendly colleagues."

The university-imposed arrangements of PGM was a catalyst for facilitating professional relationships between peers. In addition, working collegially with peers built confidence to work more extensively with other peer groups. To illustrate this point, one preservice teacher commented:

> I think working in pairs like this enabled everyone to be close to each other; everyone felt that they had a friend, and we felt close. At first, we worked together as a requirement of the program, but gradually it became auto-

matic. Everyone not only worked in their pairs, but worked together in the larger group, the whole group, not just individual pairs.

Sources of Emotional Support

Most of the preservice teachers participating in the six focus group interviews reported that they received emotional support from their peers. This support assisted them to "feel better," "reduce stress," not feel "alone," and "made the practicum go smoothly." Their peers instilled in them emotional strength to deal with the various problems they faced during the practicum. One focus group participant commented,

> I got more emotional benefit from interacting with peers.... When I encountered trouble, for example, I complained. Even though no one could help me out, there was a person [peer] who listened to it. I felt less stressed.

The nature of this emotional support was further detailed in the comments about peers comforting each other. Practicum was a stressful time for many of the preservice teachers, and although they worked as peer mentors, many considered the relationship as a friendship. One participant praised her peer's role in supporting her emotionally as follows:

> We often had some pressure; when we talked with our friends, we felt less pressure. In general, I felt supportive in any aspects. I think if there had not been friends there for us, we would have found it harder to go through this practicum. My friends made the practicum go smoothly.

It was not a surprise, therefore, that the preservice teachers valued their peers' help in dealing with tensions by listening to each other's challenges and providing emotional support accordingly. As another preservice teacher remarked:

> Apart from sharing teaching knowledge, my peers' emotional support was very important. In the beginning weeks, we faced difficulties in teaching; for example, Trang and I did not teach well, and our mentors criticized us a lot.... We felt disappointed, but we were always there to comfort each other. It, therefore, helped us feel better.

The similarities of their collective situations and levels of pedagogical development allowed these preservice teachers to empathise strongly with each other: "I had to comfort my friends and said that everyone was the same and not to worry too much. Everyone had problems, the same as each other, not to worry. I think my friends felt better." Teachers often remain isolated in classrooms with little adult interaction during teaching periods. These preservice teachers had opportunities to provide support in peer mentoring arrangements, which was largely emotional support that aimed at building confidence and sharing experiences. Emotional support from their peers at this formative stage of development provided an avenue for confidential and nonthreatening dialogue that may lead to more successful subsequent teaching experiences.

IMPLICATIONS AND RECOMMENDATIONS FOR PRACTICE

The current study provided evidence that PGM can work effectively for preservice EFL teachers in a TESOL practicum in Vietnam where the process of learning to teach traditionally featured the transfer of knowledge and experience from seasoned teachers (mentors) to preservice teachers. The PGM intervention was reported to have positive effects on preservice EFL teachers' teaching practices, including the provision of professional and emotional support and enhancement of reflection on practices. These preservice teachers embraced the PGM framework, particularly as the feedback through professional dialogue with their peers appeared to advance their classroom teaching.

As a collective connected to the same university with similar coursework experiences, the preservice teachers had commonalities among them and therefore were better able to elicit empathetic understandings from each other. Unlike the conflicting positions that can occur with supervising teachers, who in effective mentoring roles may be assessors and confidants, these preservice teachers had no conflict of interest for supporting each other's pedagogical development. They could be confidants for one another without feeling they were jeopardizing their potential opportunities within a school. Furthermore, they were not in a position to formally assess their peer's performance, hence the assessment pressure was diminished. Peers, understanding each other's stages of development, were sensitive to criticism and couched their own comments in a constructive rather than destructive way.

Facilitating PGM

PGM can open discussions to issues that are common among a particular group of preservice teachers. PGM can present another level of support when classroom teachers—in their roles as mentors—may not be readily or willingly available to guide preservice teachers' practices. However, it is important to recognise that mentoring through the PGM model must not be haphazard, unbalanced, or uninformed. If preservice teachers are to undertake PGM, they need to be educated on effective peer mentoring attributes and practices.

PGM can be further facilitated through purposeful guidance to support preservice teachers' roles as comentors. To capitalize on PGM effectiveness, preservice teachers will require a mentoring framework to guide their interactions (Hudson, Nguyen, & Hudson, 2009). Factors within the mentoring framework include: the mentor's personal attributes that can assist in facilitating the mentoring process, mentoring to the education system requirements, articulating pedagogical knowledge, and modelling of effective EFL teaching practices. For example, it is argued in this study that a preservice teacher can learn about successful personal attributes employed for mentoring (e.g., being supportive, instilling confidence and positive attitudes, and being an attentive listener), which would facilitate the mentoring process more effectively.

As another example, preservice teachers need to be astutely aware of the syllabus requirements and policies within their school. If there are discussions about an issue within their school, preservice EFL teachers need to know how to access school policies and other information that would allow them to deal with the issue. They must be able to access valid and reliable information that supports their discussions; otherwise, preservice teachers in their formative stages of learning may not necessarily be accurate in their advice and deliberations with peers. Therefore, PGMs require checks and balances to ensure the advice provided and received does not conflict with school policies and practices. A university liaison officer or school site coordinator (lead mentor) can be a *sounding board* for the peer group to clarify ideas and information.

CONCLUSION

In this study, participation in the PGM during practicum enabled preservice EFL teachers to interact positively with each other. The study provided further evidence for the position that learning does not take place in isolation but rather through interaction; in other words, learning occurs through communication and collaboration with other people in social settings. This study also raised awareness of the need for well-structured support for interaction among peers through which knowledge of effective mentoring can raise the standard of mentoring within peer groups. Teacher educators, policy makers, and teachers can use PGM as a supplementary source of learning and support for preservice teachers during practicum. A PGM program can support preservice teachers by facilitating collaborative construction of meaning through reflective insights that aim to develop effective pedagogical practices.

REFERENCES

Franzak, J. K. (2002). Developing a teacher identity: The impact of critical friends practice on the student teacher. *English Education, 34*, 258-270.

Hittleman, D. R., & Simon, A. J. (2006). *Interpreting educational research: An introduction for consumers of research*. Upper Saddle River, NJ: Prentice-Hall.

Hudson, P., Nguyen, T. M. H., & Hudson, S. (2009). Mentoring EFL preservice teachers in EFL writing. *TESL Canada Journal, 27*(1), 85-102.

Le, V. C. (2007). A historical review of English language education in Vietnam. In Y. H. Choi & B. Spolsky (Eds.), *English education in Asia: History and policies* (pp. 167-179). Seoul, South Korea: Asia TEFL.

Le Cornu, R. (2005). Peer *mentoring*: Engaging pre-service teachers in mentoring one another. *Mentoring and Tutoring, 13*, 355-366.

Morton, C. A. (2004). *The relationship among planning activities, peer coaching skills and improved instructional effectiveness in preservice special education teachers* (Unpublished doctoral dissertation). Texas A & M University, College Station, TX.

Nguyen, T. M. H., & Baldauf, R. B. Jr. (2010). Effective peer mentoring for EFL preservice teachers' instructional practicum practice. *The Asia EFL Journal Quarterly, 12*(3), 40-61.

Nguyen, T. M. H., & Luong, Q. T. (2007, September). *EFL student teachers' challenges during practicum: A case study*. Paper presented at the 2007 ETAK International Conference, Kongju National University, Kongju, South Korea.

Patton, M. Q. (2002). *Qualitative research & evaluation methods* (3rd ed.). Thousand Oaks, CA: SAGE.

Pham, H. H. (2001). Teacher development: A real need for English departments in Vietnam. *English Teaching Forum, 39*(4). Retrieved from http://www.greenstone.org/greenstone3/sites/nzdl/collect/literatu/import/Teacher's%20Edition/Hiep36.pdf

Strauss, A., & Corbin, J. (1998). *Basics of qualitative research: Techniques and procedures for developing grounded theory*. Thousand Oaks, CA: SAGE.

Vygotsky, L. S. (1978). *Mind and society: The development of higher mental processes*. Cambridge, MA: Harvard University Press.

CHAPTER 23

SHARED COMPETENCE

Native and Nonnative English Speaking Teachers' Collaboration That Benefits All

Jan Edwards Dormer

"Come to the office! The books have arrived!" One of our teachers was eagerly rounding up our teaching staff, most of whom had participated in the development of our new English workbooks for Grades 1-4. Oohs and aahs were audible as we unpacked the books, which had been delivered not from a publisher but from our local photocopy shop. To us, however, they were quite an accomplishment, not only in terms of creative work, but in terms of collaboration. I looked around the room at our teachers in this growing English school in Londrina, Brazil, by then serving around 150 students. About half Brazilians and half North Americans, we were a strong team—made stronger through our collaborative efforts.

NEST AND NNEST WORKING RELATIONSHIPS

Issues concerning native English speaking teachers (NESTs) and nonnative English speaking teachers (NNESTs) have been the subject of considerable discussion and research in recent years (e.g. Braine, 1999; Kamhi-Stein, 2004). Many schools in English as a foreign language (EFL) environments have both NESTs and NNESTs on their English-teaching staffs. After working in just such a school in Brazil, and having seen the tremen-

Coteaching and Other Collaborative Practices in the EFL/ESL Classroom:
Rationale, Research, Reflections, and Recommendations, pp. 241–250
Copyright © 2012 by Information Age Publishing
All rights of reproduction in any form reserved.

dous advantages that this can bring to the school, I conducted my doctoral research on the relationships between these two groups of teachers. I investigated school sites in both Brazil and Indonesia, examining how NESTs and NNESTs worked together and what level of satisfaction was reported by those who experienced NEST-NNEST interaction.

The fact that collaborative relationships among teachers can be beneficial is well documented (e.g. Clandinin & Connelly, 1995; Sergiovanni, 1994), and we might assume that a NEST-NNEST difference introduced into the mix would not make any difference. Caution is warranted with such an assumption, however. Tajino and Tajino (2000) investigated the working relationships between Japanese and American teachers in the Japan Exchange and Teaching (JET) Program. They suggested that the original assumption—two teachers working together would be twice as effective—has not always worked out in practice, stating that "the last decade has seen a great deal of anecdotal evidence that reveals difficulties when teachers cooperate with each other in Japanese schools" (p. 5).

De Oliveira and Richardson (2004), on the other hand, told a very different story. They claimed "unique benefits when native English-speaking and nonnative English-speaking educators form a collaborative relationship" (p. 295) for professional growth. Katz, Omar, and Snow (2004) also reported positive collaborative experiences when NESTs and NNESTs collaborate in curriculum development.

What Makes it or Breaks it?

Why do NEST-NNEST collaborative relationships thrive in some circumstances and cause stress in others? My research (Dormer, 2010) brought to light two key characteristics of school sites, which determined the relative success or failure of NEST-NNEST collaboration: promotion of teacher development and promotion of teacher interaction (see Figure 23.1). Schools that did not place a high value on either were characterized by *isolated frustration*. Teachers in such schools did not have adequate opportunities to get to know—let alone learn alongside or teach with—the other group of teachers on staff. They remained both *isolated* and *frustrated*. In contrast, teachers who experienced *shared competence* in their school contexts saw both teacher development and collegial interaction between NESTs and NNESTs valued and promoted. These teachers had a dramatically different perspective. They viewed the presence of NESTs and NNESTs on staff as beneficial, and expressed high levels of satisfaction with their school environments, in terms of both professionalism and personal relationships.

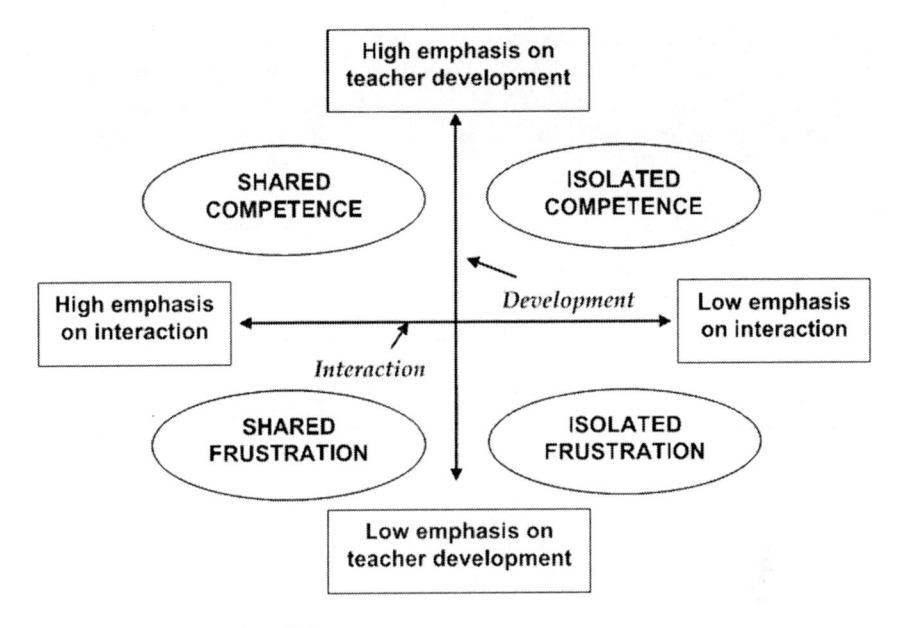

Shared Competence 243

```
                    High emphasis on
                    teacher development
                           ▲
                           │
       ┌─────────────┐     │     ┌─────────────┐
       │   SHARED    │     │     │  ISOLATED   │
       │ COMPETENCE  │     │     │ COMPETENCE  │
       └─────────────┘     │     └─────────────┘
                           │
┌──────────────┐           │ Development  ┌──────────────┐
│High emphasis │◄──────────┼──────────────►│ Low emphasis │
│on interaction│           │               │ on interaction│
└──────────────┘      Interaction          └──────────────┘
                           │
       ┌─────────────┐     │     ┌─────────────┐
       │   SHARED    │     │     │  ISOLATED   │
       │ FRUSTRATION │     │     │ FRUSTRATION │
       └─────────────┘     │     └─────────────┘
                           │
                           ▼
                    Low emphasis on
                    teacher development
```

Source: Dormer (2010, p. 271).

Figure 23.1. NEST/NNEST relational environments produced by levels of interaction and teacher development.

COLLABORATION PROMOTING SHARED COMPETENCE

What is Shared Competence?

Shared competence is a prevailing school attitude which suggests, "We value NESTs and NNESTs equally, and we want both to be successful. Furthermore, we believe the key to this success is working together and learning from one another." In such a positive and hopeful environment, NESTs and NNESTs find the courage to let down their guard, face their weaknesses honestly, work through cross-cultural differences with perseverance, and genuinely care about and help one another.

In this chapter, I will describe three types of NEST/NNEST collaborative efforts in EFL school contexts which can foster *shared competence*:

1. Collaboration in developing linguistic and cultural competence;
2. Collaboration in developing teaching skills; and
3. Collaboration in developing curriculum and materials.

Each segment will be introduced through a vignette taken from Brazil or Indonesia and will be followed by key points highlighting factors which contributed to the effectiveness of the collaborative practice. (All names are pseudonyms and the vignettes are composites of data from more than one individual.)

A Language Class: Developing Linguistic and Cultural Competence

Hannah came to Brazil to teach in our English school for a year. She arrived not knowing any Portuguese, so she was immediately placed in a Portuguese class. Her teacher was Sara, one of the Brazilian English teachers in the school. The school director set the stage for viewing the language class in a nontraditional way; by pairing Hannah and Sara, she hoped it would be a time of collaborative learning, where there was a lot of give and take of ideas.

Hannah found that she learned not only Portuguese from Sara in her classes, but also new games and other language teaching techniques which would be useful in her own English teaching. Sara, in the meantime, was learning how hard Portuguese was! She had never thought about what it must be like to learn Portuguese as a foreign language. Thus, she developed a new empathy and appreciation for people like Hannah who were willing to leave their home countries and come to Brazil and learn Portuguese.

Sara and Hannah enjoyed the many discussions about culture which emerged in their Portuguese classes, as each learned about the other's culture. At first, Sara was a little self-conscious about her own knowledge of English. After just a couple of weeks teaching Portuguese to Hannah, however, she felt secure enough to begin to ask her questions about English pronunciation and idioms. Hannah gladly answered her questions, and Sara was surprised to discover that even a native speaker didn't necessarily have all the answers or know the origin of every idiom.

Hannah and Sara soon became fast friends. They had grown to appreciate and respect each other. They had learned to trust one another and the stage had been set for further collaborative efforts.

When NESTs come to a school in an EFL setting and are immediately enrolled in classes to learn the local language with the NNESTs on staff as their teachers, there can be several positive results:

1. *NESTs learn the local language.* Studying the local language is fundamentally important for NESTs, even if they are not in the country long enough to learn it well. It helps them understand the learners and their difficulties with English and facilitates becoming part of a collaborative NEST-NNEST team.
2. *NESTs and NNESTs learn teaching techniques.* Sometimes a NEST arrives on the scene with little or no training in teaching English. When her local language class is taught by a trained NNEST, she has an ideal environment for learning language teaching tech-

niques to use in her own classes. Sometimes it is the NEST who has training in language teaching. In a language class, this NEST can suggest learning activities; thus the NNEST is able not only to learn teaching techniques, but to practice them and to receive feedback on their effectiveness.

3. *NNESTs develop empathy for NESTs.* Though they have struggled to learn English, many NNESTs have never lived for an extended period of time in a context in which they do not know the language of the surrounding environment. They seem to frequently underestimate the difficulty of learning *their* native language as a foreign language! As they teach their own language to foreigners, they begin to understand the challenges and develop empathy.

4. *NESTs and NNESTs learn culture.* Culture is a frequent topic in language classes, and learning about both cultures works to the advantage of both NESTs and NNESTs. The NESTs have a lot of culture learning to do: they must be able to live and to work in a foreign environment. However, NNESTs also usually need additional cultural understanding. What they have studied about North American culture in English textbooks may be stilted or outdated. The local language classroom provides the ideal context for the development of mutual cultural competence.

5. The path is paved for NESTs to become language resources for NNESTs. Just because there is a NEST on staff does not mean the NNESTs will feel free to use that person as a language resource. In a local language class, the tables are turned—the native speaker becomes the language learner, and the nonnative speaker becomes the authoritative native speaker. This levels the playing field between NESTs and NNESTs. Everyone is both a learner and a teacher, and everyone becomes more willing to learn from the other.

Team Teaching: Developing Teaching Skills

Collaborative language lessons are often a logical first means of interaction between NESTs and NNESTs. Ideally, this can lead to another type of collaboration: team teaching.

Susan and Hardi taught in a private bilingual school in Indonesia. Susan, an American, taught English classes for Grades 3-6. She had taken a short certificate course in teaching English as a foreign language, but had no background in teaching beyond that. Hardi, an Indonesian, was a fourth-grade teacher who was supposed to teach half of the school day in English and half in Indonesian. He had no background in education or in language teaching. There was little clear direction in the school as to how bilingual education should actually happen. The English teachers (all NESTs) came to the school only to teach their English classes and never interacted with the NNESTs (the majority of the teaching staff, who were all expected to teach bilingually). NESTs and NNESTs alike on staff were frustrated, not only with their lack of teaching skills, but also with the lack of interaction and direction in the school. It was an environment of isolated frustration (see Figure 1).

As a bilingual education consultant, I suggested that the school try the concurrent approach (Lessow-Hurley, 2000), a bilingual team-teaching technique in which both teachers remain in the classroom for the entire lesson, conducted as follows:

1. The lesson introduction is in Language A, by Teacher A
2. The main lesson is in Language B, by Teacher B
3. The lesson conclusion is in Language A, by Teacher A

Susan and Hardi were selected as coteachers for a 4-week pilot project using this approach in the fourth-grade character education class. They worked together before the project started to outline the curriculum and materials for the 4 weeks. They decided that they would switch the language blocks each week. The first week, Indonesian would be the opening and closing language and English, the main lesson language; in subsequent weeks, these roles would be reversed.

After the project began, Susan and Hardi met weekly to prepare. Susan often suggested ideas for group work or discovery learning–techniques she remembered her teachers using in school. Hardi often had ideas for skits and presentations–ways of learning which were common in Hardi's Indonesian background. While the children were benefitting from the diverse methods that each teacher brought to their teaching, Susan and Hardi were each doubling their teaching repertoires as they watched the other teach. They became comfortable enough with each other to openly discuss activities and their effectiveness. At the end of the 4-week pilot project, both came to the same conclusion: "This is hard, but worthwhile. Let's do it more!"

The language learning benefits of dual-language team teaching are many (Lessow-Hurley, 2000), for both students and teachers. In Susan and Hardi's case, NEST-NNEST collaboration equipped both teachers with more effective and diverse teaching skills.

1. *Discussions of effectiveness become commonplace and nonthreatening.* Having another teacher in the classroom so frequently helps teachers to lower their guard. It also makes discussions of teaching practices and evaluations of effectiveness a common and natural occurrence, rather than something that only happens rarely, during high-stakes observations.
2. *Minimally trained teachers acquire teaching skills through observation and reflection.* Ideally, teachers like Hardi and Susan should have opportunities to receive training to learn effective teaching practices prior to employment. However, when these ideal conditions are not present, minimally trained teachers *can* indeed learn a great

deal about teaching from observing each other teach and then reflecting on their observations of what worked and what did not. In fact, for a school without funds to send teachers for proper training, collaborative team teaching may be the next best thing. Especially if coupled with some instruction on identifying and assessing student learning, team teaching can advance teachers' development of teaching skills.

3. *NESTs learn local teaching and learning strategies.* Every NEST teaching in an EFL context needs to understand how the students are accustomed to learning. Watching local teachers and learners, NESTs discover the values and norms of the classroom. Susan was surprised to see how often Hardi engaged the students in skits and role-plays and how effectively he conducted these activities. This caused her to value and respect his suggestions more that she would have had she not seen him teach.

4. *NNESTs learn new teaching and learning strategies.* In Indonesia, many teachers have not experienced constructivist ways of learning; thus NNESTs often appreciate opportunities to learn how to use these teaching strategies. Such was the case with Hardi. By watching the group and discovery-learning techniques favored by Susan, he was able to expand his view of language learning beyond memorization and performance to deeper understanding and real communication.

5. *NESTs and NNESTs struggle together to engage in effective content-based language teaching.* The school in which Susan and Hardi taught did not provide much direction concerning how bilingual education was to happen. In the absence of clear guidelines, the team-teaching context at least provided a natural place for Susan and Hardi to discuss the teaching of language and content together–a school goal which many teachers were struggling to fulfill. Susan and Hardi began to dialogue about the difficulties of teaching language and content with other teachers as well. As a result, for the first time teachers were getting beyond the label *bilingual school*— an effective marketing tool—to addressing what such a label actually meant in the classroom.

Collaborative Production: Developing Curriculum and Materials

Our final view of NEST-NNEST collaboration in this chapter takes us back to our opening story about the teachers in Brazil who produced their own student workbooks.

> Clarice, one of the Brazilian teachers in our collaborative team, had been the first to suggest that we develop our own workbooks. She felt that she did not have enough time to do her own fun activities with her students because she was so busy trying to complete the textbook series we had adopted. However, parents insisted that their children complete the books—understandably so, given their cost. How great it would be, we dreamed, to develop our own workbooks. They would be cheaper than the purchased texts, and we could design them to meet the needs of both students and teachers.
>
> A team was assembled. Clarice wrote most of the teacher's book, providing her an opportunity to share the engaging communicative games and activities she had developed through her years teaching English to children. Ana, another Brazilian teacher, and I worked together to design an overall curriculum and a table of contents for each grade level workbook. Several Brazilian, American, and Canadian teachers took on assignments to create various lessons. Clarice edited the teaching guides which accompanied each lesson to ensure that the activities were comprehensible for Brazilian teachers. Rosana, a Brazilian teacher, contributed all the artwork that was needed. Davi, a Brazilian administrator for our school, designed the cover and managed the production of the books.
>
> Like any other project involving diverse people, cultures, and perspectives, this one had moments of stress and tension. Sometimes the Brazilians and North Americans operated on different assumptions regarding deadlines and priorities, and discussion was needed to clarify expectations. Where the content of our work was concerned, however, unity prevailed. Editing suggestions were taken in the spirit of helpfulness with which they were given. Teachers looking at rough drafts of artwork or lessons produced by other teachers were often so impressed by the quality that they wanted to use the pages right away in their classes. Since all of our teachers in the children's program were involved in the project, the extra workload of creating materials was shared by all.
>
> Today, the workbooks are used not only in Brazil, but in Indonesia as well. They are a testimony to what cross-cultural collaboration can accomplish.

Though collaboration for development can bring tremendous benefits to teachers, students and schools in any setting, when such collaboration includes both NESTs and NNESTs, some specific benefits can ensue:

1. *NESTs and NNESTs have opportunities to use their specific skills and abilities.* NNESTs who have considerable teaching experience may, like Clarice, have developed activities and techniques which work well in the local context. They may also have expertise in creating artwork, offering relevant grammar explanations, or managing the production of materials. NESTs sometimes do not have the training in language teaching that NNESTs have, but they may be able to edit materials. They may also have creative ideas for activities that are new to the local context.

2. *NESTs and NNESTs have reasons to interact, and thus to also foster learning and growth in each other.* In the absence of purposeful encounters, both NESTs and NNESTs may feel shy and awkward initiating interaction. A joint task provides a natural meeting place—a ready topic for discussion, a reason to get together both socially and professionally.
3. *NESTs and NNESTs produce materials better suited to the local context than commercial products.* Finding appropriate materials is problematic in many EFL contexts. Internationally available commercial texts are often too expensive for Indonesian schools, and so locally produced materials are used. Unfortunately, such materials are sometimes inadequate linguistically and pedagogically. In other instances, commercially produced materials are available and accessible but contain topics or images which are not well suited for the local context. In each of these cases, a good solution is NESTs and NNESTs working together to produce materials for the local environment.

CONCLUSION

We have seen three avenues for NEST-NNEST collaboration on a school staff: language classes, team teaching, and curriculum and material development projects. All three types of collaborative endeavors increase both NEST-NNEST *interaction* and *professional development*, thus creating the optimal environment of *shared competence* in the school context. Such an environment benefits both groups of teachers—and ultimately their students.

REFERENCES

Braine, G. (Ed.). (1999). *Non-native educators in English language teaching.* Mahwah, NJ: Erlbaum.

Clandinin, D. J., & Connelly, M. (1995). *Teachers' professional knowledge landscapes.* New York, NY: Teachers College Press.

De Oliveira, L., & Richardson, S. (2004). Collaboration between native and non-native English-speaking educators. In L. Kamhi-Stein (Ed.), *Learning and teaching from experience: Perspectives on nonnative English-speaking professionals* (pp. 294-306). Ann Arbor, MI: The University of Michigan Press.

Dormer, J. E. (2010). Strength through difference: Optimizing NEST/NNEST relationships on a school staff. In A. Mahboob (Ed.), *The NNEST lens: non-native English speakers in TESOL* (pp. 285-304). Newcastle upon Tyne, England: Cambridge Scholars.

Kamhi-Stein, L. (Ed.). (2004). *Learning and teaching from experience: Perspectives on nonnative English-speaking professionals.* Ann Arbor, MI: The University of Michigan Press.

Katz, A. M., Omar, M., & Snow, M. A. (2004). The development of EFL standards in Egypt: Collaboration among native and nonnative English-speaking professionals. In L. Kamhi-Stein (Ed.), *Learning and teaching from experience: Perspectives on nonnative English-speaking professionals* (pp. 155-175). Ann Arbor, MI: The University of Michigan Press.

Lessow-Hurley, J. (2000). *The foundations of dual language instruction.* New York, NY: Longman.

Sergiovanni, T. (1994). *Building community in schools.* San Francisco, CA: Jossey-Bass.

Tajino, A., & Tajino, Y. (2000). Native and non-native: What can they offer? *ELT Journal, 54*(1), 3-11.

CHAPTER 24

IN OUR SCHOOL, WE ALL TEACH ESL

The Impact of the Collaborative Work of a Teacher Study Group

Patty St. Jean Barry

The focus of this chapter is to share the ways in which a group of teachers collaborated for the purpose of better serving the English language learners (ELLs) in their school. The vehicle for this collaboration was a Teacher Study Group on Instructional Strategies for English Language Learners (subsequently referred to as the Teacher Study Group), and its purpose was to raise achievement for the many immigrant students who live in the surrounding community. Through the combined efforts of these teachers, their school became a place where all teachers, in some respect, became English as a second language (ESL) teachers. To truly understand the origins of this transformation, it is necessary to share an experience I had with an immigrant student in my monolingual reading class.

> *Many years ago, I learned a valuable lesson from a little boy named Jose. At the time, I was a reading teacher working with a second grade group in a writers' workshop. As part of the workshop, I conferenced with individual students on their writing pieces and guided them through the process. The group was comprised mostly of spirited boys, all clamoring for my attention, with the exception of one.*

Jose was a fly-under-the-radar type student, always quiet, ever obedient. I often found that by the time I checked on his progress, our class time together was almost over, and I would find that his paper was blank. Disappointed in my apparent inability to unblock this young writer, I would reluctantly watch him return to his class.

After several failed attempts to move Jose's pencil to the paper, I realized a greater effort was required on my part. On a day that my lunch period was scheduled right after his class, I asked him to stay behind. With his blank page in hand, I announced that it was time we got to work. I remember my surprise as tears welled in his eyes. I adopted a gentler tone and assured him that we would conquer this page together. I thought of Donald Graves (2006) and his advice on the importance of knowing students. What did I know about Jose that could help him move forward as a writer? What choice of topic might inspire him to face the challenge of his blank page?

I had met Jose's parents and knew they were immigrants. So I asked him, "What country do you come from?"

"Salvador," he replied in barely a whisper.

"Salvador?" I thought, feeling a little panicked. I had just heard on the news that there had been a catastrophic mudslide there. "Do you have family there?" I asked.

"My grandparents," he again answered quietly.

"Are they okay?" I asked, careful not to expose my worry in case he didn't know about the landslide. But just that thought underestimated this little boy's knowledge of the world.

"We don't know. The phones don't work."

I told him I hoped that he would hear from them soon and find out that they were okay. I asked if he remembered El Salvador, and when he nodded, I asked if he would like to tell me about it. He described the beauty of the mountains and how he loved to play in those surroundings. I said that I thought that people like me, who have not been to El Salvador, would love to read about it.

With that connection to the familiar, coupled with guidance and encouragement, Jose put a description of his far away home to paper. He seemed to find comfort in the remembrance of this place and pride in having recorded it in written form. We neatly tucked his completed piece in his folder as he left for his next class.

The following day, Jose came to visit me first thing in the morning. His arms were filled with papers, which he spilled onto the table. He brought me news stories about the mudslide, along with a map of El Salvador and a picture of its flag. The next time his group met, we shared Jose's research with the other students. I soon found that many of the children were in some way affected by this event that took place so far from their present community. Jose had opened the door for conversations that benefitted both him and his classmates. From that point on, he was much more involved in our writing community, but more important, Jose had unlocked a door of understanding for me.

A LESSON LEARNED FROM A STUDENT

The experience with Jose provided the epiphany that eventually led to the work of the Teacher Study Group. What we learned from Jose was that in some respect, all teachers need to teach ESL. This understanding takes two critical forms. First, all teachers must utilize instructional strategies commonly used by those who teach ESL, especially in schools that serve large numbers of immigrant families. The most basic of these strategies is to provide students with the opportunity to build on their own knowledge and histories, an approach to learning that was successful with Jose.

Second, in order to offer effective instruction to all students, teachers must work in collaboration. One such form of collaboration is a teacher study group, a forum for facing the variety of instructional challenges a school may face. It can serve as a safe place for new learning, a means for reflecting on classroom practices, and in this case, the path taken to become a school where all teachers address the needs of ELLs.

ALL TEACHERS AS ESL TEACHERS

Perhaps it sounds a bit overzealous to say that all teachers need to have the same instructional skills as ESL teachers; however, there are many compelling reasons that support this claim. A look at the demographics of our population reveals that the United States is experiencing the largest wave of immigration in the history of our nation. By the year 2050, 50 percent of the population will be made up of ethnic minorities and by that same year, fully one quarter of all people residing in this country will be of Latino origin (Suarez-Orozco & Paez, 2002). This trend in immigration greatly impacts U.S. K-12 public schools.

Presently, there are 10.5 million children of immigrants in U.S. schools, one quarter of whom are foreign born and three quarters are born in the U.S. These children account for one in five students in kindergarten through twelfth grade (Fix & Passel, 2003). The statistics alone suggest that all teachers need to be prepared to address the needs of the increasing number of children in schools who are English language learners.

THE ROAD TO COLLABORATIVE WORK

For the Central Islip School District in particular, located in the Greater New York Metropolitan Area, the increase in children of immigrants has been apparent. In 2005, the Mulvey School from this district became a magnet for bilingual students. English language learners were clustered in fewer buildings in an effort to concentrate bilingual/ESL teaching and support staff in centralized locations. By the 2009-2010 school year, 60 percent of the district's students required either bilingual or ESL services.

In 2006, the Mulvey School was awarded a Reading First grant, a funding stream for No Child Left Behind legislation intended to increase achievement for students in kindergarten through third grade. Reading First is a government initiative that offers professional development funding (see www2.ed.gov/programs/readingfirst/). Schools that were awarded this grant received ample funds to provide teacher training, as well as implement schoolwide assessment systems that monitor the progress of all students. The school used this opportunity to ascertain important instructional programs and materials; however, Reading First presented a major challenge. All mandatory assessments were only in English. What a quandary for schools in largely immigrant communities!

More than half of the students in the school were designated as English language learners; yet they were immersed in an English-only program. In an effort to address this challenge, many steps were taken to create a program that reflected the importance of valuing a child's native language as English is acquired. To this end, the staff needed a forum to explore the complex issues of supporting bilingual students, and they were invited to participate in the *Teacher Study Group on Instructional Strategies for English Language Learners*, referred to simply as the Teacher Study Group.

WHY WORK IN COLLABORATION?

The collaborative work of the Teacher Study Group was twofold. On the one hand, teachers worked together to increase their own knowledge and understanding of instructing students whose language and experiences were different from their own. On the other hand, and in a very practical sense, teachers needed to work collaboratively to meet curricular requirements and scheduling constraints. These two factors were the key goals of the study group.

A Framework for the Teacher Study Group

In order to build a framework for collaborative practices, the study group relied on the work of Vygotsky (1986), who established that thinking develops through social interaction mediated by language. An understanding of this concept provided alternatives for staff development and the ways in which teachers grew as professionals.

A look at a typical study group session reveals Vygotsky's (1986) theories at work. Each meeting's agenda included topics that reflected new areas of learning and interest. The group perused a variety of materials, which often included articles that were usually read at the meeting either silently or through a jigsaw activity. The lion's share of each meeting, however, focused on discussion of designated topics and connections to the classroom. The collaborative character of the study group had the capacity to create new avenues for teacher learning and professional growth.

Group learning was developed through two of Vygotsky's (1978) key concepts: the *zone of proximal development* and *mediation*. The zone of proximal development refers to the contrast between what can be accomplished independently and what can be done with the help of a more capable peer: It is in this zone that learning occurs. As teachers in the group shared their insights and experiences, they took turns assuming the role of the more knowledgeable peer, and thereby created a broader understanding of the topic for the entire group. In the same way, mediation—the way humans interact using psychological signs and tools such as language—provided an avenue for problem analysis. Through group discussion, a greater understanding of the complex issues at hand was possible.

By this group process, classroom teachers recognized that they must gain a greater understanding of the instructional strategies that benefit second language learners, and classroom and ESL teachers worked together to ensure that both curricular needs and language development were addressed in students' overall programs. Without question, Vygotsky's (1978, 1986) theories provided the theoretical framework that helped to create the environment for the Teacher Study Group to thrive.

A Teacher Study Group Format

A collaborative teacher group may assume a variety of forms. The Teacher Study Group at this particular school followed a format that suited the educational needs and practical parameters of its community; the focus of the group was also determined by the unique needs of the school. The next step was to consider a practical framework for the work of the group.

The Teacher Study Group met once monthly during a designated professional period. The teachers were given a set time during the school day dedicated to staff development that was consistently devoted to their learning. In this way, the district helped to create an atmosphere that recognized the importance of a teacher's professional growth.

During meetings, some of the many resources the group employed included journal articles, professional books, videos, and Internet websites. As time went on, members of the group also brought relevant materials to share. This practice alone served to increase basic understandings of important topics and influenced the climate of the school. However, some of the most interesting moments came when teachers shared their experiences of applying concepts learned within the group in their classrooms. This transition from theory to practice was particularly important when teachers position themselves as researchers.

The inclusive nature of the study group was one factor that had a critical impact on the climate of the school. Even though the focus of the group was on ESL strategies, those who taught general education classes were active participants. Teachers from various disciplines worked together to help bridge the gap between the monolingual and bilingual classes. One general education teacher remarked, "This group provides the support I need for the English language learners in my class." In the same way, a bilingual teacher commented that membership in the group helped to positively change teachers' attitudes towards English language learners.

The Impact of Collaborative Study

Over the time the Teacher Study Group met, a great deal transpired. As a group, they faced the challenge of striving for high achievement for all students through study and research. As a staff, they increased their knowledge about second language acquisition, identified effective strategies for second language learners, and analyzed data to both assess programs and inform instruction. These practices contributed to the school being recognized by the New York State Education Department (NYSED). In 2010, the group's school was designated as a mentor school through the S3TAIR (Supporting Successful Strategies to Achieve Improved Results) Project (see www.s3tairproject.org), a program through the NYSED that identifies schools with effective practices that support students with disabilities. This designation provided the school with funds to be used to replicate elements of their literacy program in other schools. The Teacher Study Group is one facet of the program that contributed to this accomplishment and is an aspect of the program that may be replicated by other schools.

Coteaching and Collaboration

One of the many topics explored in Teacher Study Group focused on addressing the amount of time ESL students were out of the general education classroom and its impact on students' overall educational program. They searched for alternatives to traditional pull-out programs. For answers, they turned to the work of Honigsfeld and Dove (2008), who described seven models for ESL coteaching; each model assigned a specific instructional role to both the classroom and the ESL teacher. Through these models of instruction, aspects of the curriculum are taught in a way that addresses the specific needs of individual students. This inclusive framework for delivering important ESL services illustrates the shared realization that "for the sake of our students, there is a place and time for creative collaboration among all teachers" (p. 8).

Two ESL teachers, Maura Haffey and Marc Johnson, were willing to explore the option of ESL coteaching. Even though their teaching schedules were in full swing, they began to look for ways to pilot this instructional framework. As a first step, these teachers put to paper all aspects of their ESL curriculum. They then looked to see in what ways the goals they had for their students could be addressed through our Reading First literacy program.

Maura started coteaching in two specific areas: vocabulary and phonics. First, she incorporated the vocabulary program based on the research by Beck, McKeown, and Kucan (2002) into her ESL curriculum. She pretaught the same content as the classroom teacher. The preteaching model brought a good deal of praise from the classroom teacher who noticed quite a difference in their students during subsequent lessons. Students who were often taciturn during vocabulary lessons were now the first to volunteer and answer questions. Maura also retaught phonics lessons utilizing the same multisensory explicit instruction offered in the general education setting. This approach to phonics instruction provided the modeling and scaffolding critical to second language learners and also paralleled tasks on the English proficiency exam administered to all ELL students in New York State.

Marc was able to arrange times for coteaching in the general education classroom. The first partnership he developed surrounded assessment. He administered the monthly individualized progress monitoring for his students while the classroom teacher continued literacy instruction with the rest of the class. By doing so, the children were able to be assessed on their progress and still be present for the whole group instruction. Marc also scheduled time in two classes where both he and the classroom teacher each conducted a guided reading group while the rest of the class worked at centers.

This framework was successful on several levels. First, the students received additional guided reading instruction in their classroom setting, recognized as an excellent forum for teaching strategies needed for ELLs (Avalos, Plasencia, Chavez, & Rascon, 2007). Second, key instructional areas were addressed in this manner such as: vocabulary, language conventions, grammatical structures, and comprehension strategies. All this was accomplished through an inclusive and cohesive coteaching model.

"I Been Knowin' That A Long Time"

One piece of professional literature the Teacher Study Group shared was *Meeting the Diverse Needs of English Language Learners* (Fountas & Pinnell, 2006). This resource helped to broaden a shared understanding of second language learning, particularly when its authors stated, "The term *English language learner* includes any student for whom standard academic English is not a first language" (p. 500). This definition applies to many children and is illustrated in the following teacher anecdote:

> One day, when visiting a first grade class, I was sitting next to a little boy as his teacher was reviewing a lesson. As the class checked their work, this young man could see that he had answered all of the questions correctly. Proudly, he leaned towards me and whispered, "I been knowin' that a long time."

This child's words were spoken in one of the many dialects students often bring to school; his distinct language difference provided the basis for a more enlightened understanding of what it means to be an English language learner. His words clarified the group's cumulative revelation, that classes frequently have children who do not speak standard English.

FINAL THOUGHTS

An inclusive program that incorporated instructional strategies for second language learners yielded unexpected instructional and learning benefits for all program participants. In the end, the work of the collaborative study group on second language learning not only helped to raise achievement for children in the ESL program, but also improved the educational outcomes for all students.

REFERENCES

Avalos, M., Plasencia, A., Chavez, C., & Rascon, J. (2007). Modified guided reading: Gateway to English as second language and literacy learning. *The Reading Teacher, 61*, 318-329.

Beck, I., McKeown, M., & Kucan, L. (2002). *Bringing words to life*. New York, NY: Guilford Press.

Fix, M., & Passel, J. (2003). *U.S. immigration: Trends and implications for schools.* Washington, DC: The Urban Institute.

Fountas, I., & Pinnell, G. (2006). *Teaching for comprehending and fluency.* Portsmouth, NH: Heinemann.

Graves, D. (2006). *A sea of faces: The importance of knowing your students.* Portsmouth, NH: Heinemann.

Honigsfeld, A., & Dove, M. (2008). Co-teaching in the ESL classroom. *Delta Kappa Gamma Bulletin, 74*(2), 8-14.

Suarez-Orozco, M., & Paez, M. (2002). *Latinos: Remaking America.* Berkeley, CA: University of California Press.

Vygotsky, L. S. (1978). *Mind in society: The development of higher psychological processes* (M. Cole, V. John-Steiner, S. Scribner, & E. Souberman, Trans.). Cambridge, MA: Harvard University Press.

Vygotsky, L. S. (1986). *Thought and language* (Newly revised and edited by A. Kozulin, Ed.). Cambridge, MA: The MIT Press.

CHAPTER 25

BUILDING COMMUNITIES OF PRACTICE

Support and Challenge Through Mentoring Networks

Gabriel Díaz Maggioli

BACKGROUND

This chapter documents the development of an innovative teacher collaboration initiative in the public schools sector of the Uruguayan National Educational System. Uruguay, a small country in Latin America (with approximately 3 million inhabitants), has a centralized educational system and a tradition of excellence in education. However, due to a protracted period of dictatorship (1973-1984) much of its rich cultural tradition was lost.

Since 2005, a new National Curriculum spanning Grades pre-K–12 has been in place, trying to bring back the notions of quality and inclusion to education. Teacher education—provided by the National Teacher Education College through a network of 33 campuses offering undergraduate and graduate courses in education—has become a key player in the reform through its initiative which target collaborative partnerships across the different levels of the educational system.

Coteaching and Other Collaborative Practices in the EFL/ESL Classroom:
Rationale, Research, Reflections, and Recommendations, pp. 261–269
Copyright © 2012 by Information Age Publishing
All rights of reproduction in any form reserved.

PROGRAM FOCUS

Since 2005, English language (EL) teaching has been made mandatory in public schools from age 5. However, at present there are not enough qualified EL teachers, which has prompted the educational system to hire individuals who possess a working knowledge of English to be in charge of these courses. At the same time, recruitment efforts by the National Teacher Education College have continued to increase the number of graduates in the English Department. Although enrollment in teacher education programs is completely free, many prospective teachers cannot—because of personal or economic constraints—complete the on-site, 4-year bachelor of arts in English language teaching courses and hence, graduation rates have remained relatively low. While no research supports the idea that all teaching results in student learning, there is research that indicates good teaching does result in quality learning (Good & Brophy, 1976; Marzano, 1997, 2007, 2010). If EL provisions are to be effective, they need to be of such quality that they result in productive learning for all students. It was in such a context that the Modern Foreign Languages Department at the National Teacher Education College developed a mentoring program. Within its outreach unit, the department contributed to on-the-job teacher education through the establishment of collaborative partnerships among teachers, teacher educators, and educational institutions across the country.

EVOLVING CONCEPTUALIZATIONS OF LEARNING TO TEACH

Much of the literature on teacher learning and development seems to conclude that teacher learning is not a process of enculturation but rather the result of participation in communities of practice (Borg, 2006; Clarke, 2007; Díaz Maggioli, 2004; Díaz Maggioli, in press; Hobson, Ashby, Malderez, & Tomlinson, 2009) where old-timers and newcomers interact in order to negotiate meanings (Lave & Wenger, 1991; Wenger, 1998). Thus, teacher learning comes about through participation and reification of new and old meanings made possible by community members shifting their roles within the community in order to accommodate emerging collective understandings. Seen in this light, teaching is no longer conceived as the appropriation of principles and practices from the outside in, but as participation in meaningful, collective activity, which renders teachers not as experts but as learners of teaching (Johnson, 2009).

The implications of this view of teacher learning are manifold. First and foremost, seeing teacher learning as stemming from participation implies the existence of mediated learning experiences in which experts and novices access knowledge through negotiation of meanings that are mutually relevant. Second, the traditional tension between theory and practice no longer seems sensible since in the process of negotiating meaning, novices and experts are able to rename their experiences and reconstruct their practices (Freeman, 1996) by referring—throughout their interactive processes—to both their local and professional understandings of the task of teaching. Seen from Loughran's (2006) perspective, theory and practice are two sides of the same coin which are put at stake through participation and reflection in and on action (Schön, 1991).

The intervention program designed to support the work of aspiring EL teachers in Uruguay is rooted in a community-based view of teacher learning; thus the collaborative strategy chosen for its organization and delivery was the establishment of a network of mentors. In this context, mentors are peers who have an investment in the professional development of their colleagues and provide guidance, advice, direction, and support to help mentees (in our case inexperienced teachers or teachers with no formal preparation for the job) explore their practice as a means to learning.

THE MENTOR PREPARATION PROGRAM

Given the diversity of the teaching force in Uruguay, a strategy was needed which could rapidly secure quality provisions for all students, while at the same time enhance the professional development of all teachers involved. During early 2009, the National Teacher Education College opened a Mentor Training of Trainers Program, which included a rigorous application and selection process oriented at disclosing readiness for the role.

Through a series of structured interviews and problem solving tasks, the candidates who possessed a clear orientation toward prespecified criteria for mentoring were selected. This process was followed by participation in an online course and an on-site workshop that helped the selected group build community in order to elaborate on materials for the delivery of mentor training. Of the original 43 applicants, 28 were selected based on their commitment to public education, their professional profile, and their track record of promotion of student learning. Additionally, an effort was made to acquire representatives from different regions in the country as well as the different levels of the National Public Education System.

During the semester-long online course, participants became acquainted with the theory and practice of mentoring (Díaz Maggioli, 2003, 2004; Malderez, 2009; Malderez & Wedell, 2007) and carried out a series of reflective and collaborative online tasks in preparation for the on-site course. The on-site course consisted of a 3-day retreat during which, through workshops, simulations, Socratic groups, and role plays, participants confronted their initial understandings of mentoring with actual field practices. Some of the key topics explored in the course included working with reticent colleagues, providing formative feedback, and exploring diverse collaborative strategies such as collegial development groups, peer coaching, collaborative action research, peer-journal writing, lesson study, and in-house training (Díaz Maggioli, 2004).

Following the coursework, participants formed groups charged with exploring one aspect of mentoring they had found either relevant to their reality, interesting, difficult, or intriguing. In groups, they developed a 4,000-word professional article and a proposal for a workshop session. A total of eight chapters and workshops were produced and published under the title *Mentoring in a Mint* (Díaz Maggioli & Kaplan, 2010), which became the official training manual for mentor courses.

Each of the original 28 participants organized a training of mentor trainers course for eight colleagues in their region of the country who, in turn, would train ten aspiring mentors in their local school districts. In this way, and in a very short time, a significant number of professionals knowledgeable about how to support teacher learning was established around the country, enabling inexperienced teachers at the primary and secondary levels nationwide to receive adequate support to enhance their students' learning.

Although the main emphasis of the program was on the development of a community of practice centered on mentoring, we purposefully set as a subsidiary goal, the attempt to break the barriers of balkanization and isolation (Hargreaves, 1994) so frequently present in Uruguayan schools. The decidedly sociocultural approach to the task of training mentors instantiated how the enactment of teacher support and development could be offered as well as how our concepts of language, teaching, and learning are constantly shaped and reshaped in light of our collective experience. Likewise, the familiarization of the mentor trainers with collaborative development processes was intended as a tool to add to the cohesion of the emergent learning communities while reconfiguring their understanding of professional learning.

SUCCESSES AND CHALLENGES

The endeavors of the original group of mentor trainers were followed up through a survey 6 months after the completion of their final coursework assignments. The survey was specifically designed to probe into the promotion of collaborative practices through the implementation of the mentoring network. The survey was also sent to 28 teacher educators and supervisors who had not participated in the mentoring program as a way of providing a control group.

Of the 56 potential respondents, 17 responses were received from the mentor trainers and 12 responses from the control group. Answers were collated according to their source and coded according to emerging themes and the frequency of similar responses. Mentor preparation program participants reported preference for three main collaborative development activities: (a) workshops and seminars organized with their mentees, (b) peer coaching, and (c) participation in collaborative development groups centered on an analysis of student learning artifacts. Additionally, action research was also considered as a viable option, though not as frequently noted as the professional development activities above.

The control group, on the other hand, reported joint participation in workshops, seminars, and courses as the most frequent form of collaboration, followed by peer teaching (i.e. working with a colleague in designing, teaching, and reflecting on a class) sponsored by the institution. They considered that the other strategies were far too difficult and expensive to incorporate and that mentoring, although a lofty ideal, would require too high an investment in terms of human resources.

Both groups were given an open question regarding what other collaborative development strategies they implemented. While the mentor preparation group reported using team teaching, recording lessons (either on audio or video) for collaborative reflection, and adopting joint lesson planning and lesson study, the control group's responses emphasized informal forms of collaboration resulting from years of working together with a colleague, or participation in *ad hoc* groups organized by the school's administrators.

As to what hurdles respondents experienced in terms of implementing collaborative development projects, mentor training participants reported communication problems, particularly with administrators, in terms of their role and responsibilities, as they were originally perceived as being supervisors and not mentors. In some cases, this led to the collaborative strategies in place being interrupted for lack of support from the administration. However, mentors found ways of communicating their roles and responsibilities to administrators and were able to overcome the initial obstacles. The control group, on the other hand, reported issues of trust, confidence, and lack of time and resources as the main hurdles in helping them implement collaborative development projects.

Finally, a question was posed as to what respondents found most difficult in terms of performing their collaborative roles. Participants in the mentor preparation course reported (a) finding difficulties to unpack their tacit knowledge about teaching and learning, (b) having to counteract the effects of the apprenticeship of observation (Lortie, 1975), (the power of our learning experiences that influence our teaching). In contrast, the control group reported (a) resistance to change, (b) inability to get teachers to buy into the process of collaborative development, and (c) lack of interest on the part of the teachers involved in pursuing professional development. This seems to indicate that participants in the mentor preparation course were better equipped to overcome the initial hurdles typical of innovations in education and were thus more readily able to concentrate on pedagogical issues.

All in all, the patterns that emerged from the survey validated the mentor preparation course as a strategy for collaborative teacher development. Among other comments by participants in the Mentor Training of Trainers program, expressions such as "welcome break from traditional chalk and talk" and "having a support network of colleagues to whom I can resort" figured prominently. It would seem that, by having had the chance of actively partaking in the creation of a learning community, mentor trainers have managed to resolve many of the conundrums of traditional professional development. They did so mostly by becoming acquainted with collaborative strategies, which have helped them and the teachers they work with to reconstruct their professional development practices.

IMPLICATIONS AND RECOMMENDATIONS FOR PRACTICE

Three key issues, stemming from the survey results, provide direction and recommendations for those willing to adopt a model similar to the one presented here. Additionally, these issues also suggest the limitations of the project.

The Need to Involve All Stakeholders

The fact that the role of the mentor was not made clear to administrators hindered the development of the collaborative relationships and further indicated the need to involve administrators from the very onset of the program. All of the participants in the Mentor Training of Trainers program were teachers and teacher educators, not administrators. Therefore, one critical recommendation is to develop strategies for administrative involvement in the process. To this end, some of the mentor trainers invited administrators to lead collegial development groups, while others worked side by side with administrators during class visits and peer teaching with mentees in order to exemplify best practices in language education.

The Need to Critically Assess our Teaching Practices

Another concern was the perpetuation of the apprenticeship of observation in teacher education courses. Traditional teacher education practices—those in which instructors deliver contents in lockstep—tend to reinforce the ubiquitous teacher-fronted characteristic of most language teachers in the country. In this sense, a suggestion was made to develop professional development seminars, workshops, and talks for teacher educators to become familiar with the collaborative development strategies being favored through the mentoring program.

The Need to Embrace Change as a Paradigm

Last, but not least, participants in the program reported the need to position the issue of change or innovation at the center of their endeavors by communicating why change is needed, exploring the phases teachers go through when experiencing educational change, and providing mentees with options so that they could best handle their own change process (Fullan, 2001, 2007, 2010). The collaborative strategies discussed above—and the support given to teachers through the mentoring system—seem to have minimized the natural resistance inherent to any change process. Alternatively, it can be claimed that in those cases in which resistance failed to be minimized, it was disclosed and made public so that it could be contested and explored.

CONCLUSIONS

The Mentor Training of Trainers program and its organization depicted in this chapter have helped a group of English Language Teaching professionals take one further step to enhance the quality of their teaching, while assuring better opportunities for student learning. At the center of the teachers' efforts lies the explicit intention of eliminating a culture of isolation and individualism and promoting a culture of collaboration where learning is synonymous with participation in meaningful activity. The data gathered seem to indicate that the setup of the program and its enactment have resulted in the achievement of the program objectives.

However, one should be weary of the fact that the program provided a focalized answer to a very situated reality, one which is bound to change as a result of the very innovation developed to counteract it. As such, the only logical conclusion which can be derived is that the next step will necessarily involve change. The strategies used to enhance collaboration and enable participation have been validated by participants and non participants in the innovation. However, one certainty remains. The only way to foster a more just and democratic way of life is to educate ... always educate.

REFERENCES

Borg, S. (2006). *Teacher cognition and language education: Research and practice.* London, England: Continuum.

Clarke, M. (2007). *Common ground, contested territory: Examining the roles of English language teachers in troubled times.* Ann Arbor, MI: University of Michigan Press.

Díaz Maggioli, G. (2003). Options in teacher professional development. *English Language Teaching Forum, 41*(2), 2-21.

Díaz Maggioli, G. (2004). *Teacher-centered professional development.* Alexandria, VA: Association for Supervision and Curriculum Development.

Díaz Maggioli, G., & Kaplan, G. (2010). *Mentoring in a mint.* Montevideo, Uruguay: Consejo de Formación en Educación.

Díaz Maggioli, G. (in press). *Teaching language teachers.* Lanham, MD: Rowman & Littlefield.

Freeman, D. (1996). Renaming experience/reconstructing practice: Developing new understandings of teaching. In D. Freeman & J. Richards (Eds), *Teacher learning in language teaching* (pp. 221-241). New York, NY: Cambridge University Press.

Fullan, M. (2001). *Leading in a culture of change.* Hoboken, NJ: Jossey-Bass.

Fullan, M. (2007). *The new meaning of educational change.* New York, NY: Teachers College Press.

Fullan, M. (2010). *All systems go: The change imperative for whole system reform.* Thousand Oaks, CA: Corwin Press.

Good, T., & Brophy, J. (1976). *Teachers make a difference.* New York, NY: Holt, Rinehart and Winston.

Hargreaves, A. (1994). *Changing teachers, changing times: teachers' work and culture in the postmodern age.* New York, NY: Teachers College Press.

Hobson, A., Ashby, P., Malderez, A., & Tomlinson, P. (2009). Mentoring beginning teachers: What we know and what we don't. *Teaching and Teacher Education, 25*(1), 207-216.

Johnson, K. E. (2009). *Second language teacher education: A sociocultural perspective.* New York, NY: Routledge.

Lave, J., & Wenger, E. (1991). *Situated learning: Legitimate peripheral participation.* Cambridge, England: Cambridge University Press.

Loughran, J. (2006). *Developing a pedagogy of teacher education: Understanding teaching and learning about teaching*. London, England: Routledge.

Lortie, J. (1975). *Schoolteacher*. Chicago, IL: University of Chicago Press.

Malderez, A. (2009). Mentoring. In A. Burns & J. Richards (Eds.), *The Cambridge guide to second language teacher education* (pp. 259-268). New York, NY: Cambridge University Press.

Malderez, A., & Wedell, M. (2007). *Teaching teachers: Processes and practices*. London, England: Continuum.

Marzano, R. J. (1997). *What works in Schools: Translating research into action*. Alexandria, VA: Association for Supervision and Curriculum Development.

Marzano, R. J. (2007). Leadership and school reform factors. In C. Teddlie & S. Stringfield (Eds.), *International handbook of school effectiveness and improvement* (pp. 597-614). New York, NY: Springer.

Marzano, R. J. (Ed.) (2010). *On excellence in teaching*. Bloomington, IN: Solution Tree Press.

Porter, A., & Brophy, J. (1988). Synthesis of research on good teaching: Insights from the work of the Institute for Research on Teaching. *Educational Leadership, 45*(8), 74-85.

Schön, D. A. (1991). *The reflective practitioner: How professionals think in action*. Hants, England: Ashgate.

Wenger, E. (1998). *Communities of practice: Learning, meaning, and identity*. Cambridge, England: Cambridge University Press.

CHAPTER 26

SYNERGIZING PROFESSIONAL DEVELOPMENT THROUGH VIDEO RECORDING, CRITICAL REFLECTION, AND PEER FEEDBACK

B. Greg Dunne and Sean H. Toland

The inspiration for this chapter was the aspiration of two English as a foreign language (EFL) teachers who sought to develop their individual teaching practices through collaborative reflection. Accordingly, each teacher video recorded two of his own lessons during the same semester before undertaking a six-step procedure of critical reflection for each. The underlying purpose to each step was to raise the *self-awareness* of each teacher in regard to the qualities of their lessons. The direction that unfolded for this professional development (PD) project subsequently became based on the following three premises:

1. Current theory in second language teacher education reflects the increased importance of teacher development through self-awareness (Ho, 2009; Ohata, 2007; Zepeda, 2008).
2. Video recordings provide the fullest accounts of lessons.

3. Collaborative reflection is the synergy of self-reflection and peer feedback.

EFL teaching contexts and policies can vary significantly from institution to institution. For that reason, this chapter proposes a context-independent framework that all teachers will hopefully find helpful to their own PD. Due to their irrelevance to individual teaching contexts, the observed teaching qualities themselves shall not be discussed.

THEORETICAL BACKGROUND UNDERPINNING PD

The greatest leaps in PD theory would seem to have occurred during the late twentieth century. It was during that era that issues such as teacher isolation (Edge, 1993; Lortie, 1975; Wells, 1994) and reflection (Richards & Lockhart, 1996; Schön, 1983) were most blatantly brought to the attention of teachers. Subsequent research appears to merely confirm such previous insights or report on them either in localized contexts or technology-assisted contexts. Mindful of these proceedings, the following section elaborates on the three above-stated premises.

Teacher Development Through Self-Awareness

Effective teaching had traditionally been seen to result directly from effective teacher training. Such teacher training adopted what Wallace (1991) termed the *applied science model* of teacher learning whereby teachers learned how to teach according to the assumption that effective teaching consisted of mastering a set of learnable routines and skills, such as lesson planning and classroom organization. Freeman (1994) referred to this phenomenon as *front-loading*, meaning that teacher training remained almost exclusive to preservice practices.

While not denouncing the concept of formalized teacher training, the 1990s and beyond have witnessed second language teacher education researchers deemphasize the process-product nature of training practices. Instead, recent investigations have tended to focus more on the description and understanding of how teachers learn to teach through the *self-awareness* engendered by reflecting on their own teaching (Kong, Schroff, & Hung, 2009; Ohata, 2007). Paramount to this repositioning is the stance that teaching is a dynamic process characterized by varied contexts and constant change, thus not conducive to lockstep recipes intended to outline a best way of teaching.

During class, language teachers do not merely need to demonstrate acquired learnable, low-inference skills but indeed need to engage in continuous high inference decision making. Accordingly, contemporary research (e.g., Igawa, 2008; Roffey-Barentsen & Malthouse, 2009) has emphasized the importance of Wallace's (1991) *reflective model* of teacher learning. Edge (1993) equated this model to *empowerment*, which he duly defined as "working our own way forward, based on our own understanding" (p. 1).

VIDEO RECORDING OF LESSONS

For too long, video was almost exclusively utilized as a tool for either pre-service training or as an evaluative device imposed upon in-service teachers (Bailey, Curtis, & Nunan, 2001). Yet, with a multitude of events occurring simultaneously in the classroom, teachers need to be constantly processing the lesson proceedings while contemplating ensuing lesson steps and strategies. Accordingly, teachers are often unaware of what they do when they teach (Richardson, 2007).

Video is the only medium through which teachers can later observe the full proceedings of the lesson. It "allows teachers to see the lesson as students do" (Gross-Davis, 2009, p. 472) and constitutes an objective record of the lesson (Richards & Farrell, 2005). Unlike a real-time third party observation or personal recall, video mitigates the tendency for premature interpretation (DuFon, 2002). With the hindsight that video affords, teachers are more likely to base their reflections on evidence as opposed to memory or inference. As DuFon reminds us, video also offers permanence, enabling teachers to compare with past and future recordings in order to gauge their teaching progress.

Free-of-charge, publicly available platforms such as YouTube and VideoPaper Builder enable teachers to upload recorded lessons for online storage and viewing. Video affords both a holistic approach to the lesson and a specific focus on any aspect of the lesson deemed appropriate. Video captures everything in the range of the lens and avails the teacher to multiple retrospective viewings. It indeed provides teachers with a *self-directed* learning opportunity (Kong et al., 2009). Video is, as Richards and Farrell (2005) attested, an excellent way to *self-monitor*. In essence, when we consider that *awareness-raising* is the crux of PD, video is the ultimate medium available to teachers engaging in self-initiated PD.

Even so, video possesses one more very important and as yet unmentioned virtue. Inherent to this medium is the capacity for sharing. Indeed, through VideoPaper Builder for instance, an unlimited number of entrusted colleagues from any corner of the globe can view the video, wherever and whenever they choose. Such insights from varied contexts and perspectives can stimulate valuable unanticipated feedback. Not only then is video the ultimate medium for self-reflection, it is also the ultimate medium for *collaborative* reflection.

Collaborative Reflection

A recurring theme in twentieth century PD literature was *teacher isolation* (Griffiths, 1994; Lortie, 1975; Wells, 1994). Imagery from this era could be no more vivid than in Lortie's (1975) dubbing of language teaching as "the egg-carton profession" (p. 223), due to the isolated operation of teachers in independent classrooms and workspaces. Underscoring the favored teacher training (as opposed to ongoing PD) disposition of the era, Wells (1994) lamented that engaging in PD in isolation led to "the loneliness of the long-distance reflector" (p. 11). Clearly, the awareness-raising related virtues associated with self-reflective teaching were craving for disciplined collegial cooperation.

Conveniently, there would appear to be no aspect of self-reflection that cannot alternately be conducted at a collegially collaborative level. In fact, Edge (1993) was unequivocal in his belief that self-development cannot be achieved in isolation but indeed requires input from colleagues and students. This viewpoint has since prevailed and could probably not be any more concise than in the words of Zepeda (2008): "Effective PD occurs in the company of others who support, encourage and learn along in partnership" (p. 2).

Yet some of the hurdles that earlier researchers noted can sometimes still exist. Fundamental to these hindrances is the feeling of apprehension emanating from a tradition of equating teacher observation with teacher evaluation. The sovereignty to select partners for peer feedback and other collaborative PD projects needs to remain in the hands of teachers who elect to engage in *self-initiated* PD. Integral to this freedom of choice is the element of *trust*. Unless the working relationship is characterized by trust the project may as well have not been self-initiated but instead institutionally imposed.

The need for teacher collaboration on PD projects is also evident when considering localized contextual factors. In Japan, the vast majority of university-level EFL teachers are employed on a part-time basis. In this insecure job climate, many perceive that their career prospects are largely being determined by their own PD pursuits (Toland & Dunne, 2011). This somewhat constitutes a Catch-22 situation since the PD practices needed to advance beyond part-time employment can be constrained by the lack of decision-making power that comes with being a part-time employee.

OUR COLLABORATIVE REFLECTION PROJECT

Having argued the importance of ongoing PD practices and the advantages that self-reflection, video recorded lessons, and collaborative reflection bring to them, the following sections outline how we applied these theories in our own PD practices. Integral to the procedural model adopted was the triangulation of all available sources of feedback. The final step of the model sought a synergy whereby collaborative discussion between colleagues might prove more illuminating than the simple sum of the individual insights noted in each individual step.

Awareness Raising Through Disciplined Cooperation

In the context of a non-English major, EFL course for first-year students at a women's university in Japan, two colleagues sought to raise their awareness of their teaching strengths and shortcomings. Having established *raising self-awareness* as the objective, *video* as the data collection medium and *disciplined collaboration* as the direction, in order to round off a functional model, a 6-step triangulated critical feedback model was devised as a suitable analytical framework (see Figure 26.1).

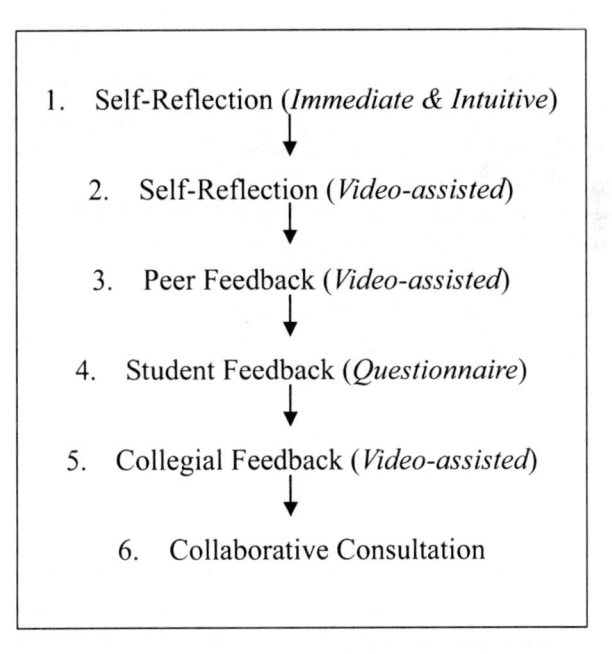

1. Self-Reflection (*Immediate & Intuitive*)
2. Self-Reflection (*Video-assisted*)
3. Peer Feedback (*Video-assisted*)
4. Student Feedback (*Questionnaire*)
5. Collegial Feedback (*Video-assisted*)
6. Collaborative Consultation

Figure 26.1. Lesson reflection model.

In terms of the project's macro planning, two more decisions needed to be made. First, should self-reflection and collegial-reflection be based around a prescription or should observers be free to offer feedback unbound by categorical bias? The latter option was settled upon as it was deemed more likely to unearth unanticipated matters for discussion. Consequently, all participating teachers were simply asked to note from three to five perceived strengths and from three to five shortcomings on each lesson that they observed.

The second decision pertained to lesson selection. The curriculum consisted of two subcourses, namely *Topics* and *Speaking*, each conducted in accordance with a task-based learning (TBL) framework (Willis & Willis, 2007). For each 45-minute *Topics* lesson, teachers were required to select one task from a pack of six commercially produced lesson tasks on a predetermined topic. In order to maximize peer-lesson familiarity, both teachers agreed to use the same task with their respective classes.

Since the lesson was essentially formulaic, it enabled a more concentrated focus on how each teacher utilized the whiteboard, the CD recording, the CD transcript, pair work, group work, worksheets, and other teaching aids. Similarly, it enabled more informed reflection regarding techniques of presentation and practice, time management, student/teacher talk time ratios, L1 (native language) versus L2 (second language) usage, teacher speaking speed and complexity, rapport, positive and negative body language, levels of student participation and adherence to TBL principles.

Immediately subsequent to the lesson, the reflection process began. Four weeks later, each teacher taught a self-designed 45-minute lesson with a focus on speaking to the same class at the same time of day in the same room as before. Apart from facilitating same-teacher comparison of the above-listed teaching considerations and the degree to which each teacher was demonstrating development in light of the collaborative feedback he had received, this lesson provided for critiques regarding original task design and sequencing.

Metareflection: Reflecting on the Critical Feedback Model

Not only does collaborative reflection enhance one's ability to teach, it also fosters one's ability to critically reflect. This symbiotic relationship subsequently intensifies the enhancement of teaching ability. In *metareflecting*, or reflecting on the researchers' framework for reflection, the following observations emerged in regard to each of the six steps.

1. Self-Reflection (Immediate and Intuitive)

The accepted initial undertaking in the reflective process is to document one's impressions of the lesson conducted. This is best done immediately following the lesson or perhaps intermittently during the lesson providing it does not impinge on the flow of the lesson itself. Appreciating that the teaching schedule may allow limited time to do this, the researchers recommend using either a digital voice recorder or a form with prepared columns for noting perceived lesson strengths and shortcomings.

2. Self-Reflection (Video-Assisted)

When viewing a recording of one's lesson and noting reflections, those reflections are likely to be more wide-ranging if one is not overly mindful of the intuitive reflections documented in step one. During the video-assisted reflection, the researchers were drawn not just to a wider array of teacher-related matters, but they indeed became more conscious of student performance.

As previously noted, the quest here is for objective reflection. On this note, the researchers also found that the more they viewed their own class on video, the easier it became for them to distance themselves and depersonalize their critiques.

3. Peer Feedback (Video-Assisted)

A PD partner offers a fresh perspective. Accordingly, it is essential that the video recording affords one's partner as full an account of the lesson as possible by capturing the teacher's action zone, whiteboard displays, and a significant representation of student performance. The researchers accomplished this by placing one tripod-mounted camcorder in a rear corner of the classroom and an auxiliary camcorder on the TV/video deck trolley in a front corner, both facing away from incoming sunlight. Remembering that communicative classrooms create much ambient noise, a digital voice recorder was carried in the teacher's chest pocket to capture close-up communication.

4. Student Feedback (Questionnaire)

Issues pertaining to consent will vary from institution to institution. In the current instance, all students claimed to be satisfied that the purpose of the recording was not to evaluate their performance but to instead research the teacher's performance, and promptly gave their consent. Yet claims and truths can differ. Also, as the *observer's paradox* (Labov, 1972) decrees, the act of observation can influence what is being watched. For these reasons, the teachers sought verification by having all students anonymously complete a short questionnaire (in their L1) upon completion of each lesson.

Students were asked how nervous the video camera made them feel at the beginning and middle of the lesson. Collectively across the four lessons in the project, 44 of 46 respondents stated they were *not nervous* at the beginning of the lesson. There were two responses of a little nervous and none stating very nervous. By the middle of the lesson all 46 responded that they were not nervous. The absence of a dedicated cameraman and the establishment of a high degree of student/teacher trust are thought to largely account for this finding.

Using a five-point scale students were also asked how each lesson compared to their teacher's previous lessons in terms of difficulty and fun. The questionnaire revealed that 80.4% ($n = 37$) of the 46 respondents reported that the difficulty level of the video recorded classes was the same as their regular lessons. In regard to the degree of enjoyment, 41.3% ($n = 19$) felt that the videotaped classes were the same as usual and 43.5% ($n = 20$) claimed that they were a little more fun than a typical lesson. Accordingly, the teachers were satisfied that the lessons under reflection were valid samples of each teacher's regular teaching. In addition to these verification questions, the questionnaire also required the students to rate the opportunity they were given to practice each of the four macro-skills so that each teacher could check the degree to which the students' impressions matched his own.

5. Collegial Feedback (Video-Assisted)

Several other teachers in the program taught the same lessons as the researchers. Two of them agreed to watch the video-recorded lessons and offered feedback. Although their feedback proved valuable and was much appreciated, it took several weeks to be returned, somewhat delaying the project. Yet, the introduction of this ongoing PD project to colleagues has generated enthusiasm and created the possibility of involving even more teachers in the future.

6. Collaborative Consultation

Rounding out the triangulation of perspectives for reflective feedback, both researchers replete with all notes procured from the preceding five steps, watched and reflected on each other's lessons together. Since one teacher was a course coordinator and the other a part-time teacher an unintended power relationship was inherent to the partnership. Accordingly, it was not until this stage that the pair could finally declare that full trust had been established and completely candid discussion could occur. Although the analysis of teaching performance and objectives will differ across contexts, the collaborative consultation step is essential for all teachers who intend to reach outcomes when attempting to determine their own teaching issues.

CONCLUSION

This chapter has argued that ongoing PD through collaborative reflection is a powerful way for any teacher to compensate for the shortcomings of traditionally front-loaded teacher training programs. By following the 6-step critical feedback model outlined, both teacher-researchers maintained that this PD experience acutely raised their self-awareness regarding numerous qualities of their teaching. The model itself emphasizes that the three most valuable PD resources accessible to teachers are themselves, their colleagues, and their students. Moreover, it illustrates how video is one powerful medium available to elicit and synergize the critical reflections of these three indispensably resources.

REFERENCES

Bailey, K. M., Curtis, A., & Nunan, D. (2001). *Pursuing professional development: The self as source.* Boston, MA: Heinle Cengage Learning.

DuFon, M. A. (2002). Video recording in ethnographic SLA research: Some issues of validity in data collection. *Language Learning & Technology, 6*(1), 40-59.

Edge, J. (1993). *Cooperative development.* Essex, England: Longman.

Freeman, D. (1994). Knowing into doing: Teacher education and the problem of transfer. In D. C. S. Li, D. Mahoney, & J. Richards (Eds.), *Exploring second language teacher development* (pp. 1-21). Hong Kong, China: City University of Hong Kong.

Griffiths, E. (1994). Keeping an eye on each other: Peer observation. In A. Peck & D. Westgate (Eds.), *Language in the mirror: Reflections on practice* (pp. 41-44). London, England: Centre for Information on Language Teaching and Research.

Gross-Davis, B. (2009). *Tools for teaching* (2nd ed.). San Francisco, CA: Jossey-Bass.

Ho, B. (2009). Training teachers of English to reflect critically. *The Journal of Asia-TEFL, 6,* 109-130.

Igawa, K. (2008). Professional development needs of EFL teachers practicing in Japan and Korea. *Journal of Shitennoji International Business University, 45,* 431-454. Retrieved from http://www.shitennoji.ac.jp/ibu/images/toshokan/kiyo45-21.pdf

Kong, S. C., Shroff, R. H., & Hung, H. K. (2009). A web enabled video system for self reflection by student teachers using a guiding framework. *Australasian Journal of Educational Technology 25,* 544-558.

Labov, W. (1972). *Sociolinguistic patterns.* Philadelphia, PA: University of Pennsylvania.

Lortie, D. (1975). *Schoolteacher: A sociological study.* Chicago, IL: University of Chicago Press.
Ohata, K. (2007). Teacher development or training? Recent developments in second/foreign language teacher education. *Language Research Bulletin, 22*(1), 1-16. Retrieved from http://web.icu.ac.jp/lrb/vol_22/Kota%20V22.pdf
Richards, J. C., & Farrell, T. (2005). *Professional development for language teachers: Strategies for teacher learning.* New York, NY: Cambridge United Press.
Richards, J. C., & Lockhart, C. (1996). *Reflective teaching in second language classrooms.* Cambridge, England: Cambridge University Press.
Richardson, J. (2007). Learning through a lens. *Tools for Schools, 10,* 1-3.
Roffey-Barentsen, J., & Malthouse, R. (2009). *Reflective practice in the lifelong learning sector.* Exeter, England: Learning Matters.
Schön, D. A. (1983). *The reflective practitioner: How professionals think in action.* London, England: Temple Smith.
Toland, S., & Dunne, B. G. (2011). Empowering teachers' professional development: Video supported reflections. In E. M. Skier & M. Walsh (Eds.), *Pan-SIG 2010 Conference proceedings* (pp. 78-91). Kyoto, Japan: JALT.
Wallace, M. J. (1991). *Training foreign language teachers: A reflective approach.* Cambridge, England: Cambridge University Press.
Wells, M. (1994). The loneliness of the long-distance reflector. In A. Peck & D. Westgate (Eds.), *Language teaching in the mirror: Reflections on practice* (pp. 11-15). London, England: Centre for Information on Language Teaching and Research.
Willis, D., & Willis, J. (2007). *Doing task-based learning.* Oxford, England: Oxford University Press.
Zepeda, S. J. (2008). *Professional development: What works.* Larchmont, NY: Eye on Education.

ABOUT THE CONTRIBUTORS

ABOUT THE EDITORS

Andrea Honigsfeld, EdD, is an associate dean in the Division of Education at Molloy College, Rockville Centre, NY. She teaches graduate education courses related to cultural and linguistic diversity, linguistics, ESL methodology, and action research. Before entering the field of teacher education, she was an English as a foreign language teacher in Hungary (Grades 5-8 and adult), an English as a second-language teacher in New York City (Grades K-3 and adult), and taught Hungarian at New York University. She was the recipient of a doctoral fellowship at St. John's University, where she conducted research on individualized instruction and learning styles. She has published extensively on working with English language learners and providing individualized instruction based on learning style preferences. She received a Fulbright Award to lecture in Iceland in the fall of 2002. In the past 8 years, she has been presenting at conferences across the United States, Great Britain, Denmark, Sweden, the Philippines, and the United Arab Emirates. She frequently offers staff development primarily focusing on effective differentiated strategies and collaborative practices for English as a second language and general-education teachers. Her coauthored book *Differentiated Instruction for At-Risk Students* (2009) and coedited book *Breaking the Mold of School Instruction and Organization* (2010) are published by Rowman and Littlefield.

Maria G. Dove, EdD, is an assistant professor in the Division of Education at Molloy College, Rockville Centre, NY, where she teaches courses to preservice and inservice teachers in the graduate education TESOL program. Having worked as an English as a second language teacher for over 30 years, she has provided instruction to English language learners in public-school settings (Grades K-12) and in adult English language programs in Nassau County, NY. During her years as an ESL specialist, she established coteaching partnerships, planned instruction through collaborative practices, and conducted ESL cotaught lessons in general-education classrooms with her fellow K–6 teachers. She has served as a mentor for new ESL teachers and coaches both ESL and general-education teachers on coteaching strategies. She has published several articles and book chapters on her experiences with coteaching, differentiated instruction, and the education of English language learners. She regularly offers professional-development workshops regarding the instruction of English language learners to local school districts as well as at state and national conferences.

ABOUT THE AUTHORS

Theresa Akerley, MEd, has taught high school science for 4 years and has been a teaching fellow, adjunct professor, and mentor teacher at the University of Vermont. She has a master's degree in special education, sought to enable her to more effectively differentiate instruction for a diverse spectrum of learners. She is eager to begin her second year of coteaching.

Patricia Page Aube, MEd, earned a bachelor of science in education from Fitchburg State College, Massachusetts, and a master's of education in mathematics and language acquisition. She began her career with Fitchburg Public Schools coteaching with an ESL teacher to address the language needs of Hmong students. Ms. Aube is currently a curriculum integration specialist supporting math and ESL teachers through curriculum development, demonstration lessons, and coaching.

Laura Baecher, EdD, is an assistant professor of TESOL at Hunter College, City University of New York. She has been an ESL teacher and teacher educator for the past 20 years. Her research interests relate to the connection between teacher preparation and teacher practice including teacher language awareness, the use of video in clinical supervision, and collaborative teaching for ELLs.

Bonnie Baer-Simahk, MEd, is the director of ELL services for the Fitchburg Public Schools, in Massachusetts, where she taught ESL for many years. She has also served as the district's early childhood director, taught kindergarten, and adult ESL as part of a job development project for Southeast Asian refugees through Catholic Social Services. A frequent provider of professional development to teachers of ELLs, Ms. Baer-

Simahk is also an adjunct instructor for Fitchburg State College and a consulting teacher for the Northeast Foundation for Children, presenting summer institutes in the Responsive Classroom Approach.

Abby P. Becker, MAEd, teaches English as a second language (ESL) at the Kent-Hall Elementary School in Homewood, Alabama. She collaborates with her fellow K-5 teachers for planning and delivering instruction in general education classrooms and, based on these collaborative efforts, was selected Teacher of the Year. Previously, she coordinated a community outreach program and taught ESL to adult learners. She regularly offers professional development workshops and presents at local, state, and national conferences.

Angela B. Bell, PhD, is an ESOL consultant and teaches for the University of Colorado at Colorado Springs and for the University of North Dakota. Her current research focuses on collaboration among mainstream and ELL teachers.

Clara Lee Brown, EdD, is an associate professor of ESL Education in the Department of Theory and Practice in Teacher Education at the University of Tennessee, Knoxville. She currently teaches courses on content-based ESL methods, assessment, and multilingualism to graduate students. Her research interests include enhancing ESL students' academic achievement in content learning and equity issues in large-scale statewide testing programs.

Colleen A. Capper, EdD, is a professor of educational leadership and policy analysis at the University of Wisconsin-Madison. She has written four books and over 120 chapters, refereed journal articles, and conference papers related to the intersection of educational leadership and equity. Her most recent book is *Leading for Social Justice: Transforming Schools for All Learners* (with Frattura, Corwin Press). She works with schools, districts, and universities across the country on ways to maximize student achievement in inclusive ways and to develop the capacity of educators to do this work.

Anne Dahlman, PhD, is an associate professor and chair of the Department of Educational Studies: K-12 and Secondary Programs at Minnesota State University, Mankato. Dr. Dahlman earned her doctoral degree at the University of Minnesota in curriculum and instruction, second languages and cultures. She has taught ESL and EFL (in Finland), German, Swedish and Finnish in the K-12 context in Finland as well as in adult education in the United States. Her research interests include culturally responsive teaching and learning, collaboration and community in teacher learning, and ESL program evaluation. She frequently serves as a consultant for staff development, curriculum reform, and program evaluation. She has published numerous journal articles and made scholarly presentations at national and international conferences.

Margo DelliCarpini, PhD, is an associate professor of TESOL and chair of the Department of Middle and High School Education at Lehman College, CUNY, New York. She is the current editor of *TESOL Journal.* She received a masters degree in TESOL and a PhD in linguistics from Stony Brook University. She has taught ESL at the pre-K-12 grade, adult, and college levels in addition to her current work as a teacher educator. Her research interests include interdisciplinary teacher collaboration and second language literacy development of older learners.

Gabriel Díaz Maggioli, EdD candidate, is a teacher who applies the lessons learned in the classroom to his roles as teacher educator, researcher and educational administrator. He is currently codirector of the School of Languages at The New School for Public Engagement, a division of The New School University. He chairs the English Language Studies Department and directs the master of arts in teaching English to speakers of other languages. He is originally from Uruguay, South America.

Shaniquia L. Dixon, EdD, has been an educator in New York City for over 17 years, where she has served as an elementary teacher, staff developer, assistant principal, principal and central administrator. She earned her EdD in urban leadership, administration and policy from Fordham University. She also serves as an adjunct graduate professor for Touro College.

Jan Edwards Dormer, EdD, has taught English and trained language teachers for the past 25 years in Canada, the United States, Brazil, Indonesia, and Kenya. She has a doctorate in education from the University of Toronto, specializing in teacher development. She currently teaches at Anderson University in the United States as well as in Kenya.

Greg Dunne, MA, began his career as a high school English teacher in his native Australia. Currently, he is a tenured instructor at Osaka Shoin Women's University, where he coordinates the EFL program. He holds a master's in applied linguistics (TESOL) degree from Macquarie University, a bachelor of education degree from the University of Tasmania and a diploma in teaching from Sydney Advanced College of Education. His research interests include teacher development, CALL, task-based learning, and World Englishes.

L. Jeanie Faulkner, MS in TESOL, spent several years in the NYC high schools, first teaching ESL in a bilingual setting. She subsequently joined Marble Hill School for International Studies, where she taught ESL and literature in a sheltered immersion program. Ms. Faulkner currently teaches business communications at Baruch College–CUNY and serves as treasurer of NYS TESOL.

Nelson Flores, MEd, is a student in the PhD program in urban education at the CUNY Graduate Center, New York, where he is currently working on his dissertation, which uses poststructural and postcolonial social theory to examine how current U.S. language ideologies marginalize language minoritized students. He also works as an adjunct lecturer in the program in bilingual education and TESOL at City College and the department of linguistics and communication disorders at Queens College.

Elise Frattura, PhD, is the associate dean for education outreach and an associate professor in the Department of Exceptional Education and Administrative Leadership in the School of Education at the University of Wisconsin-Milwaukee. Dr. Frattura researches and publishes in the area of nondiscrimination law, integrated comprehensive services for all learners, and the theoretical underpinnings of educational segregation. Dr. Frattura works with school districts across the nation to assist administrators in developing comprehensive organizational structures to better meet the individual needs of all learners.

Andrew Gladman, PhD, is coordinator of the Direct Entry English Program at the Centre for University Preparation and English Language Studies, Massey University, in Auckland, New Zealand. He was an English language and linguistics lecturer at Miyazaki International College in Miyazaki, Japan, for 5 years. He has also taught ESOL to adults and high school students in Okayama, Japan, and Bristol, England. His research interests include collaborative teaching, computer-mediated communication and textbook discourse.

Susan Goldstein, MA, received her master's in TESOL at Teachers College, Columbia University, New York. She teaches ESL in the Farmingdale School District at the primary level. Her current interests include accommodating ELLs within the reading and writing workshop models, and supporting the needs of students with interrupted formal education (SIFE) in the classroom.

Patricia Hoffman, PhD, is a professor in the College of Education at Minnesota State University, Mankato. Dr. Hoffman earned her doctoral degree at the University of Minnesota in curriculum and instruction, second languages and cultures. Dr. Hoffman taught special education and English as a second language in K-12 education and overseas. Her research interests focus on disproportionality in special education, systemic school reform, Professional Learning Communities, and culturally responsive teaching. She frequently serves as a consultant for staff development, curriculum reform, and program evaluation. She has published numerous journal articles and made scholarly presentations at national and international conferences.

Peter Hudson, is an associate professor at Queensland University of Technology. His 33-year teaching career includes 10 years as a school principal, lecturing at two universities, and various international work in Asia. He supervises five doctoral students, has over 100 refereed publications and holds three substantial grants from the Australian Government.

Yu-Ju Hung, PhD, received her doctoral degree from Indiana University in literacy, culture, and language education. She is an assistant professor in the Language Center in National Chiayi University in Taiwan. Her research interests include ESL/EFL teaching, language teacher education, online teaching, and multicultural education.

Carol J. Kinney, PhD, teaches mathematics in Bronx, New York to diverse English language learners from many countries including Dominican Republic, Yemen, and Bangladesh. Dr. Kinney continues to practice and research teaching mathematics. She has a PhD from the University of Michigan, where she taught the sociology of education and of Japan. Her dissertation examined the transition of students in lower-track high schools to work in Japan, inspired, in part, by 2 years teaching English as a foreign language in a high school in Takaoka, Japan.

Deirdre Bird Kramer, MA, is an associate professor, who has worked in the field of ESL for 35 years. A former dean, she is now working in K-12 schools by providing professional development for mainstream teachers whose schools have enrolled significant numbers of ELLs. In addition, she teaches graduate students in the ESL program at Hamline University, Minnesota.

Cynthia Lundgren, PhD, is an assistant professor in ESL in Hamline University's School of Education in Minnesota. She teaches ESL methods and second language literacy for ELLs. Previous to teaching at Hamline, she worked for the Minneapolis Public Schools as an ESL teacher, classroom teacher, and teacher mentor.

Ann Mabbott, PhD, is a professor in ESL in Hamline University's School of Education in Minnesota. She has a special interest in working with mainstream teachers who have ELLs in their classes. She started her career in ESL many years ago when she arrived in the United States speaking no English.

Rita MacDonald, MATESL, is an adjunct professor in applied linguistics at Saint Michael's College in Vermont and is the coordinator of a 5-year, $900,000 U.S. Department of Education grant, Project CREATE (Curriculum Reform for the Education of All Teachers of English Language Learners), which provides professional development for college faculty and public school teachers in educating culturally and linguistically diverse students. She is a consultant and trainer for the 27-state WIDA Consortium, training inservice teachers in the integration of English language standards into mainstream classrooms and in teacher collaboration.

Melinda Martin-Beltrán, PhD, is an assistant professor of second language education in the College of Education at the University of Maryland, College Park. She has worked as a bilingual and ESOL teacher in the United States and Latin America. Her research focuses on classroom interaction and discourse, educational equity for language minority students, sociocultural perspectives on language learning, and preparing teachers for culturally and linguistically diverse classrooms.

Greg McClure, PhD, is an assistant professor in the Department of Curriculum and Instruction at Appalachian State University, North Carolina, where he teaches courses that prepare teachers for working with linguistically and culturally diverse learners. Prior to coming to ASU, Dr. McClure worked as an ESL teacher and program director in North Carolina public schools. His teaching and research interests focus on the ways language, culture, and power intersect to influence teaching and learning.

Kelly Waples McLinden, MS, earned a bachelor of arts in linguistics from the University of New Hampshire, and a master's of education in elementary education and creative arts from Lesley University. After teaching kindergarten in Santa Ana, Costa Rica, she returned to the

United States to begin teaching in the Fitchburg, Massachusetts, public school system. In her 13 years in Fitchburg, she has been a transitional bilingual education teacher, classroom teacher, and has taught in a dual language immersion context as the English teaching partner. Ms. McLinden has also served as a mentor for newly hired ESL teachers and is currently teaching English as a second language.

Francesca Mulazzi, MS, graduated from the University of Vermont with a degree in French and Italian literature. She went on to complete a master's degree in educational leadership from the University of Oregon. After 10 years of teaching ESOL in the middle schools in Providence, Rhode Island and at the Shanghai American School, she is principal of The International School of Aruba, in the Dutch Caribbean.

James Nagle, PhD, is an associate professor of education at Saint Michael's College in Vermont, teaching middle and high school curriculum and instruction courses and educational research courses. He is a coprincipal investigator on a 5-year, $900,000 grant received from the U.S. Department of Education entitled Project CREATE (Curriculum Reform for the Education of All Teachers of English Language Learners), which provides professional development for college faculty and public school teachers in educating students who are culturally and linguistically diverse. He has published articles on preservice teacher learning, teaching culturally and linguistically diverse students, and professional learning communities.

Lan Ngo, MA, completed her master's in TESOL at Teachers College, Columbia University, New York. She teaches ESL, Grades 9-12, at The Storm King School, New York. She serves as the chair of the NYS TESOL Secondary Education Special Interest Group.

Hoa Thi Mai Nguyen, PhD, is involved in doing research at The University of Queensland, Australia. Her publications are mainly in the areas of language teaching methodology and EFL teacher education. She has experience teaching TESOL pedagogy, and training EFL teachers at both preservice and in-service levels. Recently, she received Dean's Award for Research Higher Degree Excellence 2010 at The University of Queensland.

Jon Nordmeyer, MAT, has been teaching English language learners for 20 years in the United States, The Netherlands, Turkey, Taiwan and China. He received a BA in classical archaeology from Dartmouth College and a MAT in TESOL from the School for International Training. He recently coedited *Integrating Language and Content* (TESOL, 2010), which was shortlisted for the British Council ELTons Award for Innovation in English Language Teaching.

Faridah Pawan, PhD, is an associate professor in the Department of Literacy, Culture, and Language Education at the Indiana University School of Education. She has directed several state- and federally funded programs in teachers' interdisciplinary collaboration and has published widely in the area.

Megan Madigan Peercy, PhD, is an assistant professor of second language education and culture at the University of Maryland, College Park. She has worked as an ESOL and Spanish teacher in the United States. Her research interests include teacher education regarding the teaching of language learners, methods for teaching language learners, teacher collaboration and development, and critical, sociocultural, and culturally responsive approaches to teaching culturally and linguistically diverse learners.

Lucy Portugal, MA, received her master's in TESOL at Teachers College, Columbia University, New York. She is a kindergarten ESL teacher for the Port Washington School District. Ms. Portugal's interests include student-centered language instruction and curriculum for social justice and diversity.

Judith B. O'Loughlin, MEd, a former K-8 ESOL coteacher, is a teacher trainer. Ms. O'Loughlin was the 2003 Seton Hall University Multicultural Teacher of the Year and NJTESOL-NJBE 2004 President's Leadership Award recipient. A frequent presenter at TESOL, NABE, CATESOL, and CABE, she coauthored "Leadership in Addressing Linguistic and Cultural Diversity in Low-Incidence Public School Settings" in *Leadership in English Language Teaching and Learning* (University of Michigan Press, 2008) and is the author of the *Academic Language Accelerator* (Oxford University Press, 2010).

Joanne E. O'Toole, PhD, is an assistant professor of curriculum and instruction at the State University of New York at Oswego, where she teaches in the adolescent and childhood education programs. She has substantial experience as a public school language educator and teacher mentor and has held multiple leadership roles in both fields. She lives in Liverpool, New York, surrounded by her husband, children, and grandchildren.

ABOUT THE CONTRIBUTORS

Beth Lewis Samuelson, PhD, is an assistant professor in the Department of Literacy, Culture, and Language Education at the Indiana University School of Education. Her research interests include academic literacy and conversational analysis.

Jocelyn Santana, PhD, is the principal of the Frances Perkins Academy in Brooklyn, NY. She is the author of *Dominican Dream, American Reality* (Attanasio & Associates, 2007) and coeditor of *Caribbean Connections: The Dominican Republic* (2005). She has worked as an ESL and ELA teacher, administrator, and teacher educator in New York City. She is a leadership and literacy consultant.

Martin Scanlan, PhD, is an assistant professor in educational leadership and policy analysis at Marquette University. Dr. Scanlan's teaching and scholarship focuses on educational leadership and organizational learning, particularly with regards to promoting educational opportunities for traditionally marginalized students.

Kurt A. Schneider, PhD, is currently a coadministrator of the department of teaching and learning for the Stoughton Area School District, Wisconsin, and a part-time adjunct professor at the University of Wisconsin-Madison teaching social justice courses within the Educational Leadership and Policy Analysis Department. He is a past emerging leader as well as a leadership council member for the national ASCD organization, while serving as a board member on Wisconsin's ASCD chapter (WASCD). He is also a member of Wisconsin's State Superintendent's Educational Data Advisory Committee.

Jennifer Scully, PhD, has taught ESL since 1992 to students in colleges, secondary and elementary schools in New York City. She earned her PhD in multilingual/multicultural studies from New York University in 2007 and has taught graduate students and conducted professional development since then. She writes an online column for first year K-12 ESL teachers and has published articles on teaching English learners.

Ali Fuad Selvi is a PhD candidate in the Second Language Education and Culture Program at the University of Maryland, College Park, where he serves as a graduate teaching and research assistant. He has worked as an ESOL teacher in Turkey. His research interests include the global spread of English, second language teacher education, World Englishes, and issues related to nonnative English-speaking professionals in TESOL.

Susan Spezzini, PhD, is an associate professor in the School of Education, College of Arts and Sciences, University of Alabama at Birmingham. She coordinates the master's degree program in English as a second language (ESL), teaches linguistics courses to preservice and inservice teachers, directs grant partnerships for providing professional development on the effective instruction of English language learners, and researches collaborative mentoring between ESL and mainstream teachers. During her years in Paraguay, she had taught English as a foreign language and also served as a teacher educator.

Patty St. Jean Barry, EdD, is a literacy coach for Central Islip Schools in New York, where she provides ongoing professional development targeted towards instructional concerns and school reform. She is also involved in NYS TESOL and advocates for ELLs with learning differences. Her research involves ethnographic studies with immigrant students and their families.

Andrea J. Stairs, PhD, is assistant professor of literacy education at the University of Southern Maine, where she teaches graduate courses in literacy and English as a second language. Prior to her career in higher education, she was a literacy coach and English language arts teacher in middle and high school settings. Her scholarly interests include urban teacher learning over time, choice in the English language arts/reading curriculum to meet the needs of diverse learners, and teacher research in literacy.

Christopher Stillwell, MA, has conducted workshops on peer observation, lesson study, and other forms of collaborative professional development throughout Asia and the United States. He has written chapters on these topics for several edited volumes as well as articles for *ELT Journal*. He has worked as a teacher trainer at Teachers College, Columbia University, where he received his MA. Currently, he is assistant director of curriculum of the Sojo International Language Center at Sojo University in Kumamoto, Japan.

George Theoharis, PhD, is an associate professor in educational leadership and inclusive elementary education and the director of field relations at Syracuse University. He has extensive field experience in public education as a principal and as a teacher. His interests and research focuses on issues of equity, justice, diversity, inclusion, leadership, and school reform. His book entitled *The School Leaders Our Children Deserve* (Teachers College Press, 2009) is about school leadership, social justice, and school eform. He lives in Fayetteville, NY, and has two adorable children: Ella and Sam.

Sean H. Toland, MEd, has taught English as a foreign language in Japan and Korea at every level from elementary to university. In addition to his EFL experience, he has also spent 3 years teaching high school students in two geographically remote Inuit settlements in Canada's far north. Mr. Toland holds a master's in education degree from Brock University, a diploma in education from McGill University, and an honors BA with a double major in history and religion and culture from Wilfrid Laurier University. He is currently working as an English instructor at Osaka Shoin Women's University in Osaka, Japan.

Anne B. Walker, PhD, is an associate professor of ELL education at the University of North Dakota, where she specializes in literacy, language and culture, and teacher education. Her current research focuses on rural ELL education in the United States.

Heidi Western, MATESL, is a high school ESL teacher with a master's degree in TESOL and 17 years of experience in teaching ESL. She has served on the board of Northern New England TESOL, as a consultant to the Vermont Department of Education regarding ESL teacher licensure, and has been an adjunct faculty at Saint Michael's College, Vermont. She was one of the first to embark on coteaching in her district, has been part of three coteaching teams, and is eager to begin her second year of coteaching with Theresa Akerley.

CPSIA information can be obtained at www.ICGtesting.com
Printed in the USA
BVOW040058030613

322233BV00002B/8/P

9 781617 356865